THE MAKER'S HAND

THE MAKER'S HAND
American Studio Furniture, 1940–1990

Edward S. Cooke, Jr., Gerald W. R. Ward, and Kelly H. L'Ecuyer

with the assistance of Pat Warner

MFA PUBLICATIONS

A division of the Museum of Fine Arts, Boston

■ Cover: Details of cat. no. 48.

■ Title Page: Left to right, details of cat. no. 9; Biographies, fig. 3; cat. no. 33; cat. no. 48; Biographies, fig. 35; cat. no. 15.

■ Page 4: Alphonse Mattia, *Architect's Valet,* Westport, Massachusetts, 1989. Ebonized walnut, holly, cocobollo, ebony, maple, Baltic birch plywood, dalrin; h. 79½ in., w. 25½ in., d. 20½ in. Museum of Fine Arts, Boston; Gift of Anne and Ronald Abramson 1989.126.

Published in conjunction with the exhibition "The Maker's Hand: American Studio Furniture, 1940–1990," organized by the Museum of Fine Arts, Boston, in collaboration with The Furniture Society, from November 12, 2003, to February 8, 2004.

MFA Publications
a division of the Museum of Fine Arts, Boston
465 Huntington Avenue
Boston, Massachusetts 02115

© 2003 by Museum of Fine Arts, Boston
ISBN 0-87846-662-2 (hardcover)
ISBN 0-87846-663-0 (softcover)
Library of Congress Control Number: 2003103743

Some of the introductory essay, "Defining the Field," originally appeared in *Furniture Studio: The Heart of the Functional Arts*, ed. John Kelsey and Rick Mastelli (Free Union, Va.: Furniture Society, 1999).

A grant from the Chipstone Foundation of Milwaukee, Wisconsin, assisted with the costs of photography for the catalogue.

For a complete listing of MFA Publications, please contact the publisher at the above address, or call 617 369 3438.

Designed and produced by Cynthia Rockwell Randall
Edited by Sadi Ranson
Copyedited by Patricia A. O'Connell and Sarah E. McGaughey

Available through D.A.P. / Distributed Art Publishers
155 Sixth Avenue, 2nd floor
New York, New York 10013
Tel.: 212 627 1999 ▪ Fax: 212 627 9484

FIRST EDITION
Printed and bound in Spain

CONTENTS

Director's Foreword

The Museum of Fine Arts, Boston, is home to one of the great collections of American furniture. Its holdings of early New England furniture are preeminent, but the collection also has remarkable breadth, including as it does high-style and vernacular works from North, Central, and South America. The opportunity the collection affords to our visitors to see and understand the history of American furniture as a continuum, ranging from the seventeenth century to the present, is exceptional.

Since the mid 1970s, the Museum has been in the forefront of collecting and exhibiting outstanding furniture by contemporary American studio artists, as exemplified by our innovative "Please Be Seated" program of gallery seating and the "New American Furniture" exhibition held in 1989. It was thus a natural step for us to join with The Furniture Society to present *The Maker's Hand: American Studio Furniture, 1940–1990*, the first major retrospective exhibition and catalogue to examine in depth the origins and evolution of this important aspect of twentieth-century American art.

The Maker's Hand has been written and the exhibition organized by Gerald W. R. Ward, Katharine Lane Weems Senior Curator of Decorative Arts and Sculpture, Art of the Americas, and Edward S. Cooke, Jr., Charles F. Montgomery Professor of American Decorative Arts at Yale University (and a former MFA curator), with the able assistance of Kelly H. L'Ecuyer and Pat Warner. I am grateful to them all for their fine work. I also would like to add a special note of thanks to our lenders, both the public institutions and especially the private lenders (including many of the makers themselves), who have so kindly shared works of art that they use and live with every day. Our colleagues in The Furniture Society, including Andrew H. Glasgow, its executive director, have enthusiastically supported the project in many ways. In addition, a grant from the Chipstone Foundation of Milwaukee, Wisconsin, assisted with the costs of photography for the catalogue.

The American studio furniture movement remains an ongoing and lively avenue of the arts. We are pleased to acknowledge here the foundations upon which this movement is built, as we look forward to the achievements of American furniture makers in the years ahead.

Malcolm Rogers
Ann and Graham Gund Director
Museum of Fine Arts, Boston

FOREWORD BY THE FURNITURE SOCIETY

It is with great pleasure that The Furniture Society joins with the Museum of Fine Arts, Boston, to present *The Maker's Hand: American Studio Furniture, 1940–1990*. Building on its established history of support for the studio furniture arts, the MFA confirms with this exhibition its position as the American museum with the most significant investment in our field.

The Furniture Society's mission is to "advance the art of furniture making by inspiring creativity, promoting excellence, and fostering understanding of this art and its place in society." We accomplish this goal through publications, exhibitions, and an annual conference. Our partnership with the MFA in this enterprise allows us to reach a wide audience, as we work together to present the best possible exhibition and catalogue. Telling the story of the studio furniture movement through these remarkable objects is a significant achievement, one that not only fulfills an important aspect of our mission statement but also, in the process, enriches critical discourse in the field.

I would like to acknowledge several important contributors to this project. On behalf of The Society, I would like to thank Malcolm Rogers for his support from the beginning and acknowledge his willingness to give this project so much of the Museum's attention. Much appreciation goes to Ned Cooke and Gerry Ward for their curatorial and writing acumen. Their support and understanding of this field make working with them a genuine pleasure. Jennifer Bose, Director of Exhibitions at the MFA, provided valued and ongoing support for this project and was particularly instrumental in the success of the partnership. It is important that the efforts of the makers included in this show be recognized, as well as that of the lenders, who were willing to part with treasured objects for an extended period of time. Finally, The Furniture Society's Board of Trustees, in particular Bebe Johnson, deserves special recognition for fostering this exhibition from its infancy. Without its tireless efforts, our field would be a much smaller place.

ANDREW H. GLASGOW
Executive Director
The Furniture Society

ACKNOWLEDGMENTS

During the past few years, the hard work of many people has made this book and the exhibition it accompanies a reality, and we are grateful to them all. At the Museum of Fine Arts, Malcolm Rogers, Ann and Graham Gund Director, and Katherine Getchell, Deputy Director for Curatorial Administration, have supported this project from its beginning. Pat Jacoby and Donna Clayton of External Relations worked very hard to achieve funding for the project, and Jennifer Bose and Kara Angeloni of Exhibitions and Design kept the multifaceted project on course. Keith Crippen, Julia Fuld, and other members of the design staff worked hard to make a disparate group of objects work well together harmoniously. Dave Geldart, Larry Gibbons, and the skilled craftsmen in the Facilities Department created an installation worthy of the furniture it contained.

In the Department of Art of the Americas, we are grateful for the support of Elliot Bostwick Davis, John Moors Cabot Chair, and for the assistance in myriad ways of Rebecca Reynolds, Jeannine Falino, Patrick McMahon, Courtney Rae Peterson, Angela Segalla, Katy Mrachek, and our other colleagues. The Museum's furniture conservators, especially Gordon Hanlon, Angela Meincke, and Chris White, and our Collections Care Specialist, Brett Angell, were exceptionally helpful along the way. We are grateful to the Museum's publisher, Mark Polizzotti, for his support, to Cynthia Randall for her elegant design, and to Terry McAweeney for her assistance in producing this book. Our editor, Sadi Ranson, and our copy editors, Patty O'Connell and Sarah McGaughey, made many improvements to the text, and B. J. Carrick did yeoman work in coordinating the many changes to the manuscript as it evolved. Debra LaKind guided us through the maze of permission forms involved in reproducing the work of living artists. Thomas Lang, Greg Heins, and David Mathews provided beautiful images of the Museum's objects, as well as guidance on photography issues along the way.

Pat Loiko and especially Jill Kennedy-Kernohan of the Registrar's Office skillfully and cheerfully coordinated the many loans involved in this complex project, and Julia McCarthy, Recorder, provided essential help at a critical time. Gilian Shallcross, Barbara T. Martin, Heather Cotter, Rob Worstell, Hannah Goodwin, and Lois Solomon of the Department of Museum Learning enthusiastically undertook a wide variety of programs associated with the exhibition. Dawn Griffin, Kelly Gifford, and others in Public Relations ensured that our efforts were brought to the attention of a wide audience.

In all respects, this project was a joint effort with The Furniture Society. We are thankful to its executive director, Andrew H. Glasgow, and to Bebe Johnson, Miguel Gomez-Ibanez, and many other members of that organization for their guidance and inspiration. John Kelsey and Rick Mastelli shared their extensive knowledge of the field during the early stages of the project. Glenn Adamson, curator of the Chipstone Foundation, read various versions of the manuscript, and we are most grateful to him. We also appreciate the assistance of the Chipstone Foundation and its director, Jon Prown, for their grant in support of the costs of photography for this volume.

Our greatest debt is to the makers of the furniture illustrated here, many of whom lent their works to the exhibition, and to our other private lenders, some of whom wished to remain anonymous, who were exceptionally generous in allowing us to borrow great works of art that they use, in many cases, on a daily basis. Museum colleagues also facilitated loans from their collections and assisted us in our research and writing, including Kevin L. Stayton at the Brooklyn Museum of Art; Jack Lindsey and Amanda Clifford, Philadelphia Museum of Art; Thomas S. Michie and Jayne Stokes, Museum of Art, Rhode Island School of Design; Marjorie Searl, Memorial Art Gallery; Ursula Ilse-Neuman, Museum of Arts and Design; Patricia E. Kane and David L. Barquist, Yale University Art Gallery; and Mansfield Bascom, Wharton Esherick Museum.

When she learned of the project, Daphne Farago immediately gave Wendell Castle's *Leotard Table* to the Museum. We are pleased to illustrate it here as an important example of that phase of the artist's work, which previously had not been represented in the Museum's collection. Many people helped us locate objects, answered questions, and otherwise assisted in the preparation of the book and exhibition, including Bob Aibel, Emilie Anderson, Dirk Bakker, Sylvia Bennett, Jon Brandon, Christopher Brooks, Ann D. Brown, Tim Burgard, Graham Campbell, Bruce Carlson, Laura DeNormandie, Frances Diemoz, Arthur Dion, Helen Drutt, Kay Eddy, Amy Forsythe, Donald Fortescue, Helena Foster, Peter Frid, William A. Guenther, William Hammersley, Kathleen Hanna, Daphne Harris, Sylvia Inwood, Julia Browne Jackson, Richard Kagan, Lori Kaufman, Stuart Kestenbaum, Ian Kirby, David Lamb, Jack Larimore, Jack Lavine, Albert Lecoff, Judith Lippman, Robert March, Steve Massengill, Alex Mayer, Jennifer McCarthy, Dona Z. Meilach, Alexander Milliken, Margaret Minnick, Meredyth Hyatt Moses, Grif Okie, Franklin Parrasch, Lance Patterson, Bruce Pepich, Pamela Weir Quiton, Joanne Rapp, Jack Russell, Paul Sasso, Merryll Saylan, Carol Sesnowitz, Mark Sfirri, Robert Smith, John Snidecor, Rick Snyderman, Steve Stenstrom, Michael Stone, Roy Superior, Richard Tannen, Davira Taragin, Tricia Tinling, Matko Tomicic, Ruth Walkey, Karen R. White, Gerry Williams, and Bernice Wollman.

While we relied on the sage advice and suggestions of these and other people, it was not always possible to reconcile varying opinions. The responsibility for errors and omissions remains ours.

We are particularly grateful to Kelly H. L'Ecuyer, who as a (technically) part-time research associate coordinated the exhibition and also wrote the vast majority of the sections in this book devoted to makers, schools, and galleries, compiled the chronology of exhibitions and bibliography, and contributed to the text in many other ways. In a very short time, Kelly has become well versed in the field, and her tireless work on the project (even when interrupted by the birth of her first child) was crucial in its completion. This project would also not have been possible without the essential assistance of Pat Warner, volunteer *par excellence*. Pat kept the project on track, ferreted down innumerable facts and details, and simply was a driving force behind all our efforts. We are more grateful to Pat than we can say for her dedication to this project and to the field of contemporary American crafts as a whole.

Each of us would also like to acknowledge our indebtedness to Jonathan L. Fairbanks, the Katharine Lane Weems Curator of American Decorative Arts and Sculpture, Emeritus, at the Museum, for whom we served as successive associate curators from 1985 to 1999. Since the early 1970s, Jonathan has enthusiastically supported the studio furniture movement, through his collecting for the MFA, including the innovative "Please Be Seated" program, and his many lectures, publications, and other scholarly contributions. His efforts, in addition to stimulating our own work in the field, have been a major factor in the movement's recognition by art museums, collectors, and the scholarly community at large.

As always, we are grateful to our spouses and families for their support of our endeavors and the concomitant sacrifices that this work involves.

GERALD W. R. WARD
EDWARD S. COOKE, JR.
March 2003

■ Details of Kristina Madsen's side chair, Northampton, Massachusetts, 1989. Pau ferro, maple, Baltic birch plywood, silk upholstery; h. 36 ¾ in., w. 19 in., d. 17 in. Museum of Fine Arts, Boston; Gift of The Seminarians in honor of Jonathan L. Fairbanks 1991.452.

This publication, like the exhibition it accompanies, offers a historical exploration and analysis of one of the most important aspects of twentieth-century furniture—the studio furniture movement in North America. The majority of the furniture discussed is one-off, high-end, custom work and is thus distinct from—although not always unrelated to—the pieces mass-produced by the furniture industry. These works intersect with design and sculpture, and they have an affinity with other media-based crafts such as ceramics and metals. In this book, we have chosen to refer to this type of work as "studio furniture" to distinguish it from the fashions of the industry on the whole and to further place it within a specific temporal and cultural context that is most widely known as the "studio craft movement."

Our chronicle of the more public dimension of studio furniture begins in 1940, when the work of Wharton Esherick attracted considerable attention in the "America at Home" exhibition of the New York World's Fair. It ends in early 1990, when two museum exhibitions—"New American Furniture: The Second Generation of Studio Furnituremakers" at the Museum of Fine Arts, Boston, and "Furniture by Wendell Castle" at the Detroit Institute of Arts—garnered extensive press coverage and public attention. But, before a presentation of this history, it is important to explain the term "studio furniture" and its application to such a visually diverse grouping of objects. Is this work merely a coincidental or forced postmodern assemblage of disparate individual voices? Does it coalesce into a single, coherent field?

A broad range of work is chronicled here—from the refined joinerly furniture of James Krenov and Hank Gilpin to the iconic humor of Tommy Simpson and Mitch Ryerson, as well as the cross-culturally inspired work of Thomas Hucker and Kristina Madsen and the sculptural work of Wharton Esherick and Wendell Castle. The fifty-year range of objects is also quite broad. There are, we believe, significant relationships among these works, for they are products indicative of a particular time. However, to see their coherence as a field, one must understand and question previous terminology and perspectives.

Furniture historians have traditionally tended to organize antique furniture according to formal, stylistic categories. Such groupings of relatively high-style work have been assigned names of seminal designers and rulers or nomenclature describing aesthetic intent. Thus, eighteenth-century furniture is popularly known as Chippendale or Hepplewhite, referring to the designers who codified certain styles through their publications; Louis XVI or Georgian, in honor of the magistrates whose reigns corresponded with the popularity of these styles; or Baroque or Rococo to signify dominant aesthetics in a world context. Art historians such as Meyer Shapiro have argued that products of a specific time and place tend to bear the aesthetic imprint of their origin—their moment and location. Style—which may be rooted in shared outlooks of shop masters, coherent demands of a particular client group, common printed sources,

■ George Nakashima, Conoid bench with back, New Hope, Pennsylvania, 1979. Walnut, hickory; h. 31¼ in., w. 85 in., d. 36 in. Museum of Fine Arts, Boston; Purchased with funds provided by the National Endowment for the Arts and the Deborah M. Noonan Foundation 1979.275.

or available materials—serves as the primary means of linking objects.

With the stylistic revivals of the mid-nineteenth century and the increased production that came with mechanization, style became a less important barometer. Instead, taste and workmanship arose as the prevailing criteria for the creation of objects. Following the lead of mid-nineteenth-century writers and critics, particularly John Ruskin, English taste-makers such as Charles Locke Eastlake and architects such as E. W. Godwin began to call for better-designed furniture. Godwin developed the term "Art Furniture" in the late 1860s to distinguish well-designed, custom-produced work from comparatively tawdry factory work that produced poor copies of previous styles. In America, Art Furniture ran the stylistic gamut from the Japanese-inspired work of Herter Brothers to the Modern Gothic of Kimbel and Cabus and further to the Colonial Revival work of Potthast Brothers; attention to tasteful design and quality workmanship linked these various expressions. In the late nineteenth and early twentieth centuries, Gustav Stickley, Charles Limbert, William Price, and other Arts and Crafts enthusiasts emphasized the importance of craft over decor. Good, hon-

est, structural furniture was considered to possess the greatest moral integrity and therefore would best facilitate the simple life pursued by many middle- and upper-class Americans. Furniture historians studying work from the last quarter of the nineteenth century and first two decades of the twentieth tend to categorize the work less by style and more by the prevalent intellectual charge of the time— the Aesthetic movement or the Arts and Crafts movement.

Interest in abstract notions of taste and morally charged craftsmanship had waned by the 1920s and 1930s, ushering in a renewed interest in style and appearance. Although modernism began as an intellectual investigation of design, it quickly became a new way of packaging furniture and was reduced to a style. Promoted by industrial designers, architects, and cabinetmakers, modernism privileged new materials, industrial production, and streamlined forms. Even postmodernism, the subsequent response to the perceived bleakness of the modern style, has been viewed primarily as an aesthetically coherent style that referenced historical form and detail, displaying a fondness for color.

Drawing from promotional literature of the period, furniture historians have reverted to stylistic criteria to classify twentieth-century work. In the postindustrial world, we must search for a term that is appropriate to our specific time and circumstance. It is difficult to describe the entire field of furniture discussed here simply by evoking major designers or political figures. The work of James Krenov or Sam Maloof, for instance, though widely emulated, hardly reflects enough of the field for the terms "Krenovian" or "Maloof-style" to have broad currency. Similarly, defining the furniture illustrated here in terms of aesthetic form, such as postminimalist, would be a disservice. Other aesthetic terms, such as "California Roundover" or "Northeast Academic," may be appropriate for certain regional work at a particular time, but neither provides a cohesive description of all furniture produced. They only fragment the field further.

In our time of rapid information exchange, an oversaturated market for domestic goods, and heightened interest in art and design, aesthetic pluralism is striking. Many furniture makers have used their independent status in the marketplace to explore multiple directions and to try to distinguish themselves from other craftsmen. Yet we should not take the easy path and simply refer to the contemporary furniture field as "pluralistic furniture." That would be too vague. Other contextual terms such as "art furniture," "handcrafted furniture," and "modern and postmodern furniture" also do not work, as they have been used to describe furniture in other times. What we need, then, is a term unique to our own time—not one based solely on form, aesthetic intention of the maker, or hype of the gallery. For these reasons, we favor the term "studio furniture."

What distinguishes the furniture illustrated and discussed herein is the background of the furniture makers; their interest in linking concept, materials, and technique; and the small shops in which they work. Studio furniture makers have not learned their skills through traditional apprenticeship systems but rather have mastered design and construction in college (either in dedicated college art programs such as those at the California College of Arts and Crafts or Rhode Island School of Design or in college woodworking shops such as those at Dartmouth College). There are also others who are self-taught. The latter, as well as many of the academically trained, have developed their skills through reading, attending workshops or short-term courses, constant experimentation, and comparing notes with other furniture makers. Unlike the wage-based, task-specialized, restrictive training so typical of the furniture trade, most studio furniture makers experience a longer, self-directed, and less constrained learning process.

The term "studio" evokes this type of long-term, exploratory learning while also suggesting a high degree of visual literacy as well as a vigorous conceptual approach to design and construction. Many of the makers featured in this book have had some formal education in art or design and draw their inspiration from a vast stock of images and ideas—traditional furniture or new industrial design, fine arts or popular culture, the familiarity of wood and

■ Gary Knox Bennett, telephone table, Oakland, California, 1984. ColorCore, gold-plated bronze, aluminum, walnut; h. 33 in., w. 24 in., d. 12 ⅞ in. Museum of Fine Arts, Boston; Gift of Warren Rubin and Bernice Wollman 1988.341.

■ Edward Zucca, *XVIIIth Dynasty Television*, Woodstock, Connecticut, 1989. Honduras mahogany, yellow poplar, ebony, gold leaf, silver leaf, rush, latex paint, ebonizing; h. 61 in., w. 33 ½ in., d. 42 in. Museum of Fine Arts, Boston; Gift of Anne and Ronald Abramson 1989.263.

■ Judy Kensley McKie, bench, Cambridge, Massachusetts, 1979. Mahogany, leather upholstery; h. 26 ¾ in., w. 61 ¼ in., d. 26 ⅞ in. Museum of Fine Arts, Boston; Purchased through funds provided by the National Endowment for the Arts and the Deborah M. Noonan Foundation 1979.284.

joinery or the excitement of new materials and techniques, common notions or private dreams, and so forth. What remains constant throughout the design and fabrication process is an intellectual rigor in which a maker fully invests him- or herself to realize an idea.

"Studio" also identifies the place in which this practice of furniture making occurs. Studio furniture makers use a vast array of machinery and hand tools and often employ assistants or specialists; they also tend to work in smaller spaces, organized to maximize the efficiency of the individual. Still, their level of production remains relatively low. Their spaces, approaches to work, and volume of final products lack the larger scale of a manufactory. The term "studio furniture" thus highlights the independent professionalism of these makers and their custom production, which is reflective of most aspects of today's decentralized (yet networked) social and economic culture.

The marketing of studio furniture is also unique to our time. Normal retail outlets have little relevance to the field. Studio works are distributed through more specialized and dynamic sales networks; they are showcased and sold through art and craft galleries or at craft and furniture shows. Such pieces can also be displayed at studio "open houses" where local groups of art supporters might see them; they can be commissioned by a particular client; or they can be purchased directly from the maker's own shop. Some makers sell through a number of these venues simultaneously; one finds considerable variation based on region, gallery or show visibility, and an individual maker's connections. Often, studio furniture tends to be concentrated in the region where it is made. However, some work transcends its region and becomes part of extralocal art collections, finding homes in private residences and museums. The marketing, therefore, is distinct from that of the mainstream furniture

trade, more akin to small local businesses and the fine art world. The term "studio" evokes the importance of the individual maker and the object's origin as well as the creator's artistic reputation in the marketplace.

Understanding the essence of today's studio furniture helps us to comprehend why American and Canadian craftsmen are leaders in the field. The furniture industry is more hierarchical in most countries, with a clear separation of design and production. Design schools and the intellectual processes taught there are distinct from technical schools and apprenticeship programs, given the cabinetmaking skills the students must learn in those settings. John Makepeace, Alan Peters, and the Royal College of Art have fostered a small group of furniture makers in Great Britain; elsewhere, the control of professional designers and the limited power of tradespeople who have learned through traditional apprenticeship contribute to stylistic and technical coherence. But in the United States and Canada, the emphasis on academic training or self-education, a profes-sional identity, and a dynamic, multilayered market have made studio furniture making more diverse, energetic, and prominent. From 1960 to the present, there have been constant intersections and ex-changes between American and Canadian makers, teachers, publications, and exhibitions. The borders between the two countries are more permeable than is true throughout the rest of the world.

Identifying the distinctive qualities that define studio furniture helps establish appropriate criteria for assessment. It is not enough to focus only on craftsmanship or the concept behind a piece of furniture. Instead, we must examine all aspects of the maker's intent and performance to truly grasp why and where an example fits within our definition of studio furniture. For this, we need a thorough understanding of the individual furniture maker and the contemporary field.

Having defined what constitutes studio furniture, we should also say what (in our opinion) it is not and name the types of makers and objects that have not been included in this study. Since the unification of design and craft is a central element of stu-dio furniture, we have not included furniture that is designed on paper by one person but made by others—a characteristic of large furniture companies. Similarly, the quasi-industrial production of a firm such as Thos. Moser Cabinetmakers of Maine falls outside our definition. Although inspired by the studio movement in the 1970s, Thomas F. Moser, a college professor turned woodworker, now operates a highly successful company employing at least sixty-five people in a shop covering sixty-five thousand square feet. Utilizing a computer-guided core cutter and other machines, members of the staff produce modern adaptations of Shaker, Windsor, Arts and Crafts, and other earlier styles in a Danish Modern mode. Although there are elements of congruity with studio work, the scale of this enterprise (as well as a few others like it) and the volume of the business, along with some of its working methods, place it outside our definition of the field.

At the other end of the spectrum, woodworking has long been an avocation for many Americans who have produced furniture for their own and their families' private use. While this may have been an important seasonal activity for rural craftsmen in the eighteenth century, there have been countless thousands of amateur woodworkers and hobbyists making furniture and other wooden objects in the last half of the twentieth century, often (although by no means always) in what might be called a Colonial Revival style. Although some of these objects are technically of superior quality, the essentially private nature of their production and use places them outside the definition of the field.

There is also a significant group of furniture makers whose shops produce custom-made furniture for a large clientele, but such work emphasizes the reproduction of seventeenth-, eighteenth-, and early-nineteenth-century furniture designs. Although this furniture is often breathtaking in the quality of its workmanship and materials—and even though some elements of twentieth-century taste inevitably creep into the most strenuous attempts to make a literal copy of an earlier design—the emphasis of these objects is usually an expression of the maker's regard for the standards and models of the past,

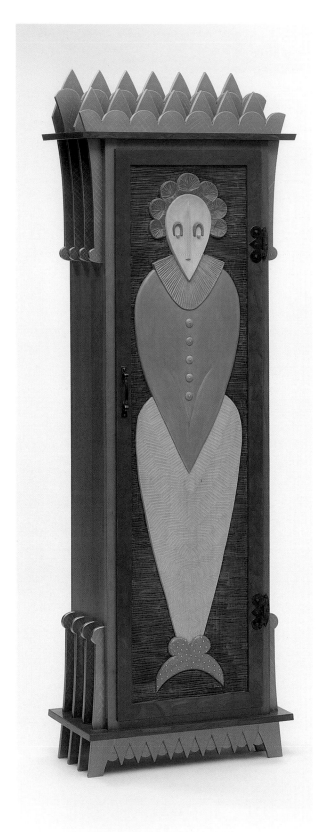

■ Mitch Ryerson, *Elizabethan Cabinet*, Cambridge, Massachusetts, 1988. Mahogany, maple, basswood, Baltic birch plywood, aromatic cedar, polychrome decoration; h. 78 in., w. 26 in., d. 13 in. Museum of Fine Arts, Boston; Gift of Anne and Ronald Abramson 1988.337.

rather than an expression of an individual's unique artistic abilities or sense of design. Many of the objects included in this exhibition and publication are somewhat indebted to historic prototypes and sources, but we have not included reproduction furniture because it does not fit within the parameters of studio furniture as we use the term in this book.

Our definition of studio furniture also does not include twentieth-century vernacular furniture makers, regional craftsmen who maintain local traditions. While the vernacular furniture made by these individuals is often outstanding, the circumstances of its creation and the traditions reflected nevertheless set it apart from the studio furniture movement. Much the same holds true for the "folk" furniture produced by twentieth-century folk artists in various guises.

An in-depth and sophisticated understanding of the practice of studio furniture is needed. Our hope is to offer insights into the varied backgrounds and approaches of the makers, the synergy of idea and technique, and the multifaceted meanings of the final product. Our intent is for this book to increase the understanding of the field for both the makers and the general public.

Toward that end, we have chosen a chronological approach for our presentation, beginning our analysis in the 1940s and 1950s, when the origins of what we identify as a movement can be discerned, moving forward through the decades into the 1980s. While the decades can be characterized by dominant themes—a reverence for wood in the 1940s and 1950s, challenged by a counterculture-based emphasis on the artistic qualities of furniture in the exciting 1960s, followed by a prevailing interest in various techniques in the 1970s, and the achievement of a level of professionalism and maturity in the 1980s—we recognize that there is a good deal of overlap and continuity in this relatively brief span of half a century. A number of the artists active during the nascent phase of the movement are still producing furniture today, for example, and many of the objects produced in the 1980s do not, in visual terms, differ dramatically from those made in the

1950s. Nevertheless, the passage of time has wrought changes—aesthetic and philosophical as well as cultural in the broadest sense—in the hearts and minds of the artists and in the general tenor of their work. Our goal here, then, is to identify and chart these major shifts, while understanding that a degree of simplification is unavoidable in any such condensation.

To supplement the essays, which are broadly thematic in approach, we have included brief biographies of forty-five makers—admittedly a minute portion of the thousands of artists active between 1940 and 1990, but, we feel, representative of those figures who have emerged as leaders in the field over the past decades. As indicated, most studio furniture makers, if not self-taught, have emerged from the academy, and even many of the self-taught woodworkers actually attended workshops and seminars in nondegree programs. For that reason, we have compiled a directory of college, university, and other educational programs that have given emphasis to studio furniture making throughout the period. A directory of galleries active before 1990 appears, too. It is followed by a select checklist of exhibitions—crucial to the development of public awareness and recognition of studio furniture—to provide a sense of the important venues and the ever-accelerating pace of furniture exhibitions during the fifty-year span. In addition, we offer a select bibliography of major works and seminal texts about studio furniture as a final resource.

■ Tom Loeser, chest, Cambridge, Massachusetts, 1988. Cherry with milk paint finish, curly maple, birch; h. 20 ⅛ in., w. 59 in., d. 16 in. Museum of Fine Arts, Boston; Gift of The Seminarians and Anonymous Gift 1988.332.

WOODWORKERS:
THE BEGINNINGS OF THE STUDIO FURNITURE MOVEMENT

In 1957, the Museum of Contemporary Crafts in New York City (now the Museum of Arts and Design) mounted an exhibition entitled "Furniture by Craftsmen." It showcased seventy-eight objects created by nearly forty woodworkers, whose locations ranged from Concord, New Hampshire, to Los Angeles. All of these craftsmen were key participants in this exciting new movement in the arts. As Thomas S. Tibbs, the museum's director, explained in his preface to the exhibition catalogue, furniture was "one of the last of the crafts to claim the solo spotlight," following in the footsteps of earlier shows of ceramics, metals, textiles, and other materials. The cover of the small catalogue was illustrated with linecuts from tool-company trade catalogues depicting chisels, a hammer, and a file, thus underscoring the handcrafted nature of the furniture pictured within.

Among the makers represented were many whose names remain familiar today—among them Wharton Esherick, Tage Frid, Sam Maloof, and George Nakashima—but the work of numerous other individuals, no longer so recognizable, was also included. All were men, except for Joyce Anderson of West Orange, New Jersey, who exhibited four pieces that she made with her husband Edgar (fig. 1). The substantial number of objects included clearly indicated that a critical mass of material had been produced by a widespread community of makers and thus was worthy of recognition in a New York venue as a phenomenon in its own right.[1]

What did the visitor to this exhibition see? From our twenty-first-century perspective, they saw furniture that speaks loudly and clearly of the 1950s—but that to many eyes would still look "modern" today. It included traditional forms of tables, chairs, and case pieces—often made of black walnut, cherry, African mahogany, or another hardwood, used in solid form or as veneered panels—along with other, more innovative forms. Most of the objects had essentially rectilinear or softly curving lines and were often supported by thin tapering legs. Although ornament and decoration appeared on a few examples, the visual appeal of the furniture was primarily a result of inherent simplicity: the rich appearance of its swirling, polished, wood-grain surfaces; its clean look; and its spare, sometimes gently contoured, forms. At first glance—especially in photographs, in which the quality of workmanship is not so evident—the objects in the exhibition do not seem to differ dramatically from more mainstream, mass-produced, furniture of the 1950s, such as (for example) the objects designed by Edward J. Wormley for the Dunbar Furniture Company of Berne, Indiana.[2] As Greta Daniel, an associate curator at the Museum of Modern Art, noted in a contemporary review of the exhibition, only a handful of objects in the show "reach new heights or solutions in design or reveal qualities that could not have been achieved by means of conventional factory production."[3] But the appearance of the work was perhaps not as significant as the *makers* and the *studio environment*

in which they were produced.

There had been a few precursors, largely on the regional level, to this 1957 show. An exhibition of contemporary New England handicrafts at the Worcester Art Museum in 1943, for example, had included two dozen pieces of furniture among a larger assemblage of objects made from materials other than wood. Most of the pieces of furniture in this Worcester show were not illustrated in the catalogue, but their descriptions suggest that they were largely in the Colonial Revival mode.[4]

A decade later, the American Craftsmen's Educational Council mounted a significant exhibition, itself a landmark, with the assistance of the Brooklyn Museum of Art and other institutions, entitled "Designer-Craftsmen U.S.A. 1953." The goal of the show was to assess on a nationwide basis "what is being done in the craft field in the United States," but again furniture was represented amid a host of objects in other materials.[5] Loren Manbeck of Massachusetts received a Grand Award (one of only four given) from the jurors for an elegant, rectilinear buffet-dining table. An extraordinary birch table with high, arching cast-aluminum legs by D. Lee DuSell of Illinois (fig. 3), a liquor cabinet by Tage Frid (see cat. no. 6), and a chair by Ronald Mathies also received awards. Works by Esherick and Nakashima were illustrated by Edward Wormley in his essay on wood in the catalogue.

Two years later, the Worcester Art Museum held another craft exhibition, this time with a decidedly more modern emphasis, but including only a few examples of furniture—by Walker T. Weed, Frank Rohloff, Alejandro de la Cruz, and Arnold J. Martin. John Risley noted in the catalogue that although a woodworker might use power tools, "in the deepest sense he has not lost the fine heritage of the colonial cabinetmaker." Such historical references to traditional American cabinetmaking were commonly used to contextualize modern craft work in these early exhibitions.[6]

The 1957 Museum of Contemporary Crafts exhibition indeed became a milestone in the history of the North American studio furniture movement. Its importance lies in the acknowledgment by a museum and by the scholarly community of the initial phase of a singular aspect of the arts that had begun about two decades earlier and continues to this day. The origins of this movement, which had coalesced and matured to the point of recognition by 1957, were rooted in the lives and creative acts of specific individuals who followed their own muse but who were also, as we can see in hindsight, affected by larger forces in American society during the early and mid-twentieth century that shaped their attitudes and values. In addition to the evidence in their work of aesthetic merit, careful craftsmanship, and stylistic innovation, the circumstances in which the pieces were created also proved important. As furniture historian Jonathan L. Fairbanks has noted, this group of individual artists and craftsmen "found personal ways in which to express their affection for wood and to make comfortable and beautiful furniture following abstract or ahistorical principles."[7]

To these pioneers of the studio furniture movement, taxonomy and terminology were important. Many, like Nakashima, chose to be called "woodworkers," while "craftsman" and "designer-craftsman" were other popular terms. Each title conveyed a sense that these individuals had skills both at the drawing board *and* at the workbench, as well as the fact that their heart, eyes, and hands were of equal importance in the creation of their work. "Designer-craftsman" also linked furniture makers with the wider, established world of good design and industrial design. Intent and meaning—both involved in the philosophy behind making furniture—were important issues to them, too. Many of these topics were discussed in 1957 at the Asilomar conference, the groundbreaking meeting of some 450 craftspeople on the Monterey Peninsula in California, devoted to exploring the place of the crafts and craftsmen in modern industrial society. Furniture makers, well represented at this meeting, were delighted to discover that they were part of a larger, national dialogue that embraced all crafts.[8]

It has long been noted, by both those who were themselves part of the movement and those on the outside looking in, that a key figure in the early days—probably *the* key artist—was Wharton Esherick (fig. 2). In fact, it is remarkable that his importance to the movement was recognized so early, that it has been consistently acknowledged by artists and authors alike, and that his influence persists. Wendell Castle, Arthur Espenet Carpenter, and Sam Maloof are but three of the many woodworkers, now influential in their own right, who recognized Esherick's impact on their lives and work, even if they never actually met the somewhat reclusive maker in person.[9]

While he stood at the beginning of the studio furniture movement, Esherick was a twentieth-century expression of a long-standing tradition of small-shop furniture making devoted to the production of custom-made or customized objects (called "bespoke" in earlier times) for wealthy clients. By the 1950s, the making of furniture in North America was well into its third century. In Boston, for example, it started in the 1630s, where the shops of Ralph Mason and Henry Messenger, among others, produced London-style joined furniture possibly embellished with turnings by members of the Thomas Edsall family. A chest of drawers with doors attributed to these craftsmen, carefully framed in oak, makes use of exotic tropical hardwoods, including snakewood veneers, applied split spindles of rosewood, and drawer knobs of lignum vitae. As such, it is superficially evocative of much twentieth-century

studio work, which also often emphasizes visible construction techniques and utilizes unusual and beautiful imported woods. The owner of such a piece in seventeenth-century Boston was probably a well-to-do merchant, who commissioned it directly from the shop. This face-to-face contact between craftsman and affluent patron is another parallel with the modern studio movement.[10]

The small-shop tradition held sway for almost two hundred years, after which time it was primarily replaced by the work of large factories, in which furniture was produced with the assistance of labor-saving, power-driven machinery (although some types of handwork and finishing have always been and remain part of factory furniture making). In the last quarter of the nineteenth century, several reform movements reacted against dehumanizing factory production, in which the artist and the maker were not only two separate people but also were often divorced from interaction with one another. The reformers argued for a reunification of designer and craftsman, placed a greater emphasis on the "artistic" aspects of furniture making, and sought,

Fig. 2. Wharton Esherick (1887–1970).

Fig. 3. D. Lee DuSell, dining table, Aurora, Illinois, about 1953. Birch, cast aluminum legs; h. 28 in., w. 83¾ in., d. 34¾ in. Collection of the artist.

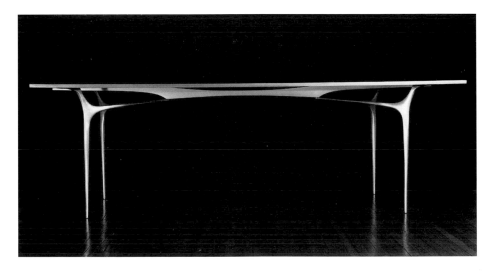

■ Fig. 4. Charles Eames, designer, Herman Miller Company and Evans Product Company, manufacturers, side chair (model DCW), Venice, California, 1946. Walnut plywood, rubber, metal; h. 28¼ in., w. 19¼ in., d. 20½ in. Museum of Fine Arts, Boston; gift of Edward J. Wormley 1975.32.

■ Fig. 5. (opposite page) George Howe, architect, Wharton Esherick, sculptor, "Pennsyl-vania Hill House" room from "America at Home" installation, New York World's Fair, 1940. From *Architectural Forum* 73, no. 1 (July 1940): 36. Photo, courtesy of Wharton Esherick Museum.

■ Cat. 1. Wharton Esherick, table and chairs, Paoli, Pennsylvania, 1940. Hickory table with black phenol top; h. 26½ in., w. 62½ in., d. 40½ in. Hickory chairs with rawhide seats; h. 32 in., w. 16½ in., d. 15½ in. Collection of Jack Lenor Larsen; courtesy of Longhouse Reserve, East Hampton, New York.

through craftwork, a balance between the intellectual and physical aspects of life. It is to the small shops of the Arts and Crafts era (with which it has many parallels) that the studio furniture movement can trace its most immediate origins, both in rhetoric and in practice.[11] Particularly important legacies of the Arts and Crafts movement include its emphasis on craftsmanship, its focus on woodworking design and construction as suitable educational and academic subjects, and the proliferation of home and small workshops—sometimes fitted with electric-powered woodworking tools. These and other developments would bear fruit in the studio furniture movement several decades later.[12]

After the First World War, the American furniture industry entered a period of stylistic dichotomy and market divergence from which it has never emerged and which is perhaps reflective of an increasingly stratified society. At one end, mass-produced factory furniture (made in such locations as Grand Rapids, Michigan; High Point, North Carolina; Jamestown, New York) remained largely fixated, stylistically, in the Colonial Revival (broadly conceived) that had started in the late nineteenth century. While some attempts were made to mass-produce more innovative designs in the 1920s and

1930s, they did not achieve much popularity. At the more expensive end of the market, "modern," machine-age furniture—often with tubular steel, chrome, and glass components and designed by immigrant or foreign artists—dominated the field. Largely resisted by middle-class consumers for domestic interiors, except for use in kitchens and other "high-tech" areas, these objects that we now generally call Art Deco or modernistic were most popular in institutional settings and among "high-brow" consumers. In the 1940s and 1950s, the husband-and-wife team of Charles (1907–1978) and Ray Eames (1912–1988) became perhaps the most important American furniture designers creating mass-produced objects in molded plywood (fig. 4), metal, and plastic. Many machine-age and Eames designs remained in production for years, and some continue even today, marketed as "originals" (from companies such as Herman Miller and Knoll) or as "knock-offs" (from other manufacturers).[13]

It was in this environment that Wharton Esherick, born in 1887, began to make furniture in the 1920s. Trained as a painter at the Pennsylvania Museum and School of Industrial Art, Esherick became dissatisfied with his work in paint and turned to woodworking, initially through carving woodcut engravings and fashioning sculpture. His efforts in sculpture and architecture, coupled with his dislike of most furniture available in the market at the time, led him to start creating his own objects. In the 1930s, responding to the general artistic trends of the time, he produced dramatic, innovative furniture in a Cubist, Art Deco mode.[14]

Much of Esherick's early work was restricted to objects for his own extraordinary home in Paoli, Pennsylvania (which he worked on throughout his life and which is a museum today) and for local customers in the greater Philadelphia area. His fame grew, however, when he worked with the architect George Howe on the design and installation of a "Pennsylvania Hill House," one of the prototype interiors (fig. 5) created for the "America at Home" display at the 1939–40 World's Fair held in New York City. This room, including an asymmetrical table with a phenol fiber top and accompanying chairs

(cat. no. 1) and the very staircase from Esherick's home, was seen by millions of people and widely publicized.[15] It was a major step, marking the transition of studio furniture from the work of a relatively isolated, perhaps even eccentric, artist to the beginnings of a movement with many practitioners that would resonate with a portion of the American public.

Esherick's table and chairs reveal some of the diverse qualities that typify Esherick's work and that defy easy categorization. The asymmetrical form of the table, its unusual black phenol top, and the exposed nature of the joinery of the objects reflect the myriad aspects of his work, including the influence of the "honest" construction of Arts and Crafts furniture, the flowing shapes of an organic style that would come to characterize Esherick's work, and the unexpected, unusual quirks of a Cubist or Expressionist sculptor.[16]

However, the potential breakthrough at the World's Fair was delayed by the onslaught of World War II. It wasn't until the postwar period that several factors coalesced to allow the work of Esherick to become an inspiration for others and the catalyst of a new movement. As the 1940s progressed, Esherick settled into a mode of free-form, sculptural expression that came to represent his work and became his hallmark for the remainder of his long and productive life. Not a teacher in the traditional sense, he led by example, letting his work, in effect, speak for him. Some of his pieces, like his walnut and cherry music stand of 1951 (cat. no. 2), became virtual icons in the studio furniture movement and inspired a host of similar works by dozens of makers. The sweeping cherry legs of this Esherick piece could be seen as wooden versions of tubular steel, and the whole object can be interpreted as a warm, soft version of modernism.

Esherick's 1950s sideboard (cat. no. 3), fashioned from assembled parts and painted blue, represents his penchant for adaptation of "found" materials and his use of color as a contrast to natural wood. He assembled a headboard and two cabinets into a new, buffet form and added a top, handles, feet, and some details. The result, like his hammer-handle chairs, wagon-wheel furniture, and other assembled objects, demonstrates Esherick's ability to manipulate prosaic materials into a pleasing, new aesthetic statement, in this case with the embellishment of a painted surface.

To many, Esherick is seen as a transitional figure between the Arts and Crafts era of the early twentieth century and the full-blown revival of the crafts movement in the 1950s, which took hold in a prosperous, optimistic society eager to rid itself of wartime shortages and to indulge in the acquisition of consumer goods. This climate during the cold-war years engendered both demand on the part of consumers and enough surplus capital to allow some individuals to pursue the risky and marginal activity of furniture making as a career rather than as a hobby.

In addition to Esherick, seminal figures in this first phase include George Nakashima (cat. nos. 4, 5, fig. 6) and Sam Maloof (see cat. nos. 9–11), each noted for an individualistic, almost instantly recognizable style produced consistently beginning in the 1950s. Other early woodworkers selected for discussion here also represent important themes that typify the early years of the movement. The Danish-

■ Cat. 4. George Nakashima, *Frenchman's Cove/Minguren I Hybrid Coffee Table*, New Hope, Pennsylvania, 1966. English walnut, rosewood; h. 17 in., w. 62 in., d. 45 in. Private collection; courtesy of Moderne Gallery.

■ Cat. 5. George Nakashima, grass-seated chair, New Hope, Pennsylvania, designed 1944; made 1971. Walnut, grass; h. 27½ in., w. 18 in., d. 18 in. Museum of Fine Arts, Boston; museum purchase with funds donated anonymously, Frederick Brown Fund, Bequest of Maxim Karolik and Gift of Estelle S. Frankfurter, by exchange, and American Decorative Arts Curator's Fund 2003.66.

■ Cat. 6. Tage Frid, liquor cabinet, Foster, Rhode Island, 1953. Rosewood veneer; h. 60 in., w. 36 in., d. 18 in. Collection of Ronald and Lawsanna Binks.

■ Fig. 6. George Nakashima (1905–1990).

born teacher and author Tage Frid (cat. no. 6), for example, created elegant, largely Neoclassical-style forms himself, but it is his emphasis on construction, promulgated through his classes at several schools and even more widely disseminated through his publications, that influenced makers from the 1950s to the present (see also chapter 3). The Spanish immigrant Alejandro de la Cruz (see cat. no. 7) and Walker Weed (see cat. no. 8), both of New Hampshire, represent a large number of craftsmen who worked independently in a historicist vein, drawing inspiration from the Early American vernacular tradition. Mary Gregory (see fig. 9, cat. no. 12), one of the first female woodworkers to enter the field, was a precursor of the gender diversity that would come to characterize the movement in its later phases. And Vladimir Kagan (see cat. no. 13) was a New York City–based designer whose shop, like Nakashima's, even in the 1950s, was staffed with a healthy number of craftsmen. In some respects, Kagan epitomized the larger-scale, more commercial aspects of the movement and the often blurry boundary between studio work and contract production.

This first generation of studio furniture makers can be defined by a return to, and reverence for,

■ Fig. 7. Hans Wegner, Y chair, Denmark, about 1950. Oak; h. 21¾ in., w. 21 in., d. 28⅜ in. Museum of Fine Arts, Boston; anonymous gift in memory of Lee Rome and Harold E. Rome, Fitchburg and New York 1987.749.

■ Cat. 7. Alejandro de la Cruz, Shaker candlestand, Canterbury, New Hampshire, about 1960–75. Curly maple; h. 25¾ in., top diam. 14¾ in. Private collection.

wood as a primary material. While wood has always been the traditional material for furniture, most early studio furniture makers carried their love for it to an extreme, especially (but far from exclusively) in the case of George Nakashima. Perhaps as a reaction against the industrial, machine-age products of the 1930s and, looking even further back, as a rejection of the heavily ornamented surfaces of much late-nineteenth-century furniture, the most prominent makers of the 1950s regarded wood with respect and made great use of its inherent qualities, eschewing both alternative materials and the use of decorative embellishments such as inlay and carving. Sam Maloof said, "If you're working in wood, you just don't want to work in anything else. Why? Well, it's the warmth, the texture, the *feel* of wood....I don't need other materials."[17] Nakashima spoke of and wrote about the "soul of a tree," a touch of Asian mysticism that was prevalent in the movement during this decade (and which still echoes among many artists and craftsmen today). According to Nakashima, "each flitch, each board, each plank can have only one ideal use. The woodworker, applying a thousand skills, must find that ideal use and then

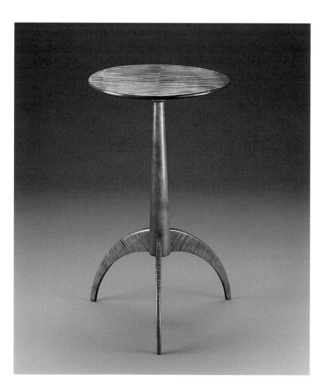

shape the wood to realize its true potential. The result is our ultimate object, plain and simple."[18] And, as Tage Frid explained, "working with a material of such natural beauty, I feel that we have to design very quietly and use simple forms."[19]

Nakashima's large coffee table, with a top of carefully selected, highly figured English walnut and butterfly cleats of rosewood (see cat. no. 4, fig. 6), reflects his belief in letting the wood speak for itself in a simple and eloquent way, with a minimum of overt, "artificial" manipulation. Nakashima went to great lengths to find, stockpile, and carefully select timbers for specific pieces, often choosing them for their decorative qualities that would enhance a specific object. He thus designed around the material, showcasing its natural properties and often leaving bark edges, checks, and other naturally occurring features of the tree intact.[20]

In retrospect, the products of these seminal furniture makers reveal a number of common stylistic characteristics (although it is always true that a movement is comprised of the work of many individuals who either often or occasionally produce highly idiosyncratic furniture that defies characterization). The key influence on the work of this period was imported Scandinavian ("Danish Modern") furniture, exemplified by the work of Danish designers such as Hans Wegner (fig. 7), and rooted in the Danish small-shop tradition.[21] Some of the simpler products of the Colonial and Federal eras ("traditional Early American"), especially Windsor chairs and Neoclassical tables and case pieces, provided a second major influence, perhaps stimulated by the interest in historic preservation and collecting Early Americana that began in the 1870s and blossomed in the 1920s and 1930s. Nineteenth-century Shaker furniture, consistently praised for its "modern" appearance, was another important historical reference point for many makers.

The maple candlestand by Alejandro de la Cruz (cat. no. 7), modeled after a Shaker prototype, reflects the strong impact of Early American furniture—including Colonial and Federal designs as well as Shaker forms—on both professional and amateur members of the studio furniture movement.

De la Cruz's workshop was located next to Canterbury Shaker Village in New Hampshire, and much of his clientele preferred furniture with historical antecedents and prototypes. Some of his work was also indebted to the eighteenth-century objects produced by members of the Dunlap family of New Hampshire cabinetmakers.[22]

Walker Weed's desk and chair (cat. no. 8), exhibited in the 1957 "Furniture by Craftsmen" show at the Museum of Contemporary Crafts, are beautiful expressions relating back to the Windsor chair and to Federal-period forms. Weed, a 1940 graduate of Dartmouth College, chose a career in cabinetwork in rural New Hampshire and was soon recognized and praised for his solid designs that were "sound and undeniably sensible in a rock-ribbed Yankee sort of way." His use of contrasting light and dark woods—evocative of Federal-period furniture from northeastern Massachusetts and New Hampshire—and "deliberate accentuation of grain" give his work striking visual appeal and expression. His flat-topped desk contains a tier of drawers at each side and is supported by slightly flaring, subtly shaped legs. The chair has a substantial, rectangular crest rail, a spindle back, and similar legs tenoned into the seat block.[23]

While the first generation of studio furniture craftsmen can fairly be associated with a reverence for wood, their attitude toward the material was not necessarily reflected in a concomitant reverence for so-called handcraftsmanship, as is often suggested. Like craftsmen in the eighteenth century, who adopted new labor-saving technology as soon as practicable, most early studio furniture makers used machines to reduce drudge labor, enabling them to make objects more quickly and efficiently (without compromising their aesthetic principles). Esherick expressed his attitude toward handicraft in an oft-quoted outburst: "This thing you call handicraft, I say, 'Stop that thing.' I use any damn machinery I can get hold of. The top of this table was all done by machine. We didn't rub it by hand. Handcrafted has nothing to do with it. I'll use my teeth if I have to. There's a little of the hand, but the main thing is the heart and the head. Handcrafted! I say, 'Applesauce!'

Stop it!"[24] The essential aspect of craft for early studio furniture makers was the maintenance of individual control over the process of fabrication from beginning to end, from the mind of the creator to the home of the consumer. The maintenance of such control allowed for the use of power machinery and, when appropriate, the incorporation of modern fastening hardware. It did not preclude the employment of a small number of day-workers (journeymen, in older days) and apprentices or the farming-out of certain tasks to specialists—as Maloof has done with his upholstery, for example.

Furniture makers of this first generation derived their training in a variety of ways. Relatively few, it seems, had benefited from the classic master-apprenticeship system that had characterized the transmission of mechanical knowledge from one generation to the next for so many centuries; those who were so trained, such as Frid and de la Cruz, had developed their skills in Europe prior to arrival in this country. Many, such as Esherick (painting), Nakashima (architecture), and Maloof (graphic design), were trained in various other art forms but were largely self-taught in the field of woodworking—learning at the bench through trial and error, occasionally benefiting from the help of a more experienced craftsman. Others came to the field

■ Cat. 8. Walker T. Weed, desk, Gilford, New Hampshire, 1957. Walnut, butternut; h. 28 ½ in., w. 54 in., d. 25 in. Block-back chair, Gilford, New Hampshire, 1956. Black walnut; h. 31 ½ in., w. 17 ½ in., d. 17 ½ in. Collection of the craftsman.

■ Fig. 8. George Nakashima, Conoid side chair, New Hope, Pennsylvania, 1979. Walnut, hickory; h. 35 ½ in., w. 19 ½ in., d. 22 ¾ in. Museum of Fine Arts, Boston; purchased through funds provided by the National Endowment for the Arts and Deborah M. Noonan Foundation 1979.274.

■ Cat. 9. Sam Maloof, rocking chair, Alta Loma, California, 1975. Walnut; h. 44 in., w. 27 ¾ in., d. 46 in. Museum of Fine Arts, Boston; purchased through funds provided by the National Endowment for the Arts and the Gillette Corporation 1976.122.

through training in the academic world, following a career path that would become so common in later years, it was almost routine.[25]

The Cranbrook Academy of Art in Bloomfield Hills, Michigan, founded in the late 1920s, became the first American institution to emphasize the links between art and design, but the emphasis at Cranbrook remained on industrial design rather than craft.[26] In 1943, the School for American Craftsmen (SAC) was inaugurated at Dartmouth College in Hanover, New Hampshire (it later migrated to Alfred University in New York and eventually, in 1950, to the Rochester Institute of Technology, where its name changed to the School for American Crafts). The SAC was the first program to offer a major in woodworking and furniture design. Established, like many other efforts in the crafts at the time, as a means of rehabilitating war veterans, the SAC soon moved to an emphasis on improving craftsmanship in American life. [27]

An important step occurred in 1948 when Tage Frid joined the faculty to teach furniture design. Frid, who had been apprenticed to a master cabinetmaker and who had also graduated from the Copenhagen School of Interior Design, brought with him an old-world emphasis on techniques and skills. SAC students, under Frid's tutelage, quickly achieved impressive results. In 1950, Henry J. Bayer of the SAC received first prize for woodworking from the American Craftsmen's Educational Council for a rectangular table with arched legs.[28] Frid's approach to woodworking was articulated in numerous articles in *Fine Woodworking* beginning in 1975, then later in book form in a three-volume set. Largely due to Frid's impact upon generations of students and amateurs alike, a preoccupation with construction techniques has become a standard part of the studio furniture movement.[29]

Two pioneers—George Nakashima and Sam Maloof—came to the field in different ways. Nakashima, who had been imprisoned during World War II because of his Japanese heritage, was trained as an architect in this country and abroad, and had some experience with the firms of Knoll and Widdicomb as an industrial designer. He settled in

New Hope, Pennsylvania, in the 1940s, where he eventually operated a small shop with as many as a dozen employees. His experiences as a production contractor for large companies were not outstandingly successful, and, as expressiveness took over his work, he began to crave control over the creation of furniture, from start to finish, in a hands-on way. Blending Japanese spiritualism and nature-worship with Yankee-style entrepreneurship, Nakashima came to produce perhaps as many as seventy-five line items, particularly chairs.

Designed in the 1940s, his grass-seated chair (see cat. no. 5) makes extensive use of pins to secure the mortise-and-tenon joints of its construction and is also unusual in its use of twisted seagrass as seating material. Its raking proportions—with the seat extended forward—and the use of three clusters of paired spindles give the chair a distinctive, modern look, setting it apart from historical prototypes. Nakashima's famous Conoid chairs (fig. 8), with their architecturally inspired cantilevered seats, were designed in about 1960 and are more closely aligned with Windsor chair forms. They differ dramatically from precedents, however, in their incorporation of so-called sled runners, which allow for the heavy chairs to be moved more easily. Like Maloof, Nakashima is perhaps best understood in the context of the beginnings of the studio furniture movement. Still, he continued to be a major component of the movement well into the 1980s.[30]

A master of the band saw, Maloof was largely self-taught in woodworking and still practices today. Since opening his first woodshop in 1948, he has succeeded through the endless variation and subtle refinement of a formula of restrained, sculptural furniture of walnut and maple that seems to have instant appeal to most consumers. Best known for his seating furniture, including benches and rockers (cat. no. 9), Maloof has produced all forms of furniture (see cat. nos. 10, 11) throughout his career. Like many other furniture makers, he built and poured much of his creative energy into his own house.[31]

Maloof's cork-topped desk of 1953 and prototype dining chair of 1952 (cat. no. 10), representing the earliest phases of his work, are somewhat tenta-

tive and restrained. They also demonstrate the influence that furniture by Finn Juhl and the Danish small-shop tradition had on Maloof. The chair, part of a commission from the famous industrial designer Henry Dreyfuss, has a sculptured walnut crest rail as well as walnut "socks" in which the light-colored maple legs are housed and ostentatiously double-pinned. Other pins and joints are made prominent, emphasizing the technical virtuosity involved in producing this early chair. Similar details are evident on the desk.

A large cradle-cabinet (or cradle hutch) of 1968 (cat. no. 11) has been termed Maloof's "most unusual" design by his biographer, Jeremy Adamson. Created for an exhibition at the Museum of Contemporary Crafts entitled "The Bed," this form represented a new venture for Maloof. The case piece is supported by short, tapered legs rising to a section housing six drawers. The swinging cradle is sensibly placed at a height where it can easily be reached. A pair of cupboards is placed over the cradle, and the whole is surmounted by a slightly projecting flat top. Despite its size, the cradle-cabinet retains an air of lightness that has been likened to Shaker furniture but also echoes the spareness and delicacy of some Chinese forms. Over time, Maloof has made five more examples, each with characteristic subtle modifications and adjustments, as well as a related desk hutch of about 1970, fashioned for his own use.[32]

Maloof's classic spindle-back walnut rocker of 1975 (cat. no. 9) defines an expression of his more fully developed oeuvre. It is part of a dozen Maloof pieces commissioned by Jonathan L. Fairbanks for the innovative "Please Be Seated" program of gallery seating at the Museum of Fine Arts, Boston. The work has a solid seat, a bit saddle-shaped for comfort, and is regarded as one of the first examples in which Maloof made use of a dado-rabbet joint to secure the legs and the long, curved rockers. The gently curved arms, wide seat, and high back make the rocker visually pleasing for its interplay of soft and sharp lines, and most people find it exceptionally comfortable.[33]

■ Cat. 10. Sam Maloof, cork-topped desk, Alta Loma, California, 1953. Maple, walnut, cork; h. 28¾ in., w. 54¼ in., d. 23 in. Prototype dining chair, Alta Loma, California, 1952. Maple, walnut, leather upholstery; h. 29¼ in., w. 19⅞ in., d. 21 in. Sam Maloof Collection.

■ Cat. 11. Sam Maloof, cradle-cabinet, Alta Loma, California, 1968. Walnut; h. 68½ in., w. 47¾ in., d. 18 in. Museum of Arts and Design; gift of the Johnson Wax Company, from "Objects: USA," 1977. Donated to the American Craft Museum by the American Craft Council, 1990 1977.2.56.

Sam Maloof is probably the best-known maker in the movement today—his excellent reputation has been fostered by the high and long-sustained quality of his work and also through his abilities as a teacher, marketer, and record keeper. His standing in the field has been enhanced by Jeremy Adamson's magisterial and exhaustive study of his work, published in 2001 to accompany a retrospective exhibition at the Renwick Gallery of the Smithsonian American Art Museum in Washington, D.C. Maloof's importance is heightened by the stimulus he provided to the movement on the West Coast, especially in its early years. He continues to be a major national figure.

Historically, furniture making has been a male-dominated craft, and this would remain true in the early years of the studio movement. Despite that fact, along with limited career opportunities for women in general in the 1950s, there were exceptions, including Mary Gregory and Joyce Anderson, whose work was often produced in conjunction with her husband Edgar. After training and teaching experience garnered at Black Mountain College in North Carolina in the 1940s (fig. 9), Gregory worked in Vermont before settling in Massachusetts in the mid-1950s. Her small shop (which had a few male employees) produced furniture, including a large walnut sideboard (cat. no. 12), in a distinctive mode that blends a variety of joinery and ornamental characteristics. Especially notable in the sideboard are the arched support at the base and the rhythmic drawer arrangement; a large cupboard for trays is also cleverly included at the back of the case.[34]

In New York, German-born Vladimir Kagan operated in a slightly different manner, beginning in 1947. The son of a Russian cabinetmaker who moved to Germany, Kagan received both academic training in architecture at Columbia University and hands-on training from his father Illi in his workshop. This combination of design and cabinetmaking skills soon allowed him to run his own successful shop, which catered to wealthy clients such as Marilyn Monroe, Gary Cooper, and Walt Disney, as well as many large corporations. While never achiev-

■ Fig. 9. Mary Gregory, modular stools or tables, 1941–46. Photographed at Black Mountain College, North Carolina, 1940s. Photo, courtesy of North Carolina State Archives

■ Cat. 12. Mary Gregory, sideboard, Lincoln, Massachusetts, about 1961–65. Walnut, white pine; h. 36½ in., w. 62 in., d. 20 in. Private collection.

■ Cat. 13. Vladimir Kagan, low-back lounge chair, New York, New York, introduced 1955. Walnut, leather; h. 32 in., w. 29 in., d. 32 in. Collection of Vladimir Kagan.

ing a level of production that could be termed industrial, his shop employed up to thirty craftsmen at one time, and Kagan's own role teetered between that of a designer (like Charles Eames) and a maker (like Sam Maloof). Kagan's shop was more of a studio than a factory, but his work, such as his low-back lounge chair (cat. no. 13), reflects some of the difficulties involved when attempting to narrowly define individual furniture makers. An exhibition of his furniture in 1980 stated that each Kagan product was "entirely and obviously hand made from beginning to end" and that "Kagan is in the workshop working with his craftsmen with each new design, and follows through with them from the sketch to completion of the piece." While Kagan clearly had the requisite skills, the large size of his shop and its level of production suggest that his efforts were directed, at least occasionally, as much toward design control and supervision as toward fabrication—in other words, toward establishing the workmanship of certainty, characteristic of the design world, rather than toward exploring the workmanship of risk, more typical of studio furniture.[35]

The marketing of furniture by Kagan and Nakashima was unusual for its time. Although some craft fairs and galleries existed, most furniture was sold directly from artist to client. Shop One in Rochester, New York, a gallery that featured many types of material, also sold furniture, due to the involvement of Tage Frid, but it was the exception rather than the rule at this early stage of the movement. Notable among the few counterparts were the Bertha Schaefer Gallery in New York City, which showed studio furniture in the context of contemporary art, and the America House shop, affiliated with the Museum of Contemporary Crafts.

From the Second World War to 1960, studio furniture clearly became a significant part of the larger revival of the crafts in America. Current observers may believe that this initial phase was dominated by a few key figures, who have become well known as "old masters," but the record of the period reveals the presence of many other pioneers whose work deserves to be rediscovered and recognized.

Despite contemporary protestations to the contrary, it is difficult not to see studio furniture as a revival of the Arts and Crafts movement, which, by the 1950s, had dissipated due to the hardships and disruptions caused by two world wars and the Great Depression. Studio furniture makers reacted against the hard-edged, metallic aesthetic of the machine age in the same way that Arts and Crafts reformers rejected the elaborate gewgaws of the high Victorian era. As mentioned earlier, both movements shared a romantic notion of the benefits of craftwork and emphasized (at least in print) the "honesty" and integrity of materials and technique as well as the importance of education through woodworking.

In spite of its viability, studio furniture remained a marginal activity in the context of society at large into the 1960s. Many factors— such as the relatively high cost of the objects (when compared with factory furniture), the necessity and concomitant difficulty of obtaining them (in most cases) directly from the artist, and the lack of periodicals in which one could learn about the objects and their makers—all made studio furniture a luxury primarily of interest to consumers who were both reasonably wealthy and uncommonly persistent. *Craft Horizons* (now *American Craft*), the sole journal of significance at the time, contained only scattered articles, advertisements, and notices of furniture-related exhibitions at this early date, and its circulation in the mid-1960s was limited to about twenty-seven thousand members of the Museum of Contemporary Crafts.[36]

Mainstream society remained more attuned to readily available, less expensive Danish Modern and Early American–style furniture, to say nothing of new "Populuxe" consumer goods that came to the market, such as televisions, enormous cars with big tail fins, and push-button washing machines and stoves. New, blue-collar phenomena such as bowling alleys, diners, and trailer parks also became preoccupations of the middle class.[37] Although little is known about the consumers of studio furniture, it seems likely that they were part of what Russell Lynes characterized as "highbrow" culture, or perhaps "upper middle-brow."[38]

In the 1960s, studio furniture, like many other aspects of American life, saw dramatic changes, deplored by some people, championed by others. The careers of many earlier makers continued and flourished, but, as we shall see, a new wave of individuals challenged and questioned what had quickly become traditional notions about skill, materials, quality, beauty, and the necessity of utility. Of paramount importance to changes in the field was the concept, growing in adherents, that studio furniture is and should be Art, not just Craft. "Artist-craftsman," rather than "designer-craftsman" or "woodworker," seemed to be the term increasingly used for purposes of self-definition among practitioners who shared this new vision as the fifties gave way to the sixties.

NOTES

1. See Museum of Contemporary Crafts, *Furniture by Craftsmen*, exh. cat. (New York: Museum of Contemporary Crafts, 1957), 7. This essay is heavily indebted to the generational approach to the studio furniture movement articulated in Edward S. Cooke, Jr., *New American Furniture: The Second Generation of Studio Furnituremakers*, exh. cat. (Boston: Museum of Fine Arts, 1989); for a discussion of the first generation, see 11–14. Many of the first-generation makers are profiled in the excellent survey by Michael A. Stone, *Contemporary American Woodworkers* (Salt Lake City, Utah: Gibbs M. Smith, 1986), including Esherick, Frid, Maloof, and Nakashima, as well as the turner Bob Stocksdale.

2. See *Dunbar: Fine Furniture of the 1950s* (Atglen, Pa.: Schiffer Publishing, 2000). See also Judith Gura et al., eds., *Edward Wormley: The Other Face of Modernism*, exh. cat. (New York: DESIGNbase/Lin-Weinberg Gallery, 1997); Cara Greenberg, *Mid-Century Modern: Furniture of the 1950s* (New York: Harmony Books, 1984); and Leslie Piña, *Fifties Furniture* (Atglen, Pa.: Schiffer Publishing, 1996).

3. Greta Daniel article in *Craft Horizons* 17, no. 2 (March–April 1957): 34–38; quotation from 35.

4. *An Exhibition of Contemporary New England Handicrafts*, exh. cat. (Worcester, Mass.: Worcester Art Museum, 1943); the furniture objects are listed on 11.

5. American Craftsmen's Educational Council, *Designer-Craftsmen U.S.A. 1953*, exh. cat. (New York: Blanchard Press, 1953), 1. The exhibition was reviewed in *Craft Horizons* 13, no. 6 (November–December 1953): 12–18.

6. Worcester Art Museum, *New England Craft Exhibition—1955*, exh. cat. (Worcester, Mass.: Worcester Art Museum, 1955), 26. The exhibition was organized by the museum, the Junior League of Worcester, and the Craft Center of Worcester.

7. See Jonathan L. Fairbanks, foreword to Cooke, *New American Furniture*, 7.

8. See an "on-the-scene" report on the conference in *Craft Horizons* 17, no. 4 (July–August 1957): 17–36.

9. See Stone, *Contemporary American Woodworkers*, 4. See also statements by Maloof and Castle in *Craft Horizons* 30, no. 4 (August 1970): 11–13; and John Marcoux's letter in *Fine Woodworking*, no. 41 (July–August 1983): 6, 8.

10. See Gerald W. R. Ward, *American Case Furniture in the Mabel Brady Garvan and Other Collections at Yale University* (New Haven: Yale University Art Gallery, 1988), cat. no. 51. See also Jonathan L. Fairbanks and Robert F. Trent, *New England Begins: The Seventeenth Century*, exh. cat., 3 vols. (Boston: Museum of Fine Arts, 1982), cat. no. 481.

11. The best survey of American furniture as a whole from the seventeenth century to the 1980s is Jonathan L. Fairbanks and Elizabeth Bidwell Bates, *American Furniture, 1620 to the Present* (New York: Richard Marek, 1981). For the Arts and Crafts movement and its complicated ideology, see Wendy Kaplan et al., *"The Art That is Life": The Arts and Crafts Movement in America, 1875–1920*, exh. cat. (Boston: Museum of Fine Arts, 1987).

12. Edward S. Cooke, Jr., "Arts and Crafts Furniture: Process or Product?" in *The Ideal Home, 1900–1920: The History of Twentieth-Century American Craft*, exh. cat., ed. Janet Kardon, 75–76 (New York: Harry N. Abrams in association with the American Craft Museum, 1993). See also *Education through Woodworking: A Series of Prize Winning Essays, Practical Hints on the Operation of Woodworking Machines, Floor Plans and Machine Specifications for Woodworking Departments* (Rochester, N.Y.: Education Department, American Wood Working Machinery Company, 1924), with an introduction by Arthur Dean.

13. See Christian G. Carron et al., *Grand Rapids Furniture: The Story of America's Furniture City* (Grand Rapids, Mich.: Public Museum of Grand Rapids, 1998); Richard Guy Wilson et al., *The Machine Age in America, 1918–1941*, exh. cat. (New York: Brooklyn Museum in association with Harry N. Abrams, 1986); Pat Kirkham, *Charles and Ray Eames: Designers of the Twentieth Century*, exh. cat. (Cambridge, Mass.: MIT Press, 1995); Linda Foa, "Knocking Off the Classics," *New York* 9, no. 3 (January 19, 1970): 54.

14. Among the voluminous, scattered literature on Esherick, see the chapter in Stone, *Contemporary American Woodworkers*, 4–17; *Half a Century in Wood: 1920–1970, The Woodenworks of Wharton Esherick*, exh. cat. (Paoli, Pa.: Wharton Esherick Museum, 1988); Robert Edwards and Robert Aibel, *Wharton Esherick, 1887–1970, American Woodworker*, exh. cat. (Philadelphia: Moderne Gallery, 1996); and *The Wharton Esherick Museum Studio and Collection* (Paoli, Pa.: Wharton Esherick Museum, 1977). There remains no major biography of this important American artist.

15. See Howe's article, for example, in *Architectural Forum* 73, no. 1 (July 1940): 31–39. For the World's Fair, see David J. Gelertner, *1939: The Lost World of the Fair* (New York: Free Press, 1995), 353–54, which indicates that final attendance for the two years of the fair was 45,000,385.

16. We are grateful to Robert Aibel of the Moderne Gallery for bringing this object to our attention and for sharing his insights into its significance.

17. Quoted in Glenn Loney, "Sam Maloof," *Craft Horizons* 31, no. 4 (August 1971): 19.

18. George Nakashima, *The Soul of a Tree: A Woodworker's Reflections* (Tokyo, New York, and San Francisco: Kodansha International, 1981), xxi.

19. Quoted in Stone, *Contemporary American Woodworkers*, 49.

20. For the historic use of wood in a related manner, known as "tree art" in earlier times, see Craig Gilborn, *Adirondack Furniture and the Rustic Tradition* (New York: Harry N. Abrams, 1987), especially "The Background: Rustic Taste in England and America," 21–48.

21. See Noritsuga Oda, *Danish Chairs* (1996; reprint, San Francisco: Chronicle Books, 1999) for a good pictorial survey of influential seating furniture.

22. Measured drawings of early American furniture were published by many authors in the middle years of the twentieth century. Among the more popular titles were Edgar and Verna Cook Salomonsky, *An Exemplar of Antique Furniture Design* (Grand Rapids, Mich.: Periodical Publishing Company, 1923); Burl N. Osburn, *Measured Drawings of Early American Furniture* (Milwaukee: Bruce Publishing Company, 1926); Verna Cook Salomonsky, *Masterpieces of Furniture Design* (Grand Rapids, Mich.: Periodical Publishing Company, 1931); John Gerald Shea and Paul Nolt Wenger, *Colonial Furniture* (New York: Bruce Publishing Company, 1935); Lester Margon, *Construction of American Furniture Treasures* (New York: Home Craftsman Publishing Corporation, 1949); Franklin H. Gottshall, *Heirloom Furniture* (New York: Bonanza Books, 1957). Evidence of the continuing importance of this aspect of furniture making is the formation in 2001 of the Society of American Period Furniture Makers (SAPFM), an organization that publishes a journal, presents awards for distinguished craftsmanship, and provides other services for this community.

23. C. B., "Walker Weed, Yankee Cabinetmaker," *Craft Horizons* 17, no. 1 (February 1957): 37–39. See also Dartmouth College Museums and Galleries, *Walker Weed: A Retrospective Exhibition, 1950–1981*, exh. cat. (Hanover, N.H.: Dartmouth College Museum and Galleries, 1981); Richard Starr, "Portfolio: Walker Weed," *Fine Woodworking*, no. 38 (January–February 1983): 66–69.

24. Quoted in "The New American Craftsman: First Generation," *Craft Horizons* 26, no. 3 (June 1966): 15–34.

25. Some resources were available for the person seeking training in "modern" (as opposed to reproduction) furniture making, primarily industrial arts textbooks and a few other "how-to-do-it" manuals. See, for example, Norman Cherner, *Make Your Own Modern Furniture* (New York: McGraw-Hill, 1951); John L. Feirer, *Advanced Woodwork and Furniture Making* (Peoria, Ill.: Charles A. Bennett Company, 1954); and John L. Feirer, *Cabinetmaking and Millwork* (Peoria, Ill.: Charles A. Bennett Company, 1967). Many more such works were published in the 1970s and 1980s.

26. *Design in America: The Cranbrook Vision*, exh. cat. (New York: Harry N. Abrams, 1983).

27. The importance of craft training for veteran rehabilitation is demonstrated in Kendall T. Bassett and Arthur B. Thurman, in collaboration with Victor D'Amico, *How to Make Objects of Wood* (New York: Museum of Modern Art, 1951), a volume in the museum's "Art for Beginners" series distributed by Simon and Schuster. The captions for many of the illustrations simply identify objects as being made "by a veteran."

28. See *Craft Horizons* 10, no. 3 (autumn 1950): 38–39.

29. See Tage Frid, *Tage Frid Teaches Woodworking*, 3 vols.: vol. 1, *Joinery*; vol. 2, *Shaping, Veneering, Finishing*; vol. 3, *Furnituremaking* (Newtown, Conn.: Taunton Press, 1979–85).

30. Derek E. Ostergard, *George Nakashima: Full Circle*, exh. cat. (New York: Weidenfeld and Nicolson, 1989); Nakashima, *The Soul of a Tree*; Steven Beyer, *George Nakashima and the Modernist Movement*, exh. cat. (Doylestown, Pa.: James A. Michener Art Museum, 2001).

31. Jeremy Adamson, *The Furniture of Sam Maloof*, exh. cat. (Washington, D.C.: Smithsonian American Art Museum, 2001), is an invaluable resource. Maloof's own book, *Sam Maloof Woodworker* (Tokyo, New York, and London: Kodansha International, 1983), with an introduction by Jonathan L. Fairbanks, did much to secure his reputation in the world at large. A paperback edition was released in 1988.

32. Adamson, *The Furniture of Sam Maloof*, 128–36.

33. Ibid., 175–76.

34. Edward S. Cooke, Jr., "Women Furniture Makers: From Decorative Designers to Studio Makers," in Pat Kirkham, ed., *Women Designers in the USA, 1900–2000: Diversity and Difference*, exh. cat. (New Haven and London: Yale University Press, for the Bard Graduate Center for Studies in the Decorative Arts, New York, 2000), 296–98.

35. Numerous promotional materials on Kagan are included in his artist's file, Department of Art of the Americas, MFA. See, in particular, *Twenty Years of Vladimir Kagan Designs: Furniture Classics for the Connoisseur* (New York: Vladimir Kagan Designs International, 1967). See also *Kagan: Three Decades of Design*, exh. cat. (New York: Galleries at FIT, 1980); and David Pye, *The Nature and Art of Workmanship* (Cambridge and New York: Cambridge University Press, 1968).

36. Circulation statistics were provided by the American Craft Museum (now the Museum of Arts and Design), based on the museum's membership figures (synonymous with circulation) at the time.

37. See Thomas Hine, *Populuxe* (New York: Alfred A. Knopf, 1986); and Andrew Hurley, *Diners, Bowling Alleys, and Trailer Parks: Chasing the American Dream in Postwar Consumer Culture* (New York: Basic Books, 2001).

38. Lynes's essay originally appeared in *Harper's* and was given even greater popularity through its translation by Tom Funk into a chart published in *Life* magazine. For a discussion of these classifications and the limitations of their applications, see Michael Kammen, *American Culture, American Tastes: Social Change and the Twentieth Century* (New York: Alfred A. Knopf, 1999), 98–99.

THE CHALLENGE OF FREEWHEELING ARTIST-CRAFTSMEN:
TRADITION AND INNOVATION IN THE 1960S

Dominating the mainstream American furniture industry of the 1960s were the long-standing Colonial Revival and the more recent, but nevertheless entrenched, International Style. Enriching this mix were other historicist trends (for example, Mediterranean and French Provincial styles) and modernist furniture designed by such notables as T. H. Robsjohn-Gibbings for Widdicomb and Edward J. Wormley for Dunbar.

In 1962, a new idiom—Pop art— entered the marketplace. Drawn largely from Italian designers, this style was also expressed in American work. "Optimistic, celebratory, free from the constraints of the past," Pop art furniture was meant to be "fun." It made use of new synthetic materials and bright colors and was inspired by the basic arts of consumerism—packaging, comic books, advertising. Pop art was part of what social commentator Tom Wolfe called the "Happiness Revolution." It became the most typical form of the 1960s in the world of design, replacing the biomorphic shapes and boomerang fad of the 1950s.[1]

American furniture manufacturers, in a decade of slow growth, found their most lucrative market in the corporate and institutional worlds, although some designs, such as Warren Platner's wirework chairs and table of the mid-sixties produced by Knoll International (fig. 1), inevitably found their way into more affluent households. The existence of multiple styles and varying ideologies characteristic of the mainstream furniture industry echoed new develop-

ments in studio furniture, which continued to occupy only a small part of the furnishings market.

As the 1950s rolled into the 1960s, the careers of many studio furniture pioneers continued to evolve and, in some cases, to prosper. The furniture of these woodworkers, with its subtle modifications by individual makers, moved forward largely along the trajectory that had been established earlier. Wharton Esherick, who was by now in his seventies, continued to produce and exhibit his sculptural forms during the last decade of his life. As the acknowledged founder of the movement, Esherick maintained a strong influence on the field. Both George Nakashima and Sam Maloof gained increasing national attention for their ongoing, ever more refined, work during the 1960s: Nakashima's coffee table (see cat. no. 4) and Maloof's large, prototype cradle-cabinet (see cat. no. 11), an ingenious blend of case and sleeping furniture, were both made in 1966.

But the tumultuous period, marked by such dramatic events as the Kennedy assassination, the Civil Rights movement, and domestic upheavals over the war in Vietnam, also witnessed a significant shift in thinking in some quarters about the essence and meaning of furniture. The 1950s emphasis may have been on making good furniture that became great art, but many in the 1960s wanted to make great art that happened to be furniture.

Each side of this debate—art versus craft—had its staunch supporters. What some (including Rose

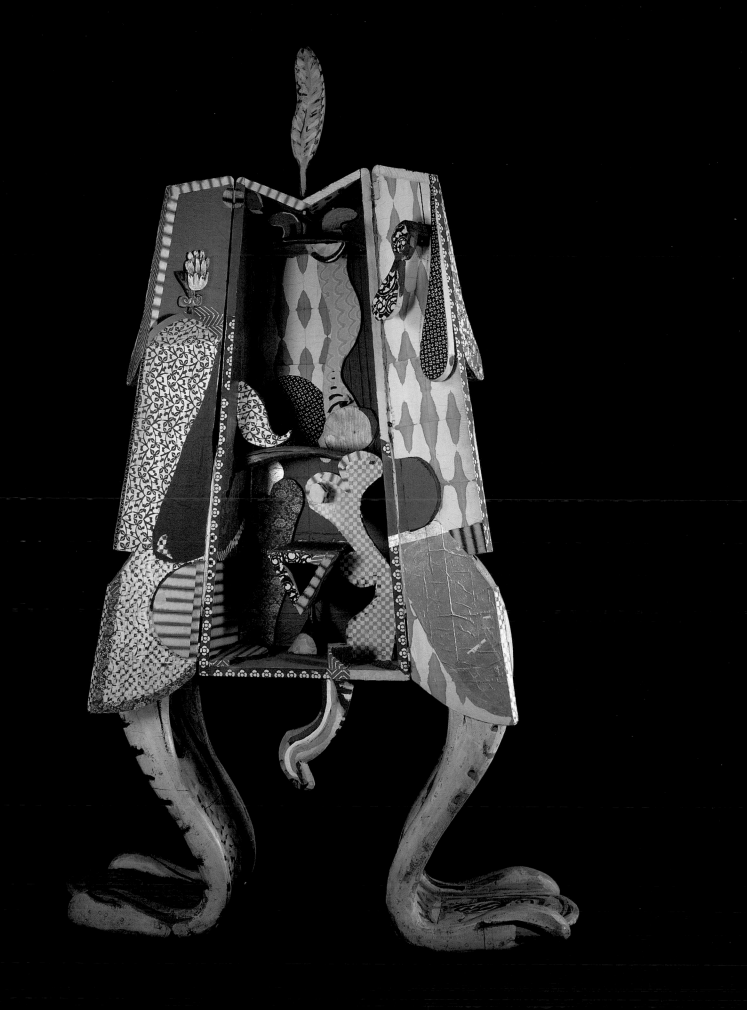

■ Fig. 1. Warren Platner, designer, Knoll International (active 1938 to present), manufacturer, dining chair, East Greenville, Pennsylvania, designed 1960–65, made about 1970. Nickel-finish steel rod with foam rubber supports and orange wool upholstery; h. 29 in., w. 26½ in., d. 22 in. Museum of Fine Arts, Boston; gift in memory of James Mills 2001.655.1.

Slivka, the influential critic and editor of *Craft Horizons* beginning in 1959) saw as freewheeling freedom of expression in these new forms, others saw as frivolous, self-indulgent, frequently bizarre creations. While some rejoiced in shedding the tedious restraints of fine materials and good craftsmanship, others lamented the loss of the ability to master a discipline. Some insisted on the maker's right to focus on personal preoccupations and tell stories with the work, to infuse it with comedy or tragedy through thematic elements; others deplored the neglect of—and lack of respect for—the consumer's needs and the rejection of utility as a commonsense, bottom-line criterion of all craft. The new spirits wished to look to the possibilities of the present and future, but others wished to retain a reverence for the achievements of the past. This polarity between tradition and innovation, between inherited culture and counterculture, was characteristic of the studio furniture movement in the 1960s.[2]

The career of the artist Richard Artschwager (b. 1923) neatly encapsulates this development as the movement became polarized. He exhibited a traditional Scandinavian-inspired piece in the 1957 "Furniture by Craftsmen" exhibition and went on to sell his furniture through Workbench, an outlet for limited-production objects in this essentially Danish Modern mode. In the early 1960s, however, he moved away from functionalist work to a more sculptural approach that celebrated inutility. He also rejected the traditional emphasis on wood, by choosing (for example) to use Formica, "the great ugly material, the horror of the age," because he "was sick of looking at all this beautiful wood."[3]

Several factors are key to understanding this sea change in attitude. One was the nature of American society as a whole in the late 1960s, an era when questioning established values and traditions in education, religion, politics, social mores (and nearly every aspect of life) was rampant, resulting in the oft-cited "generation gap." The rebellion against the war in Vietnam extended to a rejection of the "Establishment" in other areas, including notions of sexuality, drug use, and the role and status of women. In this highly charged atmosphere, it was inevitable that there would be changes in material culture and art as well.[4]

A second major change, specific to the decorative arts, was the attempt to equate craft with the so-called fine arts, especially with the values of Abstract Expressionism, such as "visual presence over function, form over material, and feeling over technique."[5] This was particularly evident in the new focus of *Craft Horizons* and in the sequence of exhibitions at the Museum of Contemporary Crafts in New York, where the emphasis was placed on new forms that were "exuberant, bold, and irreverent." Some makers no longer thought of studio furniture as a commodity in the consumer furnishings marketplace; rather, such pieces were unique works of art meant to be exhibited in galleries and acquired by art collectors. It was furniture to be looked at more than used. While this trend would accelerate in the following decades, its origins date to the 1960s.

While many studio furniture makers entering the field were self-taught, an increasing number emerged from the academy and held teaching positions that sustained them on a day-to-day basis. Making studio furniture for a living, as many people attempting to do so commented at the time, was not necessarily a lucrative enterprise. A steady teaching income helped free some artists from the constraints of the marketplace and allowed them to participate in an atmosphere more akin to the world of painters, where the goal was primarily decorative and expressive rather than functional. Furniture became more self-consciously sculptural, extraordinary, and (to some eyes) outlandish. Although excursions into "wit, irony, imagination, and fantasy" have always been a part of the history of furniture design, they seemed especially fresh in the 1960s when compared to the conservative, restrained, button-down taste of the 1950s.[6]

This new attitude, pioneered by such artists as Peter Voulkos in ceramics (fig. 2), was characteristic of all the crafts in the 1960s. It is evident in the careers of several specific individuals: for example, in the work of Wendell Castle and some of his students, including Tom Lacagnina (fig. 3) and Joe DiStefano; in the colorful, humorous, furniture of Tommy Simpson; and in the early pieces by Jon Brooks of New Hampshire. On the West Coast, in addition to Sam Maloof, Arthur Espenet Carpenter was a leading figure who helped bridge the gap between the 1950s and the 1960s with his carefully contoured work. More experimental and adventurous furniture made by a large group of California artists, including Jack Rogers Hopkins and J. B. Blunk, epitomizes the spirit of the Golden State in the tumultuous years of the late sixties, in which the choice of a crafts-oriented lifestyle was as much a political decision as it was an aesthetic choice. Other makers, such as Castle, Donald Lloyd McKinley, and Thomas Lynn, distanced themselves

completely from the "reverence for wood" by turning to materials such as plastic and aluminum to create innovative and unusual furniture.

Wendell Castle (fig. 4), born in the Midwest and trained at the University of Kansas in the 1950s, began to make furniture in 1958. In many respects, his career typifies the experience of his generation, beginning with his eclectic training. At Kansas, where he initially decided to be a sculptor, Castle was exposed to the products of industrial designers through courses and various publications, including Don Wallance's *Shaping America's Products* (1956), which is regarded as "the ultimate source of inspiration for his work" and in which he learned about the furniture of Nakashima and Esherick.[7] Esherick's designs, in particular, resonated philosophically with Castle; although he was unable to meet with Esherick, the older man's aesthetics, philosophy, and attitude toward technology all struck a responsive chord in the young artist.

After a period of experimentation with several styles, Castle moved to the Rochester

■ Fig. 2. Peter Voulkos, *Camelback Mountain*, Berkeley, California, 1959. Stoneware; h. 45 ½ in., w. 19 ½ in., d. 20 ¼ in. Museum of Fine Arts, Boston; gift of Mr. and Mrs. Stephen D. Paine 1978.690.

■ Fig. 3. Tom Lacagnina, movable-top table, Alfred, New York, 1979. Cherry; h. 26 in., w. 39 in., d. (closed) 25 in. Photo, courtesy of American Craft Council Library.

Institute of Technology in the early 1960s, where he began to teach with William A. Keyser, Jr., as successors to Tage Frid in the woodworking department. There, Castle focused on stack lamination techniques—basically gluing together multiple layers of wood and then shaping the assemblage by removing sections of the wood. Such work had a long history in furniture making and especially in wooden sculpture. By adopting this technique, Castle sought to escape the limitations of size and shape imposed by the "linear flow of wood grain." Using lamination techniques, he said, "encouraged me to challenge these age-old restrictions upon the woodworking art. By drastically increasing the overall size of the 'board' through lamination procedures, by negating the splitting factor through a process that multiplies the stability and strength many times over, I found myself freed from the necessity to operate within the confines of lines and planes. Wood, I realized, could be shaped and formed and carved in ways limited now only by my imagination!"[8]

Castle's enormous walnut *Library Sculpture* of 1965 (cat. no. 14) is a good example of the achievements made possible by stack lamination. This work, made specifically for an exhibition at the Memorial Art Gallery in Rochester, consists essentially of a double settee and desk integrated with a tall, central, twisted column containing a light, as well as an accompanying stool. Soon Castle's distinctive laminated work began to be selected for exhibitions, along with furniture by Esherick, Maloof, and Nakashima, and to be acquired by collectors and museums.[9]

Castle's laminated furniture, while innovative in design and technique, still relied for much of its visual success on the richness of traditional hardwoods, such as walnut and cherry, and thus was identified by many as a "craft product." Later in the decade, Castle introduced a line of furniture made of fiberglass-reinforced polyester that was more clearly intended to be Art. His plastic furniture, including his "Molar" series of tooth-shaped chairs and other unusual forms, such as his *Leotard Table* (fig. 5), are clearly examples of Pop art, reflecting Castle's ability to recast his furniture into different expressions at

different times. The "Molar" series was issued by Wendell Castle Associates, a production-line group formed for the purpose.[10]

Tommy Simpson's colorful, humorous, playful furniture—often characterized as "whimsical"—stands more clearly apart from the furniture of woodworkers. Trained as a painter at Cranbrook Academy of Art in Michigan, Simpson was not inhibited by any formal training in cabinetmaking but instead chose furniture as a means of self-expression. His objects, while echoing functional forms, are more clearly canvases in three dimensions that he cleverly and joyfully embellishes with iconographic elements. These decorative features often depict or allude to events in his midwestern youth, historical figures, or friends, or they may have other referential meanings.[11]

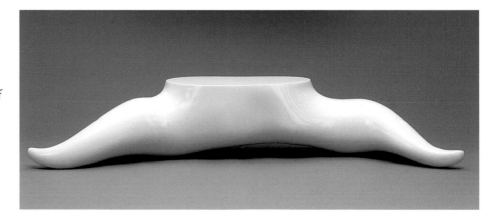

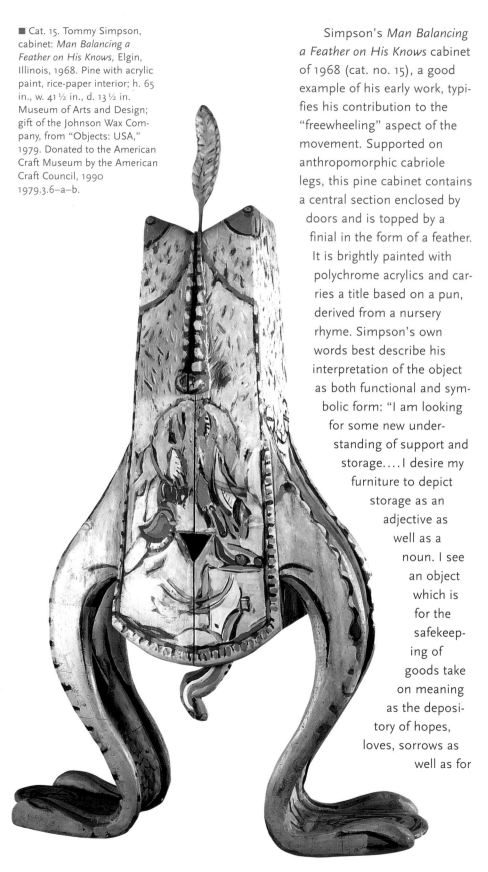

Simpson's *Man Balancing a Feather on His Knows* cabinet of 1968 (cat. no. 15), a good example of his early work, typifies his contribution to the "freewheeling" aspect of the movement. Supported on anthropomorphic cabriole legs, this pine cabinet contains a central section enclosed by doors and is topped by a finial in the form of a feather. It is brightly painted with polychrome acrylics and carries a title based on a pun, derived from a nursery rhyme. Simpson's own words best describe his interpretation of the object as both functional and symbolic form: "I am looking for some new understanding of support and storage.…I desire my furniture to depict storage as an adjective as well as a noun. I see an object which is for the safekeeping of goods take on meaning as the depository of hopes, loves, sorrows as well as for books, foodstuffs, and underwear. Furniture can expand to receive more of man's needs than be just the handler of material."[12] Pedro Friedeberg, Theodore Halkin, Kate Millet, Barbara Cohen, and others also produced similar objects for an exhibition in 1966 at the Museum of Contemporary Crafts.[13] While clearly products of their time, these pieces of "fantasy furniture" also stand as modern expressions in a long tradition of painted, vernacular furniture in this country. Such furniture is visually related to some of the (so-called) folk art of the twentieth century.

Much of the studio furniture movement has been centered on the East Coast, but a more active group on the West Coast, especially in northern California, began developing in the 1960s, joining Sam Maloof, who was located in the southern part of the state.[14] Arthur Espenet Carpenter (cat. nos. 16, 17), educated at Dartmouth College in New Hampshire, arrived in the San Francisco Bay Area in the late 1940s; with a talent for and devotion to teaching, he has since been a key figure there for half a century. His career forms a link between the makers of the 1950s and those who would come later. Five criteria—"function, durability, simplicity, sensuality, and practicality of construction"—are the hallmarks of his craft. The last characteristic—his practical use of available materials—sets him apart from the earlier "reverence for wood" group.[15]

Carpenter's wishbone chair (cat. no. 16), named for the shape of its legs, is a particularly strong example of these criteria, especially in its incorporation of surplus canvas webbing, carriage bolts, and other demonstrations of expediency and straightforward construction. Making each chair takes two and a half days; its shape has been refined over time in successive iterations. The soft edges evoke the descriptive term "California Roundover" style, coined to describe furniture by Carpenter, Maloof, and others who used a router and rasp to round and soften the edges of their furniture.[16]

His rolltop desk of 1970 (cat. no. 17) represents one of his most successful design innovations. Without formal training in woodwork, he sought an efficient and simpler means to lessen the time and

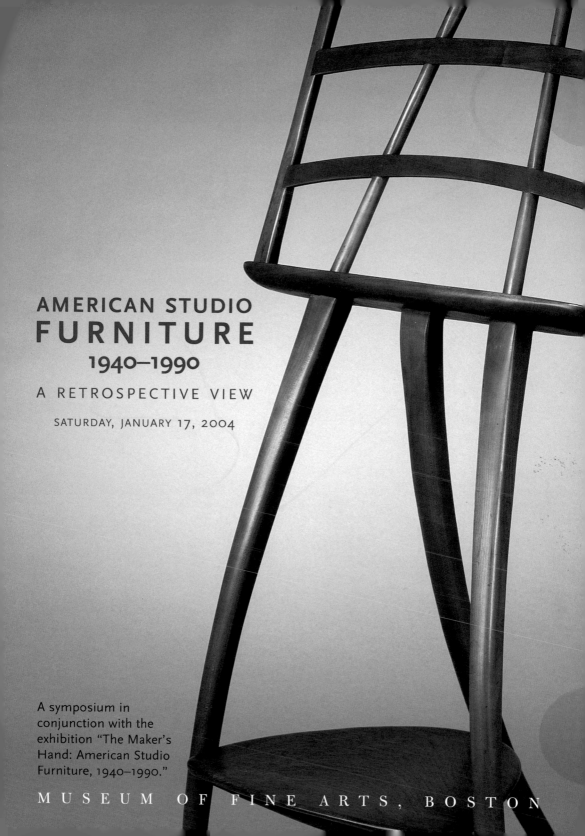

AMERICAN STUDIO
FURNITURE
1940–1990
A RETROSPECTIVE VIEW

SATURDAY, JANUARY 17, 2004

A symposium in
conjunction with the
exhibition "The Maker's
Hand: American Studio
Furniture, 1940–1990."

MUSEUM OF FINE ARTS, BOSTON

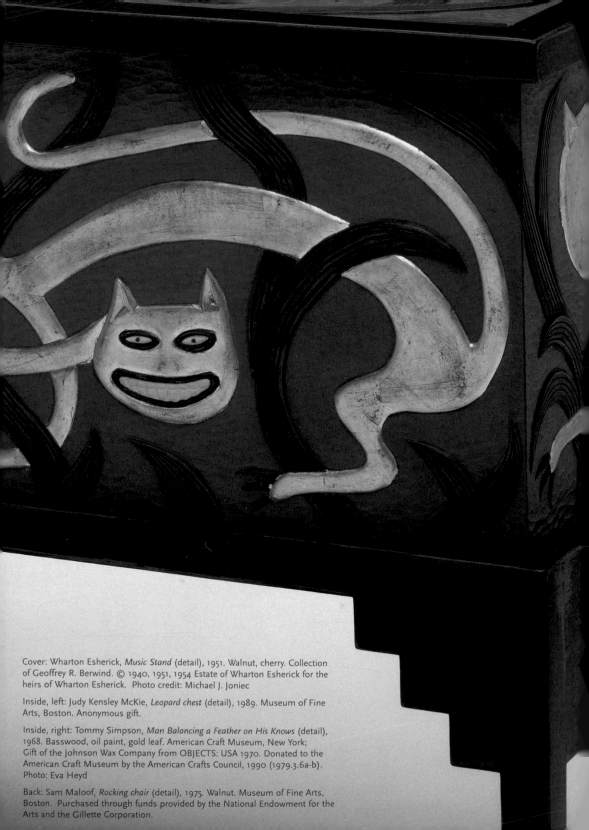

effort necessary to make a traditional drawer of dovetailed construction. His solution was to take a piece of wood and cut out a block form with a band saw, often giving it an undulating, free-form shape. He then hollows the block with the band saw, creating a space for a drawer, and slides the drawer block back into the initial block. He used this technique for drawers on this desk, in which the pigeonholes are fashioned in a similar manner. While Carpenter (who uses the name Espenet as his business name) is closely linked to the woodworker generation, he is also a free spirit; his independence and experimentation link him with the group of 1960s innovators.

Jack Rogers Hopkins, a southern California counterpart to Castle, advertised that he made "personal statements in natural materials" using the stack lamination technique.[17] Hopkins's work

■ Cat. 16. Arthur Espenet Carpenter, wishbone chair, Bolinas, California, 1970. Walnut, leather; h. 31 in., w. 21¼ in., d. 21½ in. Yale University Art Gallery 1999.70.1.

■ Cat. 17. Arthur Espenet Carpenter, rolltop desk, Bolinas, California, 1970. Walnut, mutenye, canvas; h. 40 in., w. 55¾ in., d. 32 in. Museum of Fine Arts, Boston; Museum purchase with funds donated anonymously, Frederick Brown Fund, Bequest of Maxim Karolik and Gift of Estelle S. Frankfurter, by exchange, and American Decorative Arts Curator's Fund 2003.152.

includes such fantasies as his *Womb Room*, unfortunately no longer extant (fig. 6). This giant sectional object—six feet high, thirteen feet wide, and nine feet deep—consisted of a chair, fitted with a cushion, an accompanying table, and a high billowing canopy of laminated wood. Made of Honduras mahogany, ash, and ebony, it exemplified the use of bands of woods in contrasting colors typical of Hopkins's furniture, distinct from that of other specialists in lamination. The *Womb Room* also incorporated within the design a sound system, space for books, lighting, and other creature comforts. Perhaps no other object so well represented the spirit of exuberant studio furniture of the 1960s.[18]

Hopkins's chair/table (cat. no. 18) is a more practical example of his work and illustrates the flowing, swooping feel found in so many of his objects. Other case pieces by Hopkins vividly demonstrate his mastery of arching, aerodynamic, asymmetrical, and almost preternaturally sensual forms. Many combine multiple functions into a single form, emphasizing the environmental aspect of his work.

The seating sculpture of J. B. Blunk represents an extension of or variation on the reverence for wood, particularly as found in Nakashima's work. Trained as a stoneware potter in Japan, where he was influenced by the sculptor Isamu Noguchi (1904–1988), Blunk returned to the United States in 1954 and settled near Inverness, California. By the mid-1960s, he had begun to produce furniture for local clients on a full-time basis. Working mostly in isolation, Blunk produced enormous redwood and cypress arches, benches, tables, and seating units (cat. no. 19), often monumental in size and usually textured and shaped with a chain saw. His first public commission came in 1968, from the University of California, Santa Cruz, for public seating on a campus plaza (fig. 7). To create this form, Blunk used the base of a redwood tree weighing in excess of two tons and spanning some thirteen feet in diameter. One of his sculptures was selected the next year for the "Objects: USA" exhibition and was published in the catalogue on the same spread as Tommy

Simpson's *Man Balancing a Feather on His Knows* cabinet. The two pieces evoked the dual trends of organic naturalism (Blunk's ten-foot-long redwood log only slightly modified to suggest a bench) and decorated artificiality (Simpson's pine cabinet held together with glue and wooden pegs and decorated with plastic paint).[19]

Carpenter, Blunk, and a few other northern California woodworkers, including John Kapel, John Barrow, and Miles Karpilow, formed a core of artists practicing woodworking in the region. Carpenter, in particular, created a nexus for like-minded individuals, including Tom D'Onofrio, who in 1972 would join together to form the Baulines Craft Guild. Although the basic pedagogical technique of the guild was the ancient master-apprentice relationship, the philosophy energizing the group was in perfect harmony with the 1960s counterculture theory; the goals were as much social and political as technical and aesthetic.[20]

Jon Brooks of New Hampshire is essentially an East Coast counterpart to Blunk, in terms of approach. Wendell Castle, in a brief review of

■ Fig. 6. Jack Rogers Hopkins, *Womb Room*, Spring Valley, California, 1970. Honduras mahogany, ash, ebony; h. 6 ft., w. 13 ft., d. 9 ft. No longer extant.

■ Cat. 18. Jack Rogers Hopkins, *Edition Chair*, Spring Valley, California, 1970. Honduras mahogany; h. 28 in., w. 54 in., d. 28 in. Collection of the artist.

■ Fig. 7. J. B. Blunk, seating sculpture, 1968. Redwood; h. 5 ft., w. 10 ft., d. 15 ft. University of California, Santa Cruz. Photo, private collection.

■ Cat. 19. J. B. Blunk, chair, Inverness, California, 1978. Redwood; h. 42 in., w. 34 in., d. 23 in. Private collection.

Brooks's first one-man exhibition, held at the Shop One gallery in Rochester, New York, in 1969, noted: "The basis for arriving at forms [by Brooks] is the conformation of found tree limbs. Stumps, and logs whose shapes suggest certain functions: i.e., a chair is a stump of a tree turned upside down with a section cut out to form a seat." This "anti-formal" approach is exemplified by an early Brooks carved walnut chair of 1971 (cat. no. 20), in which the maker's role (in Castle's words) is that of a "form selector" rather than a "form giver."[21] As Brooks himself noted about this walnut chair, "These things are wood objects found on earth. We are with nature one."[22]

The experimental nature of the 1960s led studio furniture makers to break with tradition not only in terms of form and technique, but also in using non-wood materials, as we have seen with Castle's plastic chairs and other objects. Thomas P. Lynn's cast aluminum seats of 1966 (fig. 8) represent a studio furniture maker's unusual use of a modern material that found more widespread acceptance in industry.

Their rootlike feet and columns, combined with irregular bicycle-like seats, make these pieces of furniture seem close to molten, cast almost as clay vessels would be. Their visibly wrought forms deny the planar, rectilinear, or smoothly rounded forms of typical aluminum pieces.[23]

The late Donald Lloyd McKinley, well known as a teacher at Sheridan College in Ontario, Canada, began to explore the expressive potential of plastics and polyvinyl chloride (PVC) in the early stages of his long career. Rather than using found materials of wood, as Esherick had done with some of his *brico-lage* furniture (see cat. no. 3), McKinley utilized cardboard shipping cylinders, white PVC tubes, and tin cans, which he regarded as "ready and inexpensive modules that were strong and light but also carried with them an amusing reference to toss-away consumer culture."[24] Amusement is certainly part of the visual appeal of a swivel-arm double-lamp with clustered table base (cat. no. 21). However, his seating furniture made from these materials, such as his chair and ottoman exhibited in 1969 in "Objects:

USA," is carefully based on a modular study of the human body and on his understanding of the applied science of ergonomics.[25]

In 1962, the Rhode Island School of Design (RISD) in Providence established a furniture program—only the second such collegiate-level program in the country (the Rochester Institute of Technology [RIT] in New York was the first). Tage Frid left RIT to teach at RISD and was replaced in Rochester by Wendell Castle. Two years later, Daniel Jackson (see chapter 3) began to teach design and woodworking at the Philadelphia College of Art (PCA), and within a short time Philadelphia had become a leading center for studio furniture and other crafts. As often happens, the effects of these inspiring and influential teachers would be felt in the work of the next generation, as the field continued to evolve in the 1970s.

Although the number of exhibitions containing studio furniture increased in the 1960s, especially at college and university galleries and in small regional shows, the opportunities for the public to become aware of the movement were still relatively restricted. The situation changed, however, with the installation of three important exhibitions in the late sixties and early seventies, much as the 1957 "Furniture by Craftsmen" exhibition encapsulated and showcased the early days of studio furniture.

In 1972, the Renwick Gallery of the National Collection of Fine Arts (now the American Art Museum) of the Smithsonian Institution in Washington, D.C., in conjunction with the Minnesota Museum of Art (now the Minnesota Museum of American Art) in St. Paul, surveyed the field in "Woodenworks: Furniture Objects by Five Contemporary Craftsmen." Organized by Lloyd E. Herman, the show was very important: it was the inaugural exhibition at the Renwick, the new crafts component in the Smithsonian's family of museums. The exhibition reflected a somewhat conservative approach, primarily representing the origins of the field rather than its growth and development (the artists selected were "all devoted to the mystery and pleasure of working in wood"). As might be expected, the show

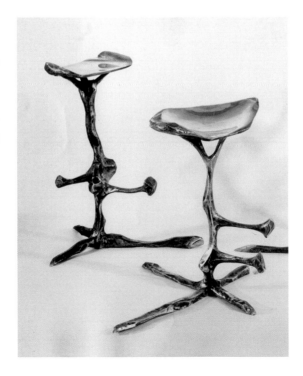

■ Cat. 20. Jon Brooks, carved seat, New Boston, New Hampshire, 1971. Black walnut; h. 35 in., w. 25 in., d. 40 in. Estate of Susan Brooks Franklin.

■ Fig. 8. Thomas Lynn, aluminum seating furniture, California, 1966. Cast aluminum. Photo, courtesy of American Craft Council Library.

■ Cat. 21. Donald Lloyd
McKinley, swivel-arm double-
lamp with clustered table base,
Mississauga, Ontario, Canada,
1969. PVC tube; h. 65 in.,
w. 17 in., d. 29 ½ in. Private
collection.

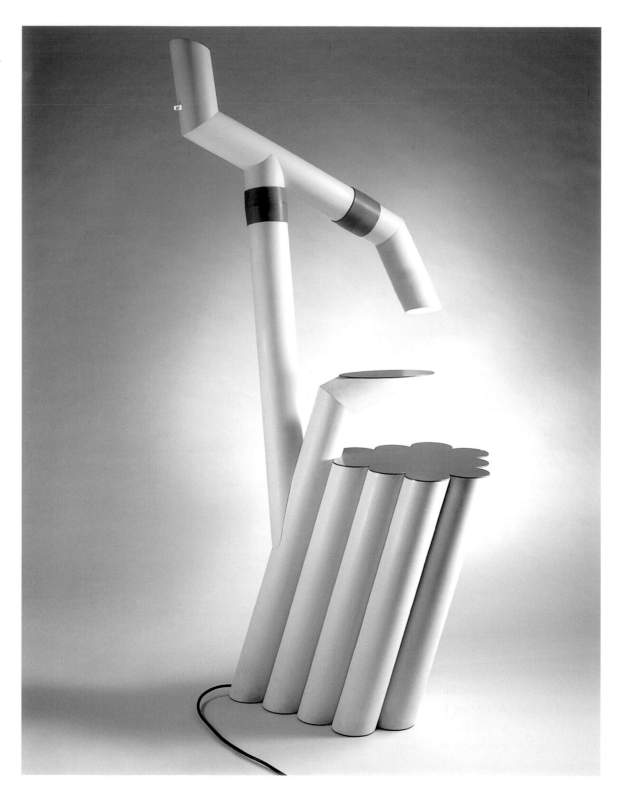

included works by Esherick, Nakashima, and Maloof, thus helping to crystallize and solidify the position of this woodworking trinity. It also embraced more sculptural works by Carpenter and Castle (and perhaps alluded to them by using the term "furniture objects," as opposed to just "furniture," in the subtitle of the exhibition and catalogue). But despite its strengths, the show did not attempt to break new ground or to recognize some of the more experimental work in the field.[26]

"Objects: USA," the slightly earlier traveling exhibition inaugurated at the Smithsonian Institution in 1969, is ironically more revealing of trends in the movement as a whole. Consisting of more than three hundred objects of nearly all types of materials, the show was funded by S. C. Johnson and Son (Johnson's Wax) and accompanied by a catalogue of the same name prepared by a New York art dealer.[27] Although not repeated on the title page, the dust jacket for the catalogue indicated the contents of the show and, in its terminology, accented the shape of the field: "Works by *Artist-Craftsmen* in Ceramic, Enamel, Glass, Metal, Plastic, Mosaic, Wood, and Fiber" (emphasis added). The exhibition contained furniture by only nine makers, along with turned wooden vessels and other small objects by Harry Nohr, Bob Stocksdale, Daniel Loomis Valenza, and Lee M. Rohde. The style of furniture exhibited included objects representative of the more traditional "reverence for wood" group: Esherick, Maloof, Nakashima, Carpenter, and Jere Osgood, a New Hampshire artist who exhibited a chest of drawers (see cat. no. 23) made of fiddleback mahogany. Almost equally represented were the more overt artist-craftspeople: Castle, whose laminated wood and plastic pieces were shown, Blunk, Simpson, McKinley, and William A. Keyser, Jr.

One of Keyser's pieces was a liquor cabinet he made in 1967 (fig. 9). It consists of a small, rectangular cabinet of benge wood at the base and a related, larger cabinet at the top; the parts are joined by a two-piece, tubular center section of metal painted in a bright red acrylic and set at a jaunty angle. In his artist's statement, Keyser noted that this object

"was an attempt to effect a semiprecarious relationship between two distinct masses." He went on to explain his philosophy in a comment that summarizes the themes of tradition and innovation in the 1960s: the "two concerns" of his work, he said, were "the conception of forms in nonutilitarian objects which sometimes might become sculpture" and "the process of applying these formal ideas to functional furniture." In his mind, the occasional moments when these two concepts are combined result in "the most successful work." By recognizing the diversity within the field and by approaching the material as art rather than (or in addition to) craft, "Objects: USA" provides us with a clear view of the variegated landscape that studio furniture had become and hints at the trends that would follow.[28]

A series of exhibitions in California similarly charted the course of the movement in the 1960s (which, by most accounts, actually came to symbolic end with the Watergate crisis that began in 1972). "California Design Eleven," held in 1971 at the Pasadena Art Museum (now the Norton Simon Museum of Art), marked the fifteenth year that the county of Los Angeles had supported the "California Design" program and its annual (later triennial) exhibitions of "both manufactured goods and crafts" made in the state. Separate juries chose the objects selected for each category. Eudorah M. Moore, in the foreword to the exhibition catalogue, noted the

■ Fig. 9. William A. Keyser, Jr., liquor cabinet, Rush, New York, 1967. Benge, with metal and plastic paint; h. 67 in. Sheldon Memorial Art Gallery and Sculpture Garden, University of Nebraska-Lincoln.

importance of furniture to the show (inasmuch as "California is the number two furniture producing and the number one furniture buying state") and emphasized the "extraordinary vitality" of the crafts in California. Without "indigenous folk art roots," in her analysis, California craftsmen were able to undertake a unique "conceptual and experimental probing of materials . . . free of the pressures of the market place." In this climate, works often became highly personal social statements. Moore cites two reasons for the nature of California crafts: the "strongly individual almost frontier syndrome of doing things oneself" and a strong educational system, especially in the state college network, emphasizing "materials exploration."[29]

The catalogue selections tell us a great deal about the mixture of approaches that characterize the 1960s. Illustrated alongside furniture designed by Charles Eames, we find craftsman-made furniture by Hopkins—including his *Womb Room* (see fig. 6), photographed outdoors—and his laminated chair, also pictured outside on a sand dune. (Sand dunes were a favorite setting for pictures; see also Randy Teeple's carved leather-seated stool and many other examples in the same volume.) Sam Maloof's upright writing desk (see cat. no. 10), "built for the ages," and Espenet's rolltop desk represent more traditional objects.

The two emphases of the early years of the studio furniture movement—on wood in the 1950s and on the artistic, free-form expressionism that evolved in the 1960s—would continue in many respects to define some of the parameters of the field. Other emphases—specifically a focus on technique—would lead the movement in new directions during the 1970s.

NOTES

1. Cara Greenberg, *Op to Pop: Furniture of the 1960s* (Boston: Little, Brown, and Company, 1999), 11–31, 97–98, and passim. For the decade as a whole, see also Philippe Garner, *Sixties Design* (Cologne: Taschen, 1996); and Tom Wolfe, *The Pump House Gang* (New York: Bantam, 1968).

2. See Edward S. Cooke, Jr., *New American Furniture: The Second Generation of Studio Furnituremakers*, exh. cat. (Boston: Museum of Fine Arts, 1989), 15.

3. See "The Object: Still Life," an interview with Artschwager and Claes Oldenburg, in *Craft Horizons* 25, no. 5 (September–October 1965): 28–30, 54. See also Cooke, *New American Furniture*, 16, for a discussion of the somewhat parallel career of H. C. Westermann (1922–1981).

4. The essays in David Farber, ed., *The Sixties: From Memory to History* (Chapel Hill: University of North Carolina Press, 1994), deal with the reactions against "cultural authority and political legitimacy" in nearly every aspect of life.

5. Cooke, *New American Furniture*, 15.

6. See ibid., 16. The history of furniture is punctuated by this interest in "fantastic" objects. See, for example, Bruce M. Newman and Alastair Duncan, *Fantasy Furniture* (New York: Rizzoli, 1989); and David Linley, *Extraordinary Furniture* (New York: Harry N. Abrams, 1996). The quotation is from Thomas Hoving's foreword to Newman and Duncan, *Fantasy Furniture*, 7. See also Dona Z. Meilach, *Contemporary Art with Wood: Creative Techniques and Appreciation* (New York: Crown, 1968), 186–87 and passim.

7. Davira S. Taragin, Edward S. Cooke, Jr., and Joseph Giovannini, *Furniture by Wendell Castle*, exh. cat. (New York: Hudson Hills Press in association with the Founders Society, Detroit Institute of Arts, 1989), 16.

8. See Wendell Castle and David Edman, *The Wendell Castle Book of Wood Lamination* (New York: Van Nostrand Reinhold, 1980); quotation from 11. See also Taragin, Cooke, and Giovannini, *Furniture by Wendell Castle*; and Michael A. Stone, *Contemporary American Woodworkers* (Salt Lake City, Utah: Gibbs M. Smith, 1986), 114–29.

9. Taragin, Cooke, and Giovannini, *Furniture by Wendell Castle*, 34–36.

10. Ibid., 36–37. See also Greenberg, *Op to Pop*, 58–59.

11. For Simpson, see Cooke, *New American Furniture*, 16–17, 112–15. See also the introduction by Pam Koob in Tommy Simpson, *Two Looks to Home: The Art of Tommy Simpson* (Boston: Little, Brown, and Company, 1999).

12. Quoted in Lee Nordness, *Objects: USA*, exh. cat. (New York: Viking Press, 1970), 269. For the symbolic meanings of case furniture, see Gaston Bachelard, *The Poetics of Space* (Boston: Beacon Press, 1964); Gerald W. R. Ward, *American Case Furniture*

in the Mabel Brady Garvan and Other Collections at Yale University (New Haven: Yale University Art Gallery, 1988); and Virginia T. Boyd et al., *Contemporary Studio Case Furniture: The Inside Story*, exh. cat. (Madison: Elvehjem Museum of Art, University of Wisconsin–Madison, 2002).

13. Thomas Simpson, *Fantasy Furniture: Design and Decoration*, exh. cat. (New York: Reinhold Book Corporation, 1966).

14. See Glenn Adamson, "California Dreaming," in *Furniture Studio: The Heart of the Functional Arts*, ed. John Kelsey and Rick Mastelli (Free Union, Va.: Furniture Society, 1999), 32–41.

15. Stone, *Contemporary American Woodworkers*, 83–85.

16. Adamson, "California Dreaming," 36.

17. Quotation is from an undated promotional flyer, Department of Art of the Americas files, MFA.

18. See Dona Z. Meilach, *Creating Modern Furniture: Trends, Techniques, Appreciation* (New York: Crown, 1975), 136–38; for additional examples of Hopkins's work, see x, 149, 150–58, 171.

19. Glenn Adamson, "California Spirit: Recovering the Furniture of J. B. Blunk," *Woodwork*, no. 59 (October 1999): 22–29. David Holtzapfel calls this approach "subtractive woodworking"; see his "Subtractive Woodworking: Furniture from Logs and Limbs," *Fine Woodworking*, no. 54 (September–October 1985): 88–93. See also Nordness, *Objects: USA*, 268–69.

20. See Adamson, "California Dreaming," 32–41.

21. *Craft Horizons* 29, no. 2 (March–April 1969): 42.

22. Quoted in University Art Gallery, State University of New York at Binghamton, *Master Craftsmen: An Invitational Exhibition, November 7–28, 1971*, exh. cat. (Binghamton: University Art Gallery, State University of New York at Binghamton, 1971), 7. Castle also exhibited three pieces in the exhibition.

23. See *Craftsmen USA 66*, exh. cat. (New York: Museum of Contemporary Crafts, 1966), x. For the use of aluminum in all manner of works of art, see Sarah Nichols et al., *Aluminum by Design*, exh. cat. (Pittsburgh, Pa.: Carnegie Museum of Art, 2000).

24. Karen R. White, *Donald Lloyd McKinley: A Studio Practice in Furniture*, exh. cat. (Ontario, Canada: Oakville Galleries, 2000), 18.

25. Nordness, *Objects: USA*, 236.

26. *Woodenworks: Furniture Objects by Five Contemporary Craftsmen*, exh. cat. (St. Paul: Minnesota Museum of Art and the National Collection of Fine Arts, Smithsonian Institution, 1972).

27. Nordness, *Objects: USA*. The wood section is 251–69; see also 243 for Castle's laminated plastic table and 236 for McKinley's PVC chair and ottoman.

28. Quoted in Nordness, *Objects: USA*, 260.

29. Pasadena Art Museum, *California Design Eleven*, exh. cat. (Pasadena: Pasadena Art Museum, 1971), 9.

TECHNOFETISHISM:
TECHNICAL VIRTUOSITY AND EXOTIC WOODS IN THE 1970S

The "California Design" exhibitions showcased continued exploration of non- or limited-function furniture, painted wood, mixed materials, and personal expression well into the 1970s; however, free-wheeling experimentation elsewhere began to subside in the early part of the decade. Even Wendell Castle, who had led the challenge in the eastern United States against straightforward furniture throughout the 1960s, turned away from his experimentation with molded plastic and reliance on stack lamination to a more elegant approach that relied on traditional joinery, like dovetails and mortise-and-tenon joints, and a variety of differently figured woods (fig. 1). Sculptural, ahistorical furniture gave way to highly refined, "serious" furniture that gained value through its maker's explicit (one might even call it obsessive) display of dexterity and use of highly figured native or tropical woods.[1]

The studio furniture field's shift from organic personal exploration toward seductive technical finesse and refined finish parallels similar transformations in other artistic media. In the world of sculpture in the late 1960s, minimalists like Robert Morris argued for a reassertion of the primacy of making art over the concern with form, thereby stressing the significance of the means of production. For Morris and Donald Judd, such an emphasis led to systematic, highly skilled, industrialized art production that resulted in pure, carefully planned forms. The new value placed on impersonal, expert industrial techniques and shiny finishes signaled the

beginning of a new poststudio world in which precision and close tolerances were celebrated over the gestural hand of the artist.[2] However, studio furniture makers were not minimalists, preferring instead to use technique as a reassertion of the primacy of the individual studio worker and a rejection of any association with the industrial world. In this way, furniture makers more closely resembled potters such as Richard DeVore, William Daley, and Robert Turner, who blended analytical design ideas with elaborate craftsmanship to reinvigorate pottery in opposition to the mass-produced ceramics of the 1970s. Like these potters, furniture makers began to focus on furniture as its own subject matter; the work was as much about furniture *making* as about furniture *function*.[3] The social basis of making, the personal connection between maker and object, object and buyer, and—symbolically—maker and buyer remained strong.

It is the reassertion of individual skill within a system of traditional, or traditionally informed, furniture techniques that unites much of the work of the 1970s. This emphasis on cabinetmaking skills and search for highly figured or exotic woods was really a fetishization, in the Marxian sense (rather than the psychosexual sense). Karl Marx asserted that everyday objects, through the value of labor, could be transformed into commodities to be worshiped, sought after, and proudly possessed.[4] For the studio furniture maker of the 1970s, explicit display of skilled workmanship became the primary means by

jigs, shop-made holding devices or patterns that allowed tools or machinery to follow a predetermined path, resulting in quick, efficient, and uniform preparation of parts. Exhibition catalogues such as *New Handmade Furniture* (1979) listed the different woodworking techniques as well as the varieties of woods used in each piece of furniture that was in the show. The universe of woods also expanded beyond the cherry and walnut that had dominated the work of the 1950s and grew to include curly and bird's-eye maple, padauk, bubinga, rosewood, cocobolo, and zebrawood. The privileging of technical virtuosity and figured wood in the critical discourse of furniture rose during the 1970s and carried through to the early 1980s.[5]

Some of the expanded repertoire of woodworking techniques can be attributed to the School for American Craftsmen at the Rochester Institute of Technology (RIT) in New York. Teaching there from 1950 to 1962, Tage Frid emphasized that a maker should "design around the construction, and not construct around the design." He grounded his students in a wide assortment of construction techniques, from machine work to hand skills, encouraged them to develop jigs to ensure accuracy and possible replication if desired, and instilled in them a cabinetmaker's work ethic. In emphasizing the workmanship of certainty, achieved through intelligent use of machines and jigs and a practiced dexterity with hand tools, Frid critiqued the self-conscious risk inherent in the work of the freewheeling 1960s. It was Frid who exerted the greatest influence on the "jigging up" of the field in the 1970s. His teaching in the late 1950s and early 1960s, before he moved to the Rhode Island School of Design in Providence in mid-1962, profoundly shaped the next generation of makers. Among the students studying at RIT during this period were Daniel Jackson, Jere Osgood, and William Keyser; all would come to play key roles in the development of studio furniture during the 1970s.[6]

Jackson, who had worked as an antiques dealer and restorer in his hometown, Milwaukee, before matriculating at RIT, found that Frid's lessons shed light on cabinetmaking practices, and he relished the ability to try different techniques. However, the

■ Fig. 1. Wendell Castle, gaming table and chairs, Scottsville, New York, 1974. Black walnut and curly maple table; h. 29 in., w. 39 in., d. 39 in. Black walnut chairs; h. 29 in., w. 22 in., d. 22 in. Photo, courtesy of the artist.

■ Fig. 2. Peder Moos, dining table and chairs, Denmark, 1944. Walnut, maple. From *Peder Moos* (Esbjerg, Denmark: Teknologisk Forlag, 1988), cat. no. 11. Photo, courtesy of the publisher.

which the work could be assessed and evaluated. Successful sales were predicated upon the ability of the viewer or buyer to see the quality of the work, recognize the hand of the maker, and sense a personal connection with that maker. Products came to be judged by the number and fineness of the dovetails, assured use of multiple shaping and joining techniques (especially bent lamination), and innovative use of tools such as the horizontal mortiser, router, and lathe. Many makers, such as Jere Osgood and Stephen Harris, developed complex

■ Cat. 22. Daniel Jackson, looking glass: *Leda, the Devil, and the Moon*, Philadelphia, Pennsylvania, 1973. Brazilian rosewood, Osage orange, luan plywood; h. 30 in., w. 40 in. Philadelphia Museum of Art; gift of the Friends of the Museum 1973.94.3.

most meaningful part of his education was a fellowship in Denmark from 1960 to 1962; he worked with Peder Moos, a skilled "furniture architect" who was exploring new decorative versions of Danish Modern style. Moos retained the structural and technical basis of Danish furniture but further explored the effects of subtly shaping and lightening members without sacrificing structural strength or compromising techniques. Moos also celebrated joinery as a decorative feature, using through tenons that he highlighted by wedging with contrasting woods, multiplying the number of tenons beyond what was necessary, and deploying keys of contrasting wood in bow-tie or barbell shapes to mitered or butted joints (fig. 2). Essential to Moos's innovations with exposed tenoning was the *langhulsbormaskine*, a horizontal boring machine that facilitated the use of spline tenons with rounded edges and permitted a pleasing bit of decorative joinery for through tenons or as connectors between two elements. When Jackson set up his first shop in Philadelphia in the

fall of 1964, he found it necessary to travel back to Denmark to purchase such a mortiser with sliding table. During the late 1960s and early 1970s, decorative joinery became one of Jackson's signatures, and he and Osgood are credited with introducing the horizontal boring machine to the American craftsman.[7]

Jackson was also one of the first studio furniture makers who assiduously collected figured wood for use in construction. Unlike George Nakashima, who stockpiled boards from around the world and used figured wood primarily for design elements, Jackson took more of a traditional cabinetmaker's approach, shaping and joining wood so that form, figure, and color reinforced one another in a way that distinguished between different functional or conceptual parts of the whole. Jackson's *Leda, the Devil, and the Moon* mirror (cat. no. 22) embodies his central and most important contributions. The use of spline tenons provides the powerful tension between the mirror's left and right as well as the upper and lower sections; their use also bestows a

■ Fig. 3. Jere Osgood, elliptical shell desk, New Milford, Connecticut, 1970. Walnut, maple; h. 48 in., w. 50 in., d. 34 in. Private collection.

■ Cat. 23. Jere Osgood, chest of drawers, New Milford, Connecticut, 1969. Fiddleback mahogany; h. 59¾ in., w. 33 in., d. 17¼ in. Collection of S C Johnson A Family Company.

■ Fig. 4. (opposite page) Jere Osgood, *Chest of Chair*, New Milford, Connecticut, 1971. Curly maple; h. 74 in., w. 72 in., d. 30 in. Courtesy of the artist.

■ Cat. 24. (opposite page) William A. Keyser, Jr., coffee table, Honeoye Falls, New York, 1978. Cherry, elm, maple, walnut; h. 16 in., w. 73 in., d. 18 in. Collection of the artist.

deep, dark energy to the carved face of the devil in the center of the lower rail. The exquisitely shaped elements attest to Jackson's keen eye for design detail and his deft carving skills. The use of the original color of Osage orange wood for the moon disk at the top of the mirror and of holly for the eyes of the swans provided a striking contrast to the richly figured rosewood frame.

Jere Osgood, a close friend of Jackson's, eagerly sought to develop new designs and techniques to lighten the structure of his furniture and to introduce more sophisticated curved lines (figs. 3, 4). Underlying Osgood's interest in curves was his concern for the intrinsic properties of wood: he believed that wood should move and curve more than it had in Frid's work of the 1950s and 1960s. Further, the

craftsperson should not violate or waste wood by removing large pieces of it to make organic forms, as Castle and Hopkins had. Instead, Osgood emphasized preplanning and the development of jigs to use and shape the wood both economically and sensitively. Toward this end, he developed two techniques in the late 1960s—compound bent-stave laminations (for carcasses) and tapered bent lamination (primarily for legs). Osgood used stave lamination to make the carcass of his 1969 chest of drawers (cat. no. 23), showcased in the touring exhibition "Objects: USA." The sides of the chest swell both front to back and bottom to top, and the drawer fronts are also bent laminations that echo the curve of the sides. The result is a sculptural piece of case furniture that presents a dynamic organic mass while still honoring the principles of fine cabinetmaking. For a 1970 elliptical shell desk (fig. 3), Osgood also developed the new tapered bent lamination to create more natural, rootlike legs. Rather than simply trimming a leg, exposing glue lines and making a weaker lamination, Osgood developed a surface planer jig to make tapered strips that were then glued in a tapered curve. While a designer, Osgood applied an engineer's thinking to cabinetmaking: "I place more emphasis on preplanning than shaping. The form comes from bending the wood into a light shell instead of removing stock. I'd rather spend my time drawing and drafting and making jigs than chopping away lumber....I feel that lamination the way I use it follows the growth patterns in a tree better than can be achieved with traditional joinery techniques using square milled-to-thickness lumber."[8]

Disciplined design and a commitment to build additively rather than subtractively was also characteristic of the work of William A. Keyser, Jr., who began teaching at RIT after receiving his MFA in 1961. In exploring the organic nature of form, he consistently sought a constructivist solution. His early work revealed an interest in distilled rectilinear parts, but he later began introducing curves into this work, using steam bending and coopering to provide gentle swells and arcs. In his teaching, Keyser consistently encouraged his students to explore a

tea cart (cat. no. 25). Relying on utilitarian ash wood as the only material, Beeken steam-bent the wheels, laminated the supporting legs, delicately hand-shaped the structural members with spokeshave and rasp, and built a dovetailed tray to produce an elegant, refined cart that bore little resemblance to undecorated wheelbarrows and farm tools incorporating similar materials and processes. Although Beeken drew inspiration from "simple work that is made in wooden ways" and believed that "time and familiarity add to the character of the things that we live around," the character of the tea cart has not emerged from loving use but rather from a visual appreciation of the technical achievement. The end result is a highly aestheticized reference to a functional form.[10]

Martha Rising explored the possibilities of compound bent laminations (bending in two planes simultaneously) in her 1980 rocker (cat. no. 26). A student in the wood program at California State University, Northridge (the one university program in which women played a significant role in the 1970s), Rising took full advantage of a program set up to explore the various expressive possibilities of wood—furniture making, turning, and sculpture. While Tom Trammel taught furniture making, students also took workshops from Sam Maloof, the sculptor Michael Jean Cooper, and the turner Jerry Glazer. It was a decentralized woodworking curriculum that spawned a wide variety of makers. Rising was most heavily influenced by the fastidious compound laminations of Cooper (fig. 5), but she consciously worked to remain within "the vocabulary of furniture and utilitarian furniture." Using maple for the lighter frame and padauk and purpleheart for darker accents, she gave "freedom, ease, and motion" to a recognizable seating form. In moving from sketch to final form, Rising remarked that "the dynamic expression of flowing lines led first to bent lamination, then to curved joinery, adding joined and shaped graphic patterns of colorful woods, and on to the bending of these flowing patterns." The viewer or user is thus able to draw on the intimacy and familiarity of a chair—its formal, functional role and material relationship to the body—while simul-

variety of construction practices in order to build a specific form, thereby upending Frid's dictum about designing around construction. Inspired by boatbuilding and early aircraft construction, in which maximum strength is achieved with minimum weight, Keyser began in the late 1970s to work with hollow cores and vacuum veneering. His 1978 coffee table (cat. no. 24) is a stunning example of this ability to construct wood shapes with asymmetrical sections. The base is a hollow form, consisting of a steam-molded plywood skin with internal ribs, accented with cherry, maple, and walnut veneers laid over the frame. This artificial twisting and lightening of wood contrasts with the naturally edged elm-log slab used for the top.[9]

Bending—either through steaming wood to increase flexibility or through laminating and gluing thin, flexible strips of wood—became one of the defining techniques of the 1970s, as makers sought to integrate technical achievement with sculptural form. Bruce Beeken, who apprenticed as a canoe builder with Carl Bausch and as a cabinetmaker with Simon Watts before studying with Jackson and Osgood at Boston University's Program in Artisanry, used both bending techniques in building his 1981

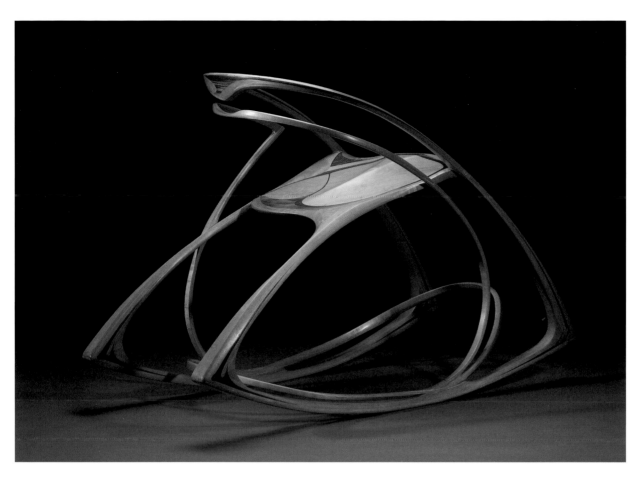

taneously noting its appeal to touch, motion, memory, and abstract notions of sitting.[11]

The interest in bending wood also influenced some makers to develop prototypes that could be put into batch production. Peter Danko (fig. 6), a studio furniture maker in the Washington, D.C., area, became interested in the design challenge of producing a chair from a single piece of wood (cat. no. 27). Drawing inspiration from cutting up and folding cardboard, he began to develop a lamination system that would permit a single-piece mold. Laying up his own plywood with ten layers of yellow poplar sheets (each one-twelfth inch thick), faced with more decoratively figured walnut and oak veneers on the exterior, Danko routed out the slots to distinguish the elements, applied glue to the sandwich, and then formed the chairs in a large particleboard press. After curing for about an hour, he

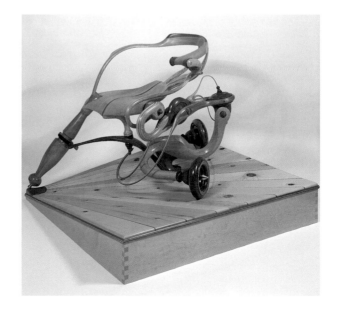

■ Cat. 27. Peter Danko,
armchair, Alexandria, Virginia,
1982. Walnut veneer, poplar,
leather upholstery; h. 30½ in.,
w. 21¾ in., d. 24 in. Museum
of Fine Arts, Boston; purchased
through funds provided by the
National Endowment for the
Arts, Ethan Allen, Inc., and the
Robert Lehman Foundation
1982.507.

■ Fig. 6. Peter Danko (b. 1949).

would remove the chair from the cauls and use a router to trim and finish the edges. The use of bent lamination to achieve the form and routing to trim and polish the edges allowed Danko to make limited production runs of this chair, while still retaining the appearance and value associated with visible crafts-manship and the maker's sensitivity to wood grain. Like Keyser, Danko recognized bending as a design problem to be explored and solved efficiently. In developing this unified, integrated structure, he sought the simplest, perfect solution.[12]

A technique that attracted more limited interest in the 1970s was turning. Stephen Hogbin, a furni-ture designer trained in England at Rycotewood College and the Royal College of Art, took up turning in 1971 because it seemed like a lathe was a "low risk means to set up with minimal equipment and try ideas in rapid succession."[13] At first he made small objects through a process of segmentation, in which he turned plates or vessels that he would then cut into segments and recombine as "fragmentals,"

where the parts were turned around, inside out, or upside down. Later he developed a large lathe—assembled from recycled pipes, an old three-quarter-ton truck rear axle and differential, and a one-horse-power motor—capable of turning elements for chairs, tables, and other sizable pieces. Laminated blocks were turned on a large faceplate and then separated and rearranged in various combinations. While the turning process did not produce the final form, it did produce the components that allowed for the creation of other designs. Hogbin's *Bird Table*, of yellow walnut (cat. no. 28), was made utiliz-ing this technique. The inspiration behind the form occurred during Hogbin's fellowship in Australia from 1975 to 1976. He described the moment of epiphany: "Walking to a political rally in Melbourne's City Square, I saw a flock of those dumb, dusty city pigeons take off. One of the pigeons in flight appeared unmistakeably to me as a turned form for a table. Occasionally ideas happen this way. It is as if the subconscious short-circuits and the flash

■ Cat. 28. Stephen Hogbin, *Bird Table*, Melbourne, Australia, 1976. Yellow walnut; h. 16 in., w. 35½ in., d. 10½ in. Collection of Stephen Hogbin.

■ Fig. 7. Mark Sfirri, chest, New Hope, Pennsylvania, 1975. Mahogany; h. 35 in., w. 30 in., d. 17 in. Photo, courtesy of the artist.

Fig. 8. Michael Graham, *Spiral Pipe Form*, Los Osos, California, 1980. Walnut, East Indian rosewood; h. 48 in., w. 24 in., d. 20 in. Photo, courtesy of the artist.

Cat. 29. Stephen Harris, television cabinet, Toronto, Ontario, Canada, 1978. Walnut; h. 48 in., w. 30 in., d. 36 in. Collection of Dr. Daniel Perlitz and Meri Collier.

Fig. 9. Stephen Harris (1939–1991).

passes to the conscious, where an image is presented as a potential turned form."[14] Hogbin's use of the lathe as a tool in service to furniture design inspired a number of other woodworkers in the 1970s. Using the lathe as an efficient carving tool, Mark Sfirri faceplate-turned parts of joined chairs and chest panels (fig. 7). In California, Michael Graham turned parts of his sliding, circular-drawered boxes. To construct the radial drawers and casings, he cut turned elements into sections and then, like Hogbin, rejoined them (fig. 8).[15]

Formal instruction in schools was not the sole way techniques were developed and passed along. Many young men and women turned to the crafts not simply as a form of counterculture expression but as a career. The appeal of woodworking was the satisfaction of working for one's self, knowing one's clients, and working with one's hands. There was a real immediacy that many found missing in corporate America. In cooperative shops throughout the United States and Canada, self-taught makers freely supported one another and helped build local, regional pockets of skill. In Boston, Massachusetts, in 1970, a group of social activists with little background in woodworking founded a collective named New Hamburger Cabinetworks, designing and making simple, affordable "furniture for the people." The members read all they could, asked questions of knowledgeable woodworkers, and took on a wide range of jobs in order to acquire skills and then strengthen their skill base. The political vision of the founders led to a wide range of projects from playgrounds to houses, their inexperience to a reliance on practical technical solutions, and their lack of capital to the use of recycled materials. However, with experience and its accompanying expertise, several collective members found themselves more interested in furniture and began to shift their focus in the mid-1970s. The sculptural possibilities were the attraction for some of this splinter group, while the allure and combina-

tion of exquisite joinery and richly figured wood proved intoxicating for others.[16]

Such informal learning was occurring in small shops throughout North America. One center of such activity was in Canada, at the shop of Stephen Harris in Toronto (fig. 9). Self-taught and uncompromising in his pursuit of the highest standards of workmanship, Harris eagerly learned all he could about design and construction and developed a reputation as the maker with the greatest number of jigs to guide his tools, ensure accuracy, and facilitate assembly. He also offered space in his shop to talented designers and makers such as Paul Epp, Stephen Hogbin, and Michael Fortune. The combination of his remarkable focus on formal and technical concerns with his personal integrity made Harris a consummate maker and leader within the Ontario furniture community. In his pursuit of organic, sensuous forms, he employed a variety of techniques: shaping or carving individual elements, softly terracing planes to resemble sandy ripples at low tide, or bending lower sections to provide a sense of motion or action. His television cabinet of 1978 (cat. no. 29) documents the ability of this maker to achieve grace and sumptuous, curving forms through high levels of technical perfection.[17]

Other self-taught makers were inspired by the work, especially the writings, of James Krenov, an American who had trained in Sweden and later, in the early seventies, taught in American school programs and workshop sessions. Over the course of the decade, he became the philosophical conscience of the "woodcraft" segment of the field. In his seminal 1976 book *A Cabinetmaker's Notebook*, Krenov criticized contemporary American studio furniture for being heavy-handed, superficial, and driven by fashion. He derided the 1950s emphasis on material at the expense of craftsmanship and lashed out against the insensitive treatment of wood and the harsh laminations of the 1960s. He scolded makers who lacked a "personal relationship with wood" and insisted that the maker needed to engage physically, intellectually, and emotionally with both his wood and his tools. Krenov romantically emphasized "the

language of wood" and called for delicate, sensitive work, in which sharp-edge tools (hand planes, chisels, spokeshaves, and scrapers) could be used to encourage individual expression. Eschewing economic practicality, he extolled the virtues of a "beautifully made drawer with its own whisper and its light movement and the fact that you can take it all the way out, if you have guests at home or if you just want to do so. You pull it all the way out, and you look at the back of it, and you see that someone has really cared. The back is as fine as the front. The bottom isn't plywood; there is no part that makes you say, 'Well, don't look at this; it's not important; it's at the back of this thing, you know, and you never really see it.'"[18]

Appalled by the "contrived designs and engineered woodworking" of makers eager to make a name for themselves in craft galleries and publications, Krenov revered the amateurs who expressed themselves through the subtleties and details of good craftsmanship. His 1982 elegant cabinet-on-stand (cat. no. 30) possesses all the elements of his refined cabinetmaking: a combination of several types of wood (spalted maple carcass set upon an oak frame with partridge wood pulls and cedar interiors); explicit use of hand planes to surface the boards, gouges to carve the pulls, saws and chisels to cut joints; and an aura of self-righteous fussiness. Krenov favored the cabinet form because he believed that working with wood and glass demanded exacting accuracy and patience and that the challenge of bestowing the cabinet with personal expression, of both maker and user, was rewarding. For his cabinets, design and function cohered: valuable objects or curiosities would be stored and displayed in delicate, precious furniture. The very form of the cabinet-on-stand became an archetype that would inspire many woodworkers in the late 1970s and early 1980s.[19]

The impact of the four books Krenov published between 1976 and 1981—with total sales exceeding half a million copies—documents another way in which the field expanded its technical base during the 1970s. Prior to this decade, most makers, amateur and professional alike, who sought to increase their technical base or try new approaches had little in the way of reference material to consult. The main sources were a few books of measured drawings for Shaker and Colonial-style furniture and dated textbooks for industrial arts programs. In 1970, Ernest Joyce's *Encyclopedia of Furniture Making* opened a new chapter in printed technical instruction. This thorough guide to machine and hand work was followed by the appearance of the magazine *Fine Woodworking* in 1975. Launched in response to the desires and needs of the growing number of academic and hobbyist makers, the new journal not only satisfied this audience but also significantly expanded the number of makers throughout North America. Offering a variety of articles—features on individual makers or types of objects, explications of different joinery or finishing techniques, quick tips on methods of work, reviews of tools, in-depth analysis of wood properties and species, plans and drawings for projects—along with extensive advertisements for tools, machinery, hardware, adhesives, finishes, and woods, the magazine raised the levels of conception, production, and reception of studio furniture making. Early articles focused on hand tools and their use (hand planes, hand-cut dovetails, cabinet scrapers, sharpening of edge tools); hand-rubbed finishes (French polish, varnish-oil finishes); the refurbishing of antique hand tools; and the selection, maintenance, and use of small-shop machines like the band saw or jointer. The logo of the periodical—a graphic representation of a series of dovetail pins—underscores the technical emphasis of this decade.[20]

The growth of *Fine Woodworking* and its publisher, Taunton Press, points to the large number of people who earned their living making furniture in a small shop or who seriously pursued their hobby. The journal began as a quarterly with sales of twenty thousand in 1975, grew to a bimonthly with sales of one hundred thousand by 1978, and topped a quarter of a million readers by 1985. Its success led the publishers to issue biannual compilations of work by its readers, starting in 1977. These heavily illustrated

■ Cat. 30. James Krenov, cabinet-on-stand, Fort Bragg, California, 1982. Spalted maple, oak, cedar, partridge; h. 67 in., w. 27 in., d. 11 in. Private collection.

■ Cat. 31. Evert Sodergren, *tansu* chest, Seattle, Washington, about 1984. Koa, Carpathian elm burl, marupa, brass; h. 42 in., w. 36 in., d. 16 in. Private collection.

volumes documented the diversity of expression in contemporary woodworking, the most important criteria being "good design, proper attention to the principles of wooden construction, artful use of wood, careful workmanship." In 1978, Taunton Press also began to publish books on woodworking techniques.[21]

The increasing number of furniture publications was also accompanied by a dramatic "tooling-up" as tool companies targeted the emerging market of furniture makers. Companies such as Woodcraft and Garrett Wade offered a wide variety of hand tools and published inexpensive catalogues for the eager new craftsmen. In the early 1980s, newer enterprises such as Bridge City Tool Works and Lee Valley Tools entered the marketplace. While American machinery and English or Scandinavian hand tools appeared in most of the earlier advertisements and articles, Japanese hand tools—particularly saws and chisels —gained cachet in late 1977. The magazine began to publish articles on Japanese woodworking and tools, and advertised books on Japanese joinery in the late 1970s. Such an interest in the complexity and exactness of Japanese joinery, as well as in Chinese furniture, documents the heightened interest in technical achievement and authentic hand skills that was so characteristic at the end of the decade.[22]

The influence of Asian form and cabinetmaking techniques can be seen in the work of Evert Sodergren, a fourth-generation Seattle furniture maker who learned the craft from his father. His earliest work, inspired by the "soft modernist" examples designed by Hans Wegner, Finn Juhl, and George Nelson, paralleled that of Vladimir Kagan and other designer-craftsmen of the 1950s. Based on the edge of the Pacific rim, Sodergren had developed an extensive familiarity with Asian aesthetics by repairing antique *tansu* chests, but he had not thought to make his own versions until a divorce cost him a prized *tansu* chest. As a reaction, he built his own, employing a variety of meticulous Eastern and Western techniques (for example, the carcass is dovetailed), showcasing figured woods in the sliding panel doors, and making his own metal hardware. After creating the chest for himself, he found that by

the 1970s the market was eager for the design and he could meet the demand (cat. no. 31).[23]

One result of the emphasis on technical prowess and exotic woods was the emergence of the "super object" that came at the decade's end. Frank E. Cummings III (fig. 10), a woodworker who taught at California State University, Long Beach, made furniture and turned vessels with a variety of precious materials accenting time-intensive workmanship. Inspired by the spiritual meaning of everyday objects in Africa, where he had also taught, and by the religious significance of the simple, well-made Shaker furniture, Cummings sought to reinvest meaning in the common object. One form he focused upon was the tall-case clock (cat. no. 32), a type that attracted many other woodworkers as well. Constantine's, a wood merchant in New York, offered plans for clocks with wooden works, and many makers recognized the mechanical challenge of creating accurate gears of wood, the aesthetic challenge of framing a clock and its works in an original or well-designed case, and the cultural reliance on accurate time. Cummings chose imported ebony for the case frame as well as ivory and African blackwood gears for his clock. He carved different piercings in each of these gears, making the final object an explicit repository of the maker's time.[24]

In 1976, Wendell Castle also began a series of what he called "illusions," pieces of furniture with integrally carved accessories that in his case resulted in a wood still-life (cat. no. 33). For these trompe l'oeil objects, Castle used a recognizable furniture form, like a chair or table, as the stage, but he employed stack lamination to build up carved objects lying on these pieces of furniture. While the interest in verisimilitude in an unusual medium linked Castle's work with the carved surrealistic work of Fumio Yoshimura, Castle was always quick to point out that his work in hardwood rather than softwood required more technical skill and thus comprised a higher level of performance. Yet his oeuvre is linked in concept and execution to the works of Robert Bourdon (fig. 11) and John McNaughton (fig. 12), and even to the imaginary laminations of Robert Strini and Michael Jean Cooper (fig. 5). These works,

■ Fig. 10. Frank E. Cummings III (b. 1938).

■ Cat. 32. Frank E. Cummings III, clock, Long Beach, California, 1979–80. Ebony case; ivory, African blackwood gears; h. 68 in., w. 24 in., d. 16 in. Collection of Frank E. Cummings III.

■ Cat. 33. Wendell Castle, *Table with Gloves and Keys*, Scottsville, New York, 1983. Honduras mahogany; h. 35 in., w. 40 in., d. 16 in. Collection of Barbara Lee.

and the technical refinement necessary for their effects, emphasize the high value assigned to time and the skill that was necessarily lavished on a successful object during this period.[25]

At the same time he was finishing up his illusionistic works, Castle also began to explore historical work in the Art Deco style, particularly that of Emile-Jacques Ruhlmann, in which rich veneers and exacting workmanship combined to celebrate the "fine art of the furniture maker." Viewing himself as the successor to Ruhlmann, Castle developed pieces of furniture that were clearly related to French examples of the 1920s, highlighted well-finished veneers, and showcased high standards of workmanship throughout the exterior and interior. His first example in this line, a lady's desk with two chairs (fig. 13), combined imported English sycamore with the patterned decoration of black epoxy that suggested ebony inlay. What really set this desk and chairs apart was the exacting standard of craftsmanship of the bottom and interiors of the desk, putting it in stark contrast to most furniture before the 1920s, in which the nonvisible work was often simple or rough. In celebrating craftsmanship and knocking down the hierarchies among primary show surfaces and secondary interior framing, Castle drew attention to the technofetishism of the period.[26]

The strength of the dominant concern with technique and materials can be charted not only through exemplary practitioners and publications or suppliers that fed the interest but also through responses to it. Some women furniture makers, such as Rosanne Somerson and Wendy Maruyama, felt marginalized by the male-dominated insistence on macho-technical wizardry. To gain acceptance, these women built furniture with complex laminations, visible joinery, and highly figured wood that satisfied those externally imposed criteria. Only later were they able to follow their own interests in exploring personal narrative or decoration.[27]

The case of Robert Whitley, a third-generation cabinetmaker in Pennsylvania, offers additional insight into the values and open membership in the field during the 1970s. Brought up as a furniture

■ Fig. 11. Robert Bourdon, *Texas Taste*, Texas, 1976. Honduras mahogany. Photo, courtesy of Dona Z. Meilach.

■ Fig. 12. John McNaughton, *The Breakfast Table*, Terre Haute, Indiana, 1979. Oak, coffee bean, pine, walnut, cherry, maple; h. 40 in., w. 28 in., d. 28 in. Photo, courtesy of Dona Z. Meilach.

■ Fig. 13. Wendell Castle, lady's desk with two chairs, Scottsville, New York, 1981. Curly English sycamore, purpleheart, ebony, Baltic birch plywood, curly English sycamore veneer, plastic inlay; desk, h. 40⅜ in., w. 41½ in., d. 22¼ in.; chair, h. 34¾ in., w. 21 in., d. 26 in. Private collection.

■ Fig. 14. Robert Whitley, *Throne Chair*, Solebury, Pennsylvania, 1978. Walnut, ebony, maple; h. 34¼ in., w. 25 in., d. 26 in. Photo, courtesy of the artist.

restorer and maker of period reproductions, Whitley gained significant "manual dexterity, technical knowledge, and aesthetic judgment"[28] and earned a reputation as a "Master Craftsman," securing commissions from the White House and the National Park Service. Yet he also managed to pursue his own line of original designs geared toward the emerging market for studio furniture. Unlike Alejandro de la Cruz, however, Whitley consciously sought to situate himself within the emerging market for contemporary studio furniture by developing designs inspired by the work of Sam Maloof, Mark Lindquist, Thomas Lacagnina, and others, and by aggressively marketing his own work. Throughout his promotional literature, Whitley stressed his detailed knowledge and careful harvesting of wood, his kit of tools (including more than 480 different types of chisels, as well as the latest in electric-powered equipment), and his painstaking, careful workmanship. In his brochure for the Whitley rocker—his version of a Sam Maloof rocking chair—Whitley organizes his discussion along headings that chronicle the various techniques—turning, spokeshaving, steam bending, finish sanding, assembly, and finishing. His *Throne Chair* (fig. 14), shown in the 1979 exhibition "New Handmade Furniture" in New York, featured richly figured woods (curly and bird's-eye maple and crotch walnut) and decorative joinery, such as the butterfly keys that reinforce the butt joint of the two boards that comprise the seat. Whitley's attention to the authentic in craftsmanship, his tireless marketing of his technical skill, and his ability to cross over from Colonial reproduction to contemporary styles confirm the ultimate value that was placed on technique, the expanding demand for well-made contemporary work, and the variety of practitioners who were active in the 1970s. It was a catholic community of makers in which Whitley, Krenov, Osgood, and Castle worked from a common ground that was defined by technique and wood.[29]

In Oakland, California, the furniture maker Garry Knox Bennett, who distrusted institutional power and therefore defined himself not within a national trend but rather in opposition to other practitioners, began to critique the studio furniture field.

From his perspective, there were numerous furniture camps in America, including the tight academic work of the School for American Crafts at the Rochester Institute of Technology and the Rhode Island School of Design, the practical naturalism of Sam Maloof and Art Carpenter in California, and the designer-craftsman approach of John Nyquist in southern California and Walker Weed in New Hampshire. It was not merely a case of regional aesthetic sensibility—East Coast Hard-Edge versus California Roundover—but rather a disparity of basic philosophies. Bennett did not begrudge the designer-craftsman woodworker such as Maloof or Carpenter or some of the East Coast academic work, but he *did* develop a particular antipathy toward the technological determinism of Tage Frid and the romantic idealism of James Krenov. To Bennett, the former's approach stifled creative design, precluded humor or social commentary, and contributed to a certain kind of "fussy," overly serious furniture that he felt characterized much of the work made by students. Bennett also believed that Krenov's preciousness was misplaced in a postindustrial world and began to rail against wood-obsessed "techno-weenies."[30]

To provide form to his critique of "woodcraft," Bennett undertook the making of a pair of cabinets that he showed at the Elaine Potter Gallery in 1979. One cabinet (cat. no. 34) featured his most technically sophisticated work to date: imported exotic padauk for the carcass, finger-jointed drawers, dovetailed carcass, bent laminated rails for the glazed doors, and secret latches. To fabricate this chest, Bennett sought out the help of other local furniture makers. Don Braden, who had apprenticed with Art Carpenter and then returned to work in urban Oakland, cut the dovetails of the carcass, and Dean Santner, a self-taught maker who made boxes and designed modular wooden furniture, provided the expertise for the finger joints and lamination. In the upper door of the cabinet Bennett drove a bent, silvered sixteen-penny nail and then surrounded the nail with a series of hammer marks on the polished, richly grained surface. Such a subversive act grew from his impassioned reaction against the technical obsession of Krenov's "woodcraft" and the sophisticated joinery flaunted by many recent graduates of East Coast furniture programs. It also signaled his unwillingness to accept the means as an end unto itself: "I wanted to make a statement that I thought people were getting a little too goddamn precious with their technique. I think tricky joinery is just to show, in most instances, you can do tricky joinery." To balance the "tight" padauk cabinet, Bennett also made a "loose" twin, a redwood and yellow poplar carcass with painted decoration (fig. 15). This cabinet served the same function, but the intent of the design was totally different and more in keeping with his own vision. The emphasis was not on cabinetmaking wizardry but on transcending the fixation on wood and instead exploring color and revealing the relationship of color to mass.[31]

The obsession with technical prowess and exotic woods, against which Bennett rebelled, emerged during a period in which American culture also began to undergo significant shifts away from the idealistic and freewheeling style of the 1960s. Recently, scholars have begun to analyze the 1970s more rigorously, pointing out the fallacy of the popular label "Me Decade." Instead, these revisionists paint a nuanced portrait of the period as one in which rebellion was more circumspect than it had been in the previous ten years. Many individuals did not merely "drop out" but rather sought meaningful pursuits by individual acts of rebellion against centralized authority. Studio furniture making was one such option, and entry to the field remained wide open to anyone who sought authentic experiences: graduates of college programs, artists, or even self-taught individuals. Perhaps the widespread displays of technical virtuosity characteristic of this decade can be attributed to the desire to legitimize a serious alternative lifestyle.

Policy changes of the decade also contributed to renewed interest in furniture and furniture craftsmanship. President Richard Nixon increased the budget of the National Endowment for the Arts (NEA) eightfold and redirected those funds from elite arts organizations (mainly concerned with painting and music) to more regional and local popular art forms, including folk art and the decorative

■ Cat. 34. Garry Knox Bennett, *Nail Cabinet*, Oakland, California, 1979. Padauk, glass, lamp parts, copper; h. 74 in., w. 24 in., d. 17 in. Collection of Garry and Sylvia Bennett.

■ Fig. 15. Garry Knox Bennett, painted cabinet, Oakland, California, 1978. Yellow poplar, cherry, glass, paint, dye; h. 74 in., w. 24 in., d. 17 in. Private collection.

arts. As a result, many regional contemporary furniture exhibitions came to be funded through the NEA. Such policies also contributed to bicentennial celebrations and exhibitions, such as "American Art 1750–1800: Towards Independence" at the Yale University Art Gallery, which brought attention to the furniture of colonial America and celebrated the integrity of craftsmanship. NEA funds, matched with private or corporate grants, also enabled the American Craft Museum (now the Museum of Arts and Design) to mount "New Handmade Furniture" in 1979 and the Museum of Fine Arts, Boston, to purchase seating furniture by Sam Maloof, Tage Frid, George Nakashima, Wendell Castle, and Judy McKie. While the 1970s showed increased growth in the studio furniture field, the following decade would usher in a shift in the hierarchy of makers and a dramatic expansion in the marketplace.[32]

NOTES

1. This transformation is illustrated by comparison of Dona Z. Meilach's *Creating Modern Furniture: Trends, Techniques, Appreciation* (New York: Crown, 1975), which showcases much of the freewheeling work of the previous fifteen years, with the Taunton Press's first two design compilations, *Fine Woodworking Biennial Design Book* (Newtown, Conn.: Taunton Press, 1977) and *Fine Woodworking Design Book Two* (Newtown, Conn.: Taunton Press, 1979). The Taunton Press books feature many more refined examples of contemporary furniture.

2. Robert Morris, "Some Notes on the Phenomenology of Making: The Search for the Motivated," *Artforum* 8, no. 8 (April 1970): 62–66; *Donald Judd Furniture: Retrospective*, exh. cat. (Rotterdam: Museum Boymans-van Beuningen, 1993), 7–21; and Caroline Jones, *The Machine in the Studio* (Chicago: University of Chicago Press, 1996), esp. 344–73. Christine Mehring kindly provided helpful sources on the value of workmanship in art production of this period.

3. For a discussion of ceramics during this period, see Garth Clark, *American Ceramics 1876 to the Present* (New York: Abbeville Press, 1987), esp. 160–71.

4. The classic text on socioeconomic fetishism is Karl Marx, "The Fetishism of Commodities," in *Capital* (1867; reprint, London: Dent, 1974), but see also Walter Benjamin, "The Work of Art in the Age of Mechanical Reproduction" in Hannah Arendt, ed., *Illuminations* (New York: Harcourt, Brace and World, 1968), and Jean Baudrillard, *The Mirror of Production* (St. Louis, Mo.: Telos Press, 1975).

5. On the captions for exhibition catalogues, see *New Handmade Furniture: American Furniture Makers Working in Hardwood*, exh. cat. (New York: American Craft Museum, 1979). In the introduction to the publication, the curator Paul Smith explains, "The application of extensive skills and experiences to the intricacies of

the handmade process has enabled the artists to extract new qualities from their traditional materials."

6. Quotation from Tage Frid, *Tage Frid Teaches Woodworking: Joinery: Tools and Techniques* (Newtown, Conn.: Taunton Press, 1979), 3. On Frid's teaching, see John Kelsey, "Tage Frid," *Fine Woodworking*, no. 52 (May–June 1985): 66–71; Jonathan Binzen, "Tage Frid: Woodworking Master and Mentor," *Home Furniture* 4 (fall 1985): 30–35; and Hank Gilpin, "Professor Frid," *Fine Woodworking*, no. 146 (winter 2000–2001): 80–85. Terms "workmanship of certainty," "workmanship of risk," and "workmanship of habit" are drawn from David Pye, *The Nature and Art of Work-manship* (1968; reprint, New York: Van Nostrand Reinhold, 1971); and Philip Zimmerman, "Workmanship as Evidence: A Model for Object Study," *Winterthur Portfolio* 16, no. 4 (winter 1981): 284–307.

7. On Jackson, see *A Tribute to Daniel Jackson* (Washington, D.C.: Franklin Parrasch Galleries, 1989); and Nancy Corwin, "Vital Connections: The Furniture of Daniel Jackson," *American Craft* 50, no. 3 (June–July 1990): 50–55 and 74–75. A helpful catalogue on Peder Moos is *Pedermoos* (Esbjerg, Denmark: Teknologisk Forlag, 1988). For the operation of the horizontal slot mortising machine, see *Tage Frid Teaches Woodworking: Joinery: Tools and Techniques*, 171–72; and Daniel Jackson, "Hand Shaping," *Fine Woodworking*, no. 3 (summer 1976): 25.

8. Quotation from Michael Stone, *Contemporary American Woodworkers* (Salt Lake City, Utah: Gibbs M. Smith, 1986), 149. See also Jere Osgood, "Bent Laminations," *Fine Woodworking*, no. 6 (spring 1977): 35–38; Jere Osgood, "Tapered Lamination," *Fine Woodworking*, no. 14 (January–February 1979): 48–51; and Jere Osgood, "Bending Compound Curves," *Fine Woodworking*, no. 17 (July–August 1979): 57–90.

9. William Keyser, "Steam Bending: Heat and Moisture Plasticize Wood," *Fine Woodworking*, no. 2 (fall 1977): 40–45; "Portfolio: W. A. Keyser," *Fine Woodworking*, no. 15 (March–April 1979): 52–55; *William Keyser: Wood Furniture, Sculpture, and Ecclesiastical Objects*, exh. cat. (Rochester, N.Y.: Bevier Gallery, 1978).

10. Edward S. Cooke, Jr., *New American Furniture: The Second Generation of Studio Furnituremakers*, exh. cat. (Boston: Museum of Fine Arts, 1989), 32–35; and Tanya Barter, John Dunnigan, and Seth Stem, *Bentwood*, exh. cat. (Providence: Rhode Island School of Design, 1984), 20–21.

11. Quotations from Barter, Dunnigan, and Stem, *Bentwood*, 20–21; see also, Oakland Museum of Art, *California Woodworking*, exh. cat. (Oakland, Calif.: Oakland Museum of Art Special Gallery, [1980]): 1, 11; and Meryll Saylan, "A Slightly Different History" (manuscript of a lecture delivered at the Wood Turning Symposium, Minneapolis Institute of Arts, October 26, 2001).

12. John Kelsey, "A One-Piece Chair," *Fine Woodworking*, no. 20 (January–February 1980): 46–47; and *Bentwood*, 26–27.

13. Edward S. Cooke, Jr., "From Manual Training to Freewheeling Craft: The Transformation of Wood Turning, 1900–76," in *Wood Turning in North America since 1930*, exh. cat. (New Haven: Yale University Art Gallery and Wood Turning Center, 2001), 48. See also Stephen Hogbin, *Wood Turning: The Purpose of the Object* (Sydney: John Ferguson Proprietary and Crafts Council of Australia, 1980); and Donald Lloyd McKinley, "The Wood-Turned Forms of Stephen Hogbin," *Craft Horizons* 34, no. 2 (April 1974): 28–32, 64.

14. See Dona Z. Meilach, *Creating Modern Furniture* (New York: Crown, 1975), 168–69, for a description and illustration of the process, including a drawing of the improvised lathe. See also Stephen Hogbin, "Turning Full Circle: An Exploration of Segmented Forms," *Fine Woodworking*, no. 21 (March/April 1980): 56–60. Quotation from Hogbin, *Wood Turning*, 55.

15. See Dick Burrows, "Furniture from the Lathe," *Fine Woodworking*, no. 59 (July–August 1986): 37–39; Oakland Museum of Art, *California Woodworking*, 9, 16; and Wood Turning Center and Yale University Art Gallery, *Wood Turning in North America since 1930*, 108, 115.

16. Roseanne Somerson, "Cooperative Shop," *Fine Woodworking*, no. 7 (summer 1977): 26; and Edward S. Cooke, Jr., "Coming of Age in Boston: New Hamburger Cabinetworks and Studio Furniture," *Art New England* 11, no. 1 (December 1989–January 1990): 10–13, 49. On furniture making as the political strategy of an individual lifestyle during this period, see Glenn Adamson, "California Dreaming," in *Furniture Studio: The Heart of the Functional Arts*, ed. John Kelsey and Rick Mastelli (Free Union, Va.: Furniture Society, 1999), 32–42.

17. Hart Massey, *Stephen Harris: Designer/Craftsman* (Toronto: Boston Mills Press, 1994); and Tom Hurley, "Furniture-Making in Toronto," *Fine Woodworking*, no. 73 (November–December 1988): 44.

18. Quotation from James Krenov, *A Cabinetmaker's Notebook* (New York: Van Nostrand Reinhold, 1976), 14–15. See also his *The Impractical Cabinetmaker* (New York: Van Nostrand Reinhold, 1979), 6–10. Useful insights into Krenov's philosophy and influence include Michael Stone, "The Quiet Object in Unquiet Times," *American Craft* 44, no. 1 (February–March 1984): 39–43; Glenn Gordon, "James Krenov: Reflections on the Risks of Pure Craft," *Fine Woodworking*, no. 55 (November–December 1985): 42–49; and James Krenov, *With Wakened Hands: Furniture by James Krenov and Students* (Bethel, Conn.: Cambium Press, 2000).

19. See James Krenov, "Showcase Cabinets," *Fine Woodworking*, no. 18 (September–October 1979): 44–50.

20. Krenov's four books published by Van Nostrand Reinhold include *A Cabinetmaker's Notebook* (1976), *The Fine Art of Cabinetmaking* (1977), *The Impractical Cabinetmaker* (1979), and *James Krenov, Worker in Wood* (1981). See also Ernest Joyce, *The Encyclopedia of Furniture Making* (New York: Drake, 1970). Also helpful in this regard is Paul Roman, "Founder's Note," and Jonathan Binzen, "The First Years of *Fine Woodworking*," *Fine Woodworking*, no. 146 (winter 2000–2001): 6–7 and 46–51.

21. Binzen, "The First Years of *Fine Woodworking*." The quotation on the jurying criteria is from *Fine Woodworking Design Book Two* (Newtown, Conn.: Taunton Press, 1979), 6.

22. On the changes in tools, see Roger Holmes, "Tools: Then and Now," and John Lively, "A Woodworker's Journey of Discovery," in *Fine Woodworking*, no. 146 (winter 2000–2001): 71–77 and 96–97. The first *Fine Woodworking* advertisement for a Japanese tool, placed by the Japan Woodworker Catalogue company in Alameda, California, appeared in series 9 (winter 1977). Soon after, Woodcraft Supply sold Japanese saws; they had already published Kip Mesirow's *The Care and Use of Japanese Woodworking Tools* in 1975. In the late 1970s and early 1980s, *Fine Woodworking* published articles by a number of California woodworkers on Japanese planes, saws, and joinery, and then, in 1984, Taunton Press published Toshio Odate's *Japanese Woodworking Tools: Their Tradition, Spirit, and Use*. For a discussion about the synergies between professionals, hobbyists, publications, and tool manufacturers in wood turning, see Edward S. Cooke, Jr., "Turning Wood in America: New Perspectives on the Lathe," in *Expressions in Wood: Masterworks from the Wornick Collection*, exh. cat. (Oakland: Oakland Museum of California, 1996), 39–46.

23. We are indebted to Margaret Minnick for sharing information on Evert Sodergren. See also Portland Art Museum, *Works in Wood by Northwest Artists*, exh. cat. (Portland, Ore: Portland Art Museum, 1976); and Scott Landis, "Design in Context: Woodworkers of the Northwest," in *Fine Woodworking Design Book Five* (Newtown, Conn.: Taunton Press, 1990), 168–69.

24. For information on Cummings, see *Wood Turning in North America*, 48, 52, 124, 126, and 165. On the interest in clocks, see John Lord, "Wooden Clockworks," *Fine Woodworking*, no. 10 (spring 1978): 44–51; and Rosanne Somerson, "It's About Time," *Fine Woodworking*, no. 22 (May–June 1980): 74–75. For a discussion of the super object in turning, see Glenn Adamson, "Circular Logic: Wood Turning 1976 to the Present," in *Wood Turning in North America*, 116–28. Garth Clark used the term "super object" to describe the ceramic sculptures made by Marilyn Levine, Richard Shaw, and others in the 1970s: *American Ceramics*, 153–60.

25. On Castle's illusionistic work, see Davira Taragin, Edward S. Cooke, Jr., and Joseph Giovannini, *Furniture by Wendell Castle*, exh. cat. (New York: Hudson Hills Press in association with the Founders Society, Detroit Institute of Arts, 1989), 54–59. For other examples of this genre of carved furniture, see Dona Z. Meilach, *Woodworking: The New Wave* (New York: Crown, 1981), 137–55.

26. On Castle's exposure to Art Deco work and his responses to it, see Patricia E. Bayer, ed., *The Fine Art of the Furniture Maker*, exh. cat. (Rochester, N.Y.: Memorial Art Gallery, 1981) and Taragin, Cooke, and Giovannini, *Furniture by Wendell Castle*, 60–65.

27. On the struggles of women against technical emphasis, see Edward S. Cooke, Jr., "Women Furniture Makers: From Decorative Designers to Studio Makers," in Pat Kirkham, ed., *Women Designers in the USA, 1900–2000*, exh. cat. (New Haven and London: Yale University Press for the Bard Graduate Center for Studies in the Decorative Arts, New York, 2000), 290–303.

28. *Robert Whitley, Master Craftsman* (Solebury, Pa.: Robert Whitley Studio, about 1978).

29. *Robert Whitley, Master Craftsman*; Carol Conn, "Robert Whitley: Working with Truth in Wood," *American Craft* 40, no. 2 (April–May 1980): 24–27 and 84; and *The Whitley Rocker* (Solebury, Pa..: Robert Whitley Studio, 1978). It is noteworthy that Mark Lindquist, who spurred the wood turning field to maturity at this time, conceived of and directed the latter publication.

30. Edward S. Cooke, Jr., "Garry Knox Bennett: The Urban Cowboy as Furniture Maker," in Ursula Ilse-Neuman et al., *Made in Oakland: The Furniture of Garry Knox Bennett*, exh. cat. (New York: American Craft Museum, 2001), 15–42.

31. The quotation is from Stone, *Contemporary American Woodworkers*, 140.

32. Helpful recent books on the 1970s include Bruce Schulman, *The Seventies: The Great Shift in American Culture, Society, and Politics* (New York: Free Press, 2001); as well as David Brooks, *Bobos in Paradise: The New Upper Class and How They Got There* (New York: Simon and Schuster, 2000).

THE PROFESSIONALIZATION OF STUDIO FURNITURE: THE 1980S

■ Details of Judy Kensley McKie's *Leopard Chest*, Cambridge, Massachusetts, 1989 (see cat. no. 39).

Garry Knox Bennett's 1979 cabinets were just one part of what would prove to be a pivotal year in the studio furniture making movement. That May, the landmark exhibition "New Handmade Furniture: American Furniture Makers Working in Hardwood" opened at the American Craft Museum (now the Museum of Arts and Design) in New York. Intended to highlight the makers' "sensitive love for the beauty of natural woods," the show actually encompassed a wide variety of work, including examples by woodworkers like Sam Maloof and Joyce and Edgar Anderson, sculpture-oriented artist-craftsmen such as Jon Brooks and Tom Lacagnina, and technically accomplished furniture makers like Jere Osgood and Bruce Beeken, as well as stack-laminated and illusionistic work by Wendell Castle and John McNaughton. Most striking and fresh were the playful carved works of Judy Kensley McKie and the informal mixed-media work of Bennett (fig. 1). Such an ecumenical assemblage united the geographically disparate parts of the field and revealed the stratigraphy of its historical development.[1] It also foreshadowed new directions. The story of the 1980s is one of conscious professionalization, in which a group of makers, predominantly academically trained and connected, began to dominate the studio furniture field.

As the work of the fifties through the early seventies showed, many types of furniture makers could produce custom pieces that would satisfy the cultural demands of the period. Makers could be amateurs and professionals, designer-craftsmen and artist-craftsmen, traditionalists, or avant-garde makers. In the 1980s, changing notions of furniture design, a sufficient quantity of academic makers who shared common experiences and concerns, and a new commercial interest in the marketing of studio furniture began to reshape the field. The challenge for studio furniture makers in the 1980s was to convince potential buyers that they had a desirable skill or talent that distinguished their work from the many other types of furniture available at the time. Sociologists refer to this "negotiation of cognitive exclusiveness" as part of the process in which market professions seek to sell conceptual skills and talents rather than simply tangible products.[2] During this decade, the makers, marketers, and enthusiasts for the studio furniture movement began consciously and unconsciously to establish criteria for inclusion in this new group. This professionalization raised public visibility and contributed to a golden age of buying, but there were some unforeseen results as well. It privileged dramatic work that was often colorful, graphically strong, or fashionable, the photographic image of which could be used to secure gallery interest or attract buyers; academic furniture makers, who had acquired specific technical and creative skills and developed impressive resumes; and commercial galleries, which sought out the credentialed academic maker in order to establish a strong national market. Quiet traditional work, self-taught makers, and local exhibitions, on the other hand, faced uphill struggles in the eighties.[3]

■ Fig. 1. Garry Knox Bennett, clock with four drawers, Oakland, California, 1979. Cherry, acid-etched galvanized steel; h. 51 in., w. 12 in., d. 12 in. Photo, courtesy of the artist.

The late 1970s and particularly the early 1980s proved advantageous to studio furniture makers. Broad-based efforts were made in art, architecture, and design to overturn the hegemony of modernism, particularly its abstraction, formal emphasis, and disdain for contextual reference. Although these efforts have often been lumped together under the rubric of postmodernism, the recent stylistic meaning of that term has blurred the various impulses for such reform.

Of primary importance in art was modernism's crisis of certainty. The need to constantly invent an avant-garde position had become self-absorbed, circular, and alienated from normal activity. Instead of pursuing a constant dialectic for radical criticism and renewal, many artists drew from performance art of the 1960s and began to explore more humanistic, inclusive work that incorporated the past rather than rejected it. Their productions explored techniques and materials rather than denying them and engaged aspects of function rather than rejecting utility. Sculptors from fine arts backgrounds such as Scott Burton and Donald Judd conceived of art objects that became furniture through the rigors of a design process and attention to fabrication. Clearly outside the realm of industrial design or the half-hearted attempts of some commercially minded artists to make fashionable furniture, the art furniture movement of the 1970s and 1980s gained vitality from its conceptual clarity, characteristic of sculpture of this period, and from the execution of this idea with a sensitivity to technique and materials typical of craft. As Rick Kaufman, founder of the New York gallery Art et Industrie, explained, "We're trying to redefine the object for the future." In sculpture, the 1980s can be referred to as "the decade of the object," and furniture found a comfortable niche within this formulation.[4]

Many of the prominent makers of this new art furniture had solo shows, but New York galleries such as Max Protetch, Art et Industrie, and the Gallery of Applied Arts became the most important showcases of the genre. For much of this work, there were no boundaries established by media, as was often the case with craft galleries or exhibitions. Rather, the work included a wide variety of materials (such as metal, glass, plastic, stone, concrete, and wood) as well as a broadening of surface treatments (including rough-cast concrete, polished granite, painted steel, anodized aluminum, ebonized wood, or varnished wood), all juxtaposed in unorthodox ways. Among the closely watched artists showing at some of the New York galleries were Forrest Myers, Terence and Laura Main, James Evanson, and Dakota Jackson; other studio furniture makers often made pilgrimages to New York to see the latest work of these artists. The intense interest in the blurred boundaries between sculpture and furniture making even stretched to inspire studio makers in other media, such as Albert Paley in iron and steel (fig. 2) and John Lewis in glass. Not restricted by machinery, labor costs, and marketing to a narrow line of products, American studio craftspeople and artists took chances and explored new variations in an aggressive effort at combining art, design, and craft. Instead of emphasizing abstract design, functional art reaffirms the humanizing elements that combine emotion and intellect: the object's stance, the change in its appearance as one approaches, its feel and use, the level of physical or psychological comfort it affords, and the quality of its workmanship. Furniture, in particular, has evoked a wide variety of responses—ranging from symbolic or metaphoric utility to traditional styling.[5]

Architects also began to question the modernist emphasis on pure form and explicit function. Instead of viewing ornament as debased, something merely applied, architects began to recognize that ornament could be integrated into the meaning of structure and serve as an important component in its symbolic dimension. In *Complexity and Contradiction in Architecture* (1966), the architect Robert Venturi articulated the first critique of modernism's disdain for ornament. Venturi pointed out that ornament and style were not absolute entities, frozen in time with constant appearances and meanings, but instead possessed a variety of ever-changing associative levels, some of which were ambiguous or contradictory. The complexity of meanings provided decorated structures with a richness that engaged the viewer or user and resulted in an emotional and intellectual effect different from the cerebral effect of modernism. In *Complexity and Contradiction* and a second book, *Learning from Las Vegas* (1972), Venturi emphasized the need to draw ideas and inspiration from the varieties of Classical and popular cultural expression. By the late 1970s, many other architects had embraced Venturi's point of view, using Classical and vernacular forms and decoration to infuse their designs with iconographic vitality and heightened emotional meaning. The best of such work did not merely apply accurate historical details to modern forms but rather reinterpreted the past in the process of composition, thereby integrating ornament and structure. The resulting work showed a clear link with traditional design, while remaining timely.[6]

The effect of the new conceptual directions was also reflected in the marketplace for home furnishings. In the 1950s and 1960s, most people purchased mass-produced, standardized objects that were restyled every few years in an effort to stimulate consumption. The various manifestations of the modern style, Good Design, or Pop furnishings were the perfect product for these passive consumers. In the 1970s, however, consumers began to play a more active role in the market, and some makers of domestic goods offered individualistic, distinctive objects designed to appeal to materialistic users and buyers. As the design historian Victor Margolin described it, "design for consumption" gave way to "design for use."[7] To humanize design and endow objects with more intellectually and emotionally affecting presences, small firms and individuals explored and experimented with juxtaposition of old and new materials, color, texture, and ornament.

From 1979 to 1982, the Italian critique against modernism gained great popular recognition. Architects and designers associated with Studio Alchymia, especially Ettore Sottsass (fig. 3) and Andrea Branzi, challenged the expressive poverty and presumptive arrogance of modern aesthetics by recasting design as a form of nonverbal communication that depended upon decorative appearance for meaning. Their furniture was made with industrial materials such as plastic laminates, sheet metal,

and neon, but these materials were integrated or juxtaposed with more traditional materials to create new contexts and relationships. This material expression, along with an emphasis on playfulness, color, and compositional sense based upon the assemblage of decorated units, became the trademark of Alchymia and its better-known successor, the Memphis Design Group. Unlike the former's emphasis on experimental prototypes, the latter was distinguished by its commitment to industrial materials and factory production and also by its enormous impact on international design from 1981 to 1983.[8]

Because designers hold such an important position in the hierarchy of the Italian furniture industry—nearly all firms regardless of size depend upon architects or designers—the Memphis designers were able to quickly produce a large number of New Design pieces to show throughout the world. Yet while this New Design extended certain intellectual and aesthetic parameters, it did not challenge the basic structure of existing modernist furniture production. Implicit within New Design was an emphasis on immediate excitement, a disregard for lasting and quality workmanship, and an expectation of continuing design obsolescence. As New Design subsumed Pop work, the vocabulary changed, but much of the grammar and syntax remained static. Like beanbag chairs and other disposable furniture of the 1960s, the Memphis work remained "semiworks of art," whose color, iconoclastic forms, and sculptured shapes were intended to communicate a hip lifestyle.[9]

In America, the reaction against modern furniture design was not as constrained as it was in Italy, since its design and production were not as centralized within a rigid hierarchy. Although architects and designers in the United States have worked with the furniture industry to produce work very similar to Italian New Design, studio furniture makers were well positioned to take advantage of the new currents. Their independence from industry afforded them the freedom, unavailable to practitioners of Italian New Design, to select their own materials and to change or refine a design while in process.

■ Fig. 2. Albert Paley, plant stand, Rochester, New York, 1988–89. Mild steel, brass, slate; h. 56 ½ in., w. 25 ½ in. Museum of Fine Arts, Boston; purchased through funds provided by the National Endowment for the Arts and The Seminarians 1989.78.

■ Fig. 3. Ettore Sottsass, designer, Memphis Design Group, manufacturer, room divider: *Carlton*, Milan, Italy, 1981. Particleboard, plastic laminate; h. 77¼ in., w. 74¼ in., d. 16⅛ in. Museum of Fine Arts, Boston; Gift of John P. Axelrod 1999.171.

■ Cat. 35. Garry Knox Bennett, ColorCore desk, Oakland, California, 1984. ColorCore, aluminum, rosewood, 24-carat gold plate; h. 30½ in., w. 90 in., d. 30 in. Collection of Bernice Wollman and Warren Rubin.

The results included considerable richness, excitement, and ambiguity. But unlike the designer-craftsman of the 1950s or the technically obsessed maker of the 1970s, the professional furniture maker of the 1980s used technique or material merely as a means. In 1983, the Oakland furniture maker Gail Fredell Smith had warned, "While technical proficiency is a means to freedom of creative thought and work, it is not necessarily a prerequisite for creativity nor does it guarantee success. Woodworking will not come of age until woodworkers stop thinking of technique and woods as ends unto themselves, and start producing pieces of aesthetic value and conceptual substance."[10]

These external changes in the design world had a profound impact on makers in the 1980s. Italian design was influential to Tom Loeser "not so much because I like the stuff, but because it opened up the field, and made more things possible and accepted." Memphis not only expanded the possibilities of furniture but it "eliminated the fear of doing timely or trendy work simply for the fun and need to express something," according to Wendy Maruyama. Maruyama also echoed the beliefs of art furniture sculptors, stating, "I see furniture as an archetypal object that can also be expressive of the times.

Furniture is capable of setting a certain mood and reflecting common ideals in our lives." A willingness to parallel or intertwine with specific concerns and fashions of the time distinguished much of the work from this decade.[11]

Memphis exerted its greatest impact on furniture making by encouraging experimentation with materials, introducing whimsy and color. Garry Knox Bennett, the West Coast iconoclast, worked with different materials to achieve formal and surface variation while relying upon a consistent technical approach, one that revolved around the band saw, table saw, and router. In fact, he gravitated toward materials such as plywood, aluminum, brass, plastic, and Formica/Colorcore because they could be worked with the same kit of woodworking tools. His incorporation of a broad material palette in a field defined by a reverence for a single material—wood—made Bennett a pioneer whose star rose further in the mid-1980s, when his work and approach were highlighted in two exhibitions that emphasized the use of alternative materials: "Material Evidence: New Color Techniques in Handmade Furniture" (1984) and "Furniture in the Aluminum Vein" (1986).[12]

Following the lead of the Memphis Design Group's loosening-up of furniture design through

the integration of plastic laminates, sheet metal, and neon with wood, along with an emphasis on the role of colorful compositional units, the Formica Corporation and the Gallery at Workbench organized an exhibition to encourage studio furniture makers to explore the many possible uses of the recently developed ColorCore, a color-permeated laminate. Bennett's judicious use of various materials had attracted the attention of Bernice Wollman and Judy Coady at the Workbench Gallery, who invited him to participate in the "Material Evidence" exhibition. The show featured work by such nationally known makers as Wendell Castle and Judy McKie, but it was the partner's desk of ColorCore, aluminum, and rosewood (cat. no. 35) created by Bennett that became the lead object in the catalogue and the highlight of show publicity. In the desk, Bennett cleverly inverted the hierarchy of materials: he hid the richly grained rosewood by using it for drawer linings and featured ColorCore and aluminum for the visible exterior surfaces. He also displayed his sophisticated craftsmanship not only in his woodworking but also in his detailed metalwork, especially the gold-plated cylinder detail where the laminate wedge supports the desk, and meticulous machine work. Bennett made the serrated drawer front by routing laminations of different sheets of ColorCore. This enduring symbol of the exhibition has been recognized as the pivotal object in his career.[13]

Bennett himself was more directly involved in "Furniture in the Aluminum Vein," organized by his close friend Norman Petersen and sponsored by the Kaiser Aluminum Company. The two men envisioned the show as an opportunity to showcase a distinctive Bay Area approach to studio furniture: a serious ecumenical design pursuit that included many practitioners of visual culture, a commitment to appropriate workmanship without a preciousness for material or technique, an embrace of humor without slapstick, and a celebration of contrasts. The varied "home bases" of the participants—painters like Jerry Carniglia, sculptors like Michael Jean Cooper, designers like Petersen (fig. 4), and woodworkers such as Sandor Nagyszalanczy—explicitly underlined how the field of furniture was

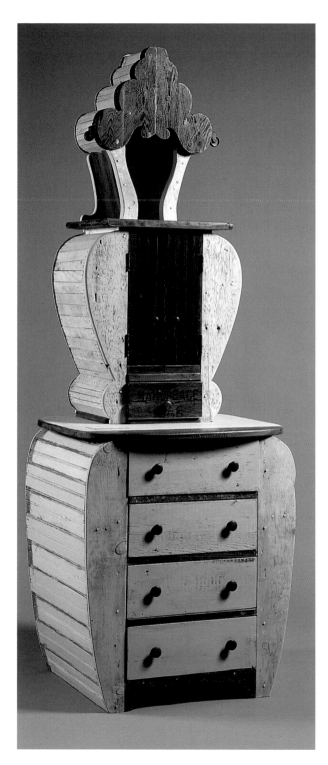

■ Fig. 4. Norman Petersen, aluminum chair, San Francisco, California, 1986. Ebonized Brazilian teak, yellow satinwood, aluminum and bronze powders, aluminized lambskin; h. 46½ in., w. 18⅞ in., d. 23 in. Museum of Fine Arts, Boston; anonymous gift 1991.688.

■ Cat. 36. Stephen Whittlesey, *Caster Oyle Cabinet*, West Barnstable, Massachusetts, 1987. Salvaged pine, poplar, oak; h. 80 in., w. 28 in., d. 24 in. Collection of Barbara Lee.

open to all makers in the Bay Area and that it was not solely wood-obsessed.[14]

The use of recycled materials, including wood, became more acceptable and commonplace during this decade. Stephen Whittlesey, trained as an artist but with extensive experience as a carpenter, collected architectural and marine salvage with interesting patinas (from layers of paint or uneven weathering). He then drew from this stockpile of found wood for formal elements, assembling these into vague furniture forms (cat. no. 36). Functionally, Whittlesey's work shared an irreverence with the work of Sottsass and other Memphis designers, but his use of found wooden objects, the ever-present flotsam and jetsam of modern life, was the flip side of the Italian use of modern mass-produced materials, the flotsam and jetsam of the future.[15]

Incorporation of common materials also characterizes some of the work of Mitch Ryerson during this period. Inspired by the New Design's emphasis on everyday vernacular objects and materials and its celebration of color, Ryerson became intrigued by the formal possibilities of common items such as washboards and plastic milk crates and the colorful potential of packaging labels, and he sought to combine these elements with a fine woodworking approach. He drew on this interest in everyday objects and color most successfully in a series of children's rockers that he made just after the birth of his first child (cat. no. 37). Based on personal experience, Ryerson incorporated off-the-shelf washboards for the back of the rocker, labels from boxes of laundry soap for the seat rails, and clothespins for the spindles underneath the arms (he turned and shaped the legs to resemble large clothespins) to comment on the mounds of laundry that overwhelmed new parents like himself and his wife. This underlying element of autobiography or self-conscious narrative was another new quality of studio furniture making during the 1980s.[16]

The broader definition of furniture in the eighties allowed studio furniture makers greater license in expressing a range of emotions beyond the previously dominant design mode, which was more seri-

■ Cat. 37. Mitch Ryerson, child's rocker with washboard back, Cambridge, Massachusetts, 1986. Maple, cherry, clothespins, washboard, oil paint; h. 26 in., w. 12 in., d. 21 in. Collection of Owen Ryerson.

■ Cat. 38. Edward Zucca, *Shaker Television*, Putnam, Connecticut, 1979. Maple, basswood, zebrawood veneer, Shaker seat tape, gold leaf; h. 36 in., w. 24 in., d. 18 in. Collection of Bernard and Sherley Koteen.

ous in nature. Whimsy or playful humor, evident in Ryerson's rockers, also characterizes much of the work of Edward Zucca and Judy Kensley McKie. The former, who had studied with Daniel Jackson at the Philadelphia College of Art, was a pioneer in exploring the humor of furniture within a tradition of cabinetmaking. His *Shaker Television* of 1979 (cat. no. 38) is basically a chest featuring a drawer made with mortise-and-tenon and dovetail joints, traditions of joinery very much in the Shaker style. Yet Zucca uses other Shaker elements in unusual and surprising ways within this familiar vocabulary: Shaker seat tape becomes the "speaker grille" in the lower section, Shaker knobs are used as the line of "control knobs" on the right side of the front, and a Shaker label is stenciled to the carcass in gold leaf just below the knobs. As the culmination of this spoof, he inlaid a zebrawood panel to serve as the screen because he felt that if the Shakers had had televi-

sion, they would have preferred to watch static.[17]

Stylized flora and fauna, elegantly rendered, imbue the work of Judy McKie with animation and personality, permitting flights of imagination, evoking humor, or providing thoughtful entertainment (fig. 5). Initially trained as a painter, McKie felt more satisfied as a woodworker in the New Hamburger Cabinetworks cooperative. After developing her technical skills by making straightforward, functional furniture, she began to use her drawing skills to explore new ways in which she might introduce a sense of living energy into her work and focused primarily on animal imagery. She started by carving relief panels, but at the end of the 1970s she was working in the round, carving structural members of her furniture; she even used paint to evoke an ancient history and tell a story or make the wood resemble ceramic or other media. She focused on neither the preciousness of the wood nor the significance of the technique but instead carved, colored, or bleached her chosen medium, using the most expedient form of construction. Her 1989 *Leopard Chest* (cat. no. 39) showcases the success of her work. She carved the basswood panels on all four sides, then applied layers of shellac, japanned boule, and paint. She rubbed the stiles and rails with cotton to achieve an aged look and then highlighted the leopard motif with burnished gold leaf.[18]

Paint also became a popular means to conceal wood grain and to celebrate the decorative quality of furniture. Although Wharton Esherick had occasionally used paint and Tommy Simpson had focused on painted surfaces, most studio furniture makers active in the third quarter of the century did not want to detract from the beauty of the wood, instead designing to showcase or enhance it. Suddenly in the 1980s, makers deployed automobile enamel, milk paint, casein paint, or aniline dyes to make pictures, create illusions, clarify structure, or create a tension between painted and natural parts. One of the leaders in the use of paint was Michael Hurwitz, who employed milk paint in conjunction with textures created by carving or sawing as a means of suggesting change or development of meaning over time. The series of bowls he fabricated, then shaped

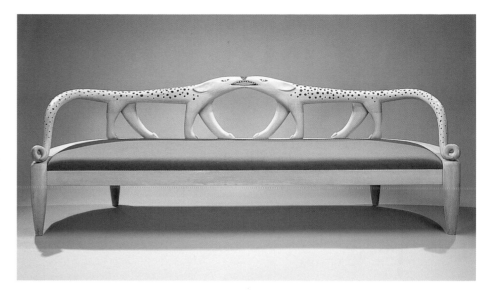

■ Cat. 39. (opposite page) Judy Kensley McKie, *Leopard Chest*, Cambridge, Massachusetts, 1989. Bass-wood with oil paint and gold leaf; h. 33 ⅜ in., w. 49 ⅞ in., d. 18 in. Museum of Fine Arts, Boston; anonymous gift 1991.444.

■ Fig. 5. Judy Kensley McKie, *Leopard Couch*, Cambridge, Massachusetts, 1983. Bleached and burned mahogany; h. 30 ½ in., w. 90 in., d. 25 in. Collection of Frances and Sidney Lewis.

■ Cat. 40. Michael Hurwitz, vessel, Cambridge, Massachusetts, 1983. Mahogany, milk paint; h. 14 ¾ in., w. 13 ⅝ in., d. 6 ⅜ in. Collection of Anne and Ronald Abramson.

with carving gouges and colored with milk paint for the 1983 exhibition "Color/Wood" and later (cat. no. 40), spawned a wide interest in painted texture and milk paint. The suggestion of an Asian sensibility and slight variation in color saturation give this object a powerful presence that far exceeds its size.[19]

Paint was integral to the work of Tom Loeser, who initially tried solid glossy enamels before turning to the softer effects of sponged enamels or milk paints more appropriate for custom furniture. Like Peter Danko (see cat. no. 27), Loeser tried to parlay stable plywood and router shaping to design a chair for limited production (cat. no. 41). Rather than concentrating on the technology of bending as Danko had, Loeser left the plywood elements flat and instead focused upon the mixed use as chair and wall ornament, the ingenuity of a folding mechanism that allowed flexibility, and the painted surface decoration, which unified the different planes and linked the chair to its hanging bracket. The paint scheme was also a means of distinguishing between the matched blanks. While Loeser attributes his original concept for a hanging chair to the Shaker practice of hanging chairs on wall hooks, he pokes fun at the craft history and function by making his example a wall decoration that also happens to serve as a perching chair.[20]

While many studio furniture makers cast their eye toward popular imagery and contemporary colors for inspiration, other academic makers looked rigorously at the past or at non-Western impulses. Many of the self-taught woodworkers painstakingly copied Colonial and Federal furniture in museums and books on antiques, but the studio furniture maker distilled elements of the historical prototypes like a *bricoleur*, breaking down familiar forms and ideas into elemental parts, then combining or recasting these parts with a contemporary grammar to produce a new expressive object. A great number of studio furniture makers in the 1980s examined furniture history and blended elements of the past with a more contemporary perspective, simplifying forms and accentuating tactile elements, deploying a variety of materials or decorative techniques, or creolizing disparate traditions.[21] Among the subtlest of such practitioners was Timothy Philbrick (fig. 6), who served an apprenticeship with John Northrup, a Rhode Island cabinetmaker specializing in reproductions and antique repair. With this skill base, Philbrick went on to study at the Program in Artisanry at Boston University. There he learned how to update traditional work through recombining small historical details in new ways and by using a wide array of currently desirable woods like curly maple and pearwood, while still maintaining the proportions and feel of traditional work. His Grecian sofa (cat. no. 42) preserves the lines of an early-nineteenth-century sofa, but the different legs, rounded shaping rather than relief carving on the rails, and curly maple mark it as a contemporary product not to be confused with examples from the past.[22]

Richard Scott Newman, who studied at the Rochester Institute of Technology and worked for Wendell Castle, took a more ornamental approach with his historically influenced furniture. Drawn to

■ Cat. 43. Richard Scott Newman, demilune table, Rochester, New York, 1990. Maple, ebony; h. 34 in., w. 46 in., d. 20 in. Collection of David J. Leveille.

■ Cat. 44. John Dunnigan, *Versailles Table*, West Kingston, Rhode Island, 1982. Black lacquered maple, purpleheart, ivoroid; h. 25 in., diam. 16 in. Collection of John Dunnigan.

the use of contrasting woods, inlay, carving, cast mounts, and engraved metal on French eighteenth-century work, Newman developed a series of chairs and tables that permitted the viewer a connection to the understandable and naturally evolved decorative past rather than the shocking, provocative present. His magisterial demilune tables (cat. no. 43) featured intricate, highly figured veneers, gilded mounts, and fluted legs achieved with uncommon precision through the use of a router jig, yet the overall impression of such a table was decidedly modern. The combinations of materials and colors linked the work to the aesthetics of the 1980s.[23]

A third, more playful approach to historical forms can be seen in the work of John Dunnigan, who combined an interest in traditional furniture with a willingness to use new materials to explore the conceptual underpinnings of the past. For a

1982 group exhibition with many of the technical virtuosi of the 1970s, Dunnigan developed a small table with circular top, tapered legs, and inverted pyramid feet (cat. no. 44). With these elements, related loosely to Federal-period designs, as well as a proportional system based on the golden mean, Dunnigan remained true to the past. Yet he updated the form in a rather innovative fashion, painting the legs and skirt so that wood grain can be seen only on the top, casting the feet and a molding between the top and the skirt out of pink plastic, and then placing the plastic so that it stood outside the perimeter of the table with Classical proportions.[24]

Other makers looked at non-Western tradition to seek inspiration for meaning in contemporary furniture. Thomas Hucker, who learned furniture making through apprenticeship with a European-trained cabinetmaker, later studied with Jere Osgood at

■ Cat. 45. Thomas Hucker, bench, Smithville, Tennessee, 1982. Beefwood, cast bronze; h. 16 ¼ in., w. 91 ½ in., d. 18 ½ in. Museum of Fine Arts, Boston; purchased through funds provided by the National Endowment for the Arts, Ethan Allen, Inc., and the Robert Lehman Foundation 1982.417.

■ Fig 7. Rosanne Somerson
(b. 1954).

■ Cat. 46. Kristina Madsen,
cabinet-on-stand, Easthampton, Massachusetts, 1989.
Wenge, ebony, obsidian; h. 56
in., w. 36 in., d. 15 in. Private
collection.

■ Cat. 47. Rosanne Somerson,
upholstered bench, Westport,
Massachusetts, 1986. Pearwood, soft curly maple, leather;
h. 22 ¾ in., w. 57 ½ in., d. 22 ¼
in. Museum of Fine Arts,
Boston; gift of Anne and
Ronald Abramson 1987.40.

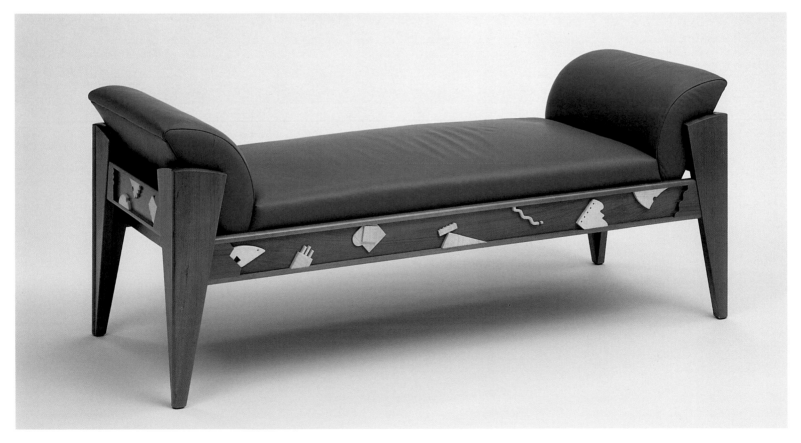

Boston University. Initially, Hucker worked closely within Osgood's design sensibility and emphasis on bent lamination to celebrate technical virtuosity. However, he developed his own interest in Japanese craftsmanship and aesthetics while attending the Urasenke School of Tea Ceremony in Boston. This experience encouraged him to use Japanese forms, details, and approaches not in a derivative fashion but in a fresh way that built upon his earlier exploration of technique. His 1982 bench (cat. no. 45) reveals this new mature vision: the exposed joinery and use of cross-braces to support a delicate, thin top calls to mind the romantic work of James Krenov, but Hucker's use of sword-shaped rails and a simple rectangular top decorated only by the rhythm of the clipped braces reveals a different interest in the designed elements of the form. This internalizing of Japanese aesthetics and the incorporation of bronze bases place this bench squarely in the 1980s.[25]

Kristina Madsen is another studio furniture maker who looked to the Pacific for new ways to personalize furniture. In the mid-1980s she became fascinated with the richly textured, shallow carved surfaces of Maorian and Fijian clubs. The seeming ease of the craftsmen who made these domestic and ritualistic objects, the beauty of the graphic patterns created with shallow relief carving, and the levels of cultural meaning inherent in the abstract designs inspired Madsen to update the free workmanship of the gouge-carved geometric patterns by using a router. She would rout shallow grooves into boards and then cut up and reassemble those boards to establish different geometric rhythms and patterns. In some ways, this approach carried Stephen Hogbin's notion of turned fragmentals (see cat. no. 28) into the furniture field, but Madsen did it in a manner that also recombined the approaches and techniques of different cultures. Using the latest electric-powered tools, she bestowed simple, elegant Western forms like cabinets (cat. no. 46), tables, and benches with personal expression derived from the interrelated marks and patterns typical of the Maori carving tradition. Her conception of texturing, far from mere borrowing, results in intricate sur-

faces that provide a visual vitality to move the viewer's eye over the piece.[26]

Another strong aesthetic direction in studio furniture of the 1980s was a graphic sensibility. Rosanne Somerson (fig. 7), a graduate of the Rhode Island School of Design who had studied at Peters Valley Craftsmen (now Peters Valley Craft Education Center) in New Jersey, originally built large, technically challenging furniture in response to the values of the 1970s. In the mid-1980s, she began to work on a smaller scale and to incorporate playful and expressive detailing. She became particularly interested in creating timeless functional pieces of furniture with simple traditional joinery that would ensure years of enjoyment, relying on subtle uses of paint, carefully applied ornament, and upholstery materials to bestow her work with personal expression. Her use of different materials and surface treatments encourages "a discovery process, possibly through visual connections, alignments, misalignments, or combinations of materials, sometimes with surprises in function or secrets." In the middle part of the decade, she made a series of benches (cat. no. 47), day beds, and couches in which she used different surface treatments (paint, bleach, or natural finish) and different upholstery fabrics (woven cottons, leather) to achieve variations. For her 1986 bench, she used a simple pearwood frame, accented with applied, bleached-maple shapes that acted as "jewels," and then relied on the color of the leather upholstery to provide the strongest visual impact, underscoring the bench's function.[27]

A different sort of visual effect can be found in the work of John Cederquist, who uses fixed-point perspective to explore the relationship between reality and illusion. A graduate of the Long Beach State College in California, he originally relied on bentwood lamination and incorporated molded leather to make containers and seating furniture in the 1970s. In the 1980s, he freed himself from an interest in the technical challenges of form and focused instead on the image of furniture. Working on plywood façades, he began to use veneering, inlaying, and painting to make pictures of furniture with a single "correct" view and multiple different or incorrect views. Yet his chairs still serve seating functions, and his case furniture retains drawers, thereby blurring the boundary of being and representation. In *Le Fleuron Manquant* (cat. no. 48), Cederquist combines this surrealistic interest in function and image with narrative. Intrigued by the story of a Rhode Island desk and bookcase that had been packed up and loaned to an exhibition but then returned without a central finial, Cederquist created the image of a Newport high chest in which different parts are crated. Behind the two-plane façade, he has also constructed parallelogram drawers that slide out on an angle that follows the correct point of view. The visual play of this chest of drawers made it the most illustrated object of the 1989 "New American Furniture" exhibition at the Museum of Fine Arts, Boston.[28]

While the newly articulated interest in objects, the lightening of design, and the theorizing of historical or traditional expression provided important external influences on the studio furniture field in the 1980s, certain changes within its constituency also had an impact. One of the primary trends of this period was the increased number of academic furniture makers and the cross-fertilization between them. In the 1950s, the School for American Craftsmen at the Rochester Institute of Technology (RIT) was the only real university program. Intended to develop graduates "who work not only as designers, modelmakers, foremen and artisans, but also as experimenters in the use of materials and methods," RIT hired Tage Frid to bring the Danish notion of designer-craftsman to the American academy. He set the agenda there until 1962, when he left to take up a position at the newly founded program at the Rhode Island School of Design (RISD). The RISD program in furniture making and design was just one of several established in the 1960s and 1970s.[29]

During Wendell Castle's active teaching at RIT from 1963 to 1969, that program blended the designer-craftsman and the artist-craftsman approach. A greater interest in personal expression was also evident in a number of other academic institutions in which furniture programs were established or energized during the 1960s, including the Philadelphia College of Art (PCA), San Diego State University, and University of Wisconsin–Madison. Many of the instructors in these programs were former students of Frid's who had gone on to apply their technical knowledge to contemporary issues of expression. Two California State University campuses, Long Beach and Northridge, also developed particular strength in furniture design and construction, although in this case through the craft or wood departments, where sculptors, turners, and designers all interacted. In the latter part of the 1960s, student enrollment in these programs began to increase noticeably.[30]

In the mid-1970s, the California College of Arts and Crafts (CCAC) in Oakland reorganized its furniture department from a vocationally oriented shop to one more in line with a studio furniture making curriculum, and the Program in Artisanry (PIA) at Boston University was established. There, students were taught to construct around design and were offered a wide variety of ideas to envision the design as well as a broad selection of technical approaches to execute it. The combination of professors with different but compatible points of view—Jere Osgood, Daniel Jackson, and Alphonse Mattia—and a student body that combined experienced furniture makers with eager undergraduates made PIA the center of functional and expressive work. RISD attracted a similar variety of undergraduate and graduate students. In the 1980s, James Krenov's College of the Redwoods, the Wendell Castle School of Woodworking, and David Powell's Leeds Design Workshops opened to offer rigorous instruction in furniture design and construction for those individuals who might not want to attend a degree-granting institution and wished to focus only on furniture. At summer craft schools, instruction in furniture design and making, usually taught by academically trained makers, began seriously in the mid-1970s at Peters Valley Craftsmen in New Jersey and Anderson Ranch in Colorado. In the 1980s, the venerable Penland School of Crafts in North Carolina and Haystack Mountain School of Crafts in Maine offered furniture sessions more regularly. One of the

■ Cat. 48. John Cederquist, *Le Fleuron Manquant*, Capistrano Beach, California, 1989. Baltic birch plywood, mahogany, Sitka spruce, purpleheart, koa veneers, pigmented epoxy, aniline dye; h. 78 ⅝ in., w. 35 in., d. 12 ½ in. Private collection.

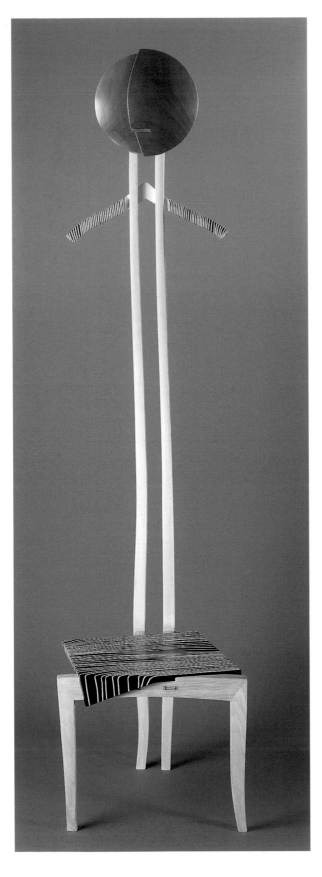

■ Cat. 49. Alphonse Mattia, *Mr. Potato Head Valet*, Westport, Massachusetts, about 1984. Bleached oak and sycamore, dyed and painted; h. 65 in., w. 20 in., d. 20 in. Collection of Anne and Ronald Abramson.

other noticeable trends from the mid-1970s to 1990 was the greater activity and visibility of graduate programs, suggesting the need for accreditation to teach and succeed in the growing field; by 1980 there were eleven such established graduate programs.[31]

The collective histories of the schools and summer programs suggest that demand for instruction and the number of overall students expanded dramatically from the late 1970s on. One result of this expansion was closer awareness of and communication among the different programs. The teachers were aware of the curriculum and approach of each school, and students often gained exposure to a wide variety of approaches through workshops and summer programs. Awareness in the academic field and common interests set up a specific set of criteria that defined acceptance within the evolving new profession. Study with one of the leaders in the field bestowed a young maker with proper credentials.

Alphonse Mattia began his education in furniture with Daniel Jackson at the Philadelphia College of Art in the late 1960s. After graduating and working for Jackson for a short time, Mattia went on to study with Tage Frid at RISD. He then taught briefly at Virginia Commonwealth University in Richmond before accepting a position as Daniel Jackson's replacement at the recently established PIA in Boston. His experience thus provided him influential connections and command of the field, which he in turn passed along to his students. From Jackson he learned to look at historical and contemporary popular modes of visual expression, to celebrate swelled and modeled shapes and exposed joinery, and to investigate narrative. As a graduate student at RISD, he increased his technical repertoire and refined his own ideas. Like his peers, Mattia began to feel frustration about the technofetishism of the field in the late 1970s and chose to explore the potential of color, the design growth possible with series, and a blend of popular culture and design. In 1983 he began a series of valets, inspired by Hans Wegner's valets of the 1950s, but preserved only the low seats and hanging support for coats. Instead, within the basic form, he used shaping techniques, paint, and a variety of motifs to animate each valet with a personality or story. This personality was further brought to life by titling each object, which became an accepted convention among academic furniture makers during this decade. Mattia's *Mr. Potato Head Valet* (cat. no. 49) featured a headrest based on the children's toy. Mattia constructed the valet using woodworking techniques appropriate for bending, shaping, and carving, but his sense of modeling and paint gave much of the surface the plastic quality of the toy. In his teaching, he encouraged students to think outside the technical limits of 1970s woodworking and instead pushed them toward personal expression using more contemporary imagery, different materials, and color. He exposed them to his own academic genealogy, while also linking them to prominent nonacademic makers in the area such as Judy McKie.[32]

Another maker whose career has knit ties among several schools is Wendy Maruyama (fig. 8). Originally introduced to furniture making while still an undergraduate at San Diego State University, Maruyama felt constrained in California and believed she should head east for graduate school. Feeling her technical skills were inadequate, she journeyed first to Virginia Commonwealth University with the intention of developing greater expertise by studying with Alphonse Mattia. When he moved to RIA, Maruyama followed. During these years, she worked very much within the 1970s stylistic approach— accomplished cabinetmaking skills visibly apparent, bent compound laminations, celebration of tropical woods, et cetera. Matriculating at RIT, Maruyama suddenly felt restricted by the highly technical furniture typical of that program at that time and grew anxious to make more expressive furniture. Although her forms remained rectilinear or angular, she began to blend wood with glass, metal, and colored epoxies. She also painted or bleached her work and drew on ideas from her personal experience and the world of popular culture around her. Her *Mickey Mackintosh Chair* of 1982 (cat. no. 50) playfully pays homage not only to Mickey Mouse but also to the Scottish designers Charles Rennie Mackintosh and his wife, Margaret Macdonald Mackintosh, an early-twentieth-century team whose work was extolled in the 1980s

■ Cat. 50. Wendy Maruyama, *Mickey Mackintosh Chair*, Smithville, Tennessee, 1982. Maple, Zolatone paint; h. 60 in., w. 30 in., d. 20 in. Private collection.

■ Fig. 8. Wendy Maruyama (b. 1952).

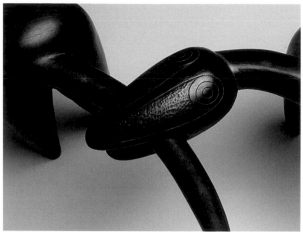

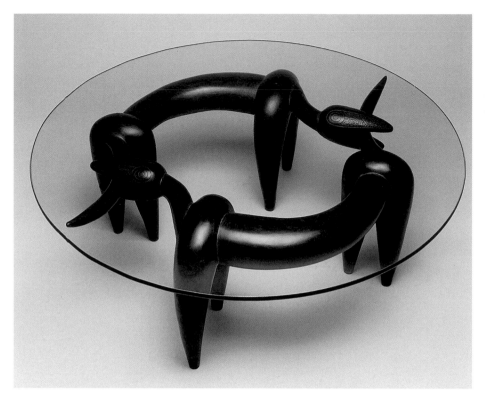

■ Cat. 51. Judy Kensley McKie, *Chase Table*, Cambridge, Massachusetts, 1987. Bronze, glass; h. 16¼ in., diam. 42 in. Collection of Sheila and Eugene Heller.

as being the best of early modern design. The chair blends historical and contemporary themes in its transformation of the signature Mackintosh tall-back chair into a pop icon by capping it with mouse ears and painting the entire chair black.[33]

In 1985, Maruyama accepted a teaching position at the recently revitalized woodworking and design program at the California College of Arts and Crafts. Like Mattia, she sought through her work and teaching to push the field forward, not embracing any one specific style but exposing the students to the same sort of ideas, techniques, and goals presented to their counterparts on the East Coast. She drew on friendships with local Bay Area makers such as Garry Knox Bennett to push her own work with color and paint; taught alongside Gail Fredell Smith, another Californian who had earned her MFA at RIT and was also exploring the possibilities of combining metal with wood; showed her work on the East Coast; and brought her East Coast friends to the Bay Area to lecture and run workshops. Increasingly, the field came to be less regionally defined and became more of a national network.[34]

The web of connections worked in both direct and indirect ways. Having been students with one another or having studied in a program genealogically connected to their own, heads of programs invited one another to lecture or conduct workshops. The gap between East and West Coast institutions and between Canada and the United States narrowed. At the same time, those makers who worked near academic centers often interacted with students or faculty of those programs. For example, McKie mentored Maruyama during the latter's time at PIA, Maruyama encouraged Bennett to incorporate more painted surfaces in his work when she taught at CCAC, and Bennett convinced McKie to cast her work in bronze (cat. no. 51).

Within the changing climate of furniture design, students finishing up in the late 1970s and 1980s often developed in ways that distinguished them from their mentors. Hank Gilpin, who studied with Tage Frid at RISD and was impressed by his instructor's practical sense of making a living as a small-shop furniture maker, developed a very different design sense. Rather than design around construction, Gilpin closely studied historical furniture to develop empirical knowledge about techniques, style, and the interrelationships between them. He downplays conception—to him "good design means solving problems" of practical use and affordability. But he draws from a wealth of visual images and ideas as a result of his historical studies. This knowledge and his understanding of wood technology have allowed Gilpin to make high-quality and unpretentious furniture with subtle handwork. Yet one of his chests of drawers (cat. no. 52) will never be confused with reproduction work. It is reminiscent of neither seventeenth-century joined oak furniture nor eighteenth-century refined dovetailed mahogany furniture. His reliance on paneled carcass construction reveals both an awareness of the way wood expands and contracts across the grain as well as an interest in exploring the decorative possibilities of the technique. He raised the plane of the panel so that it is slightly proud from the framing rails and stiles and sawed the boards used for the panel in a different manner from those used for the framing elements. The 1980s playfulness affected even his "high-style direct woodworking," as is evident in his use of native hardwood not often found in high-end eighteenth-century furniture (oak, ash, curly maple) and his interest in wood's various associations, as well as his incorporation of tropical woods like bubinga for pulls and details.[35]

William Walker, who studied with James Krenov at the College of the Redwoods, developed a style that paralleled Gilpin's. Using either local or tropical hardwoods, Walker distinguished himself from his teacher by building larger forms to fit everyday needs while retaining fine workmanship and a sense of how parts relate to one another. His desk (cat. no. 53) emphasizes the decorative properties of contrasting light and dark woods, but the shaping of the legs, the arched front skirt, and the low profile of the drawers and pigeonholes provide an overall delicate effect. Walker retains the eye for detail characteristic of his instructor, but situates the form more fully within the tradition of substantial, utilitarian furniture, rather than within the precious realm of display cabinets.[36]

■ Cat. 52. Hank Gilpin, chest of drawers, Lincoln, Rhode Island, 1988. Curly maple, Macassar ebony; h. 46 in., w. 32 in., d. 18 in. Collection of Rani C. Johnson.

Michael Fortune, who studied with Donald McKinley at Sheridan College in Ontario, Canada, picked up the design impulse of his teacher. Relishing the challenge to bring aesthetic innovation and technical knowledge together to make high-quality furniture, Fortune eagerly sought out ways to use jigs for limited-production lines of forms that possessed great decorative or finish detail. His bent lamination chairs (cat. no. 54) were Fortune's first real successful venture into this realm. Building with a sequence of thirty-eight jigs, he has introduced variation with his choice of woods and inlays. The chair is firmly ensconced in the field of studio furniture because of its detail and finish. Fortune successfully combines design innovation, technical understanding, and pleasing details.[37]

With the rise of school programs and increased interaction among students and teachers, academic furniture makers began to talk primarily among themselves about the ideas and content of their work, thereby shutting out the amateur or the self-taught. The development of a commonly under-stood language was hinted at in the October 1979 conference "Wood '79: The State of the Art," in which more than four hundred woodworkers gathered at SUNY's Purchase College to discuss design, tools, techniques, and marketing. While the audience included professionals, amateurs, students, and teachers, the agenda was decidedly dominated by the more academic makers and precluded the concerns of the traditional craftsman, hobbyist, or limited-production cabinetmaker. This fissure was to grow during the following decade as those who were excluded—earlier makers or nonacademic makers—began to critique the new work. Many first-generation woodworkers, who blazed the trail and inspired those who followed, were critical of the work so characteristic of the 1980s. Maloof, a self-taught woodworker, felt that the domination of college training had divorced the craftsperson from real-world concerns and resulted in work of great "preciousness." George Nakashima, who emphasized that design is dictated by material, found the new emphasis on personal expression misguided: "Where you start with a concept and then you try to execute it in almost any material…it's the wrong use of wood." The emphasis on concept first, then technique and material, was to Nakashima "just simply crap."[38]

Two articles in particular point out the fissure precipitated by the increasing professionalization of the field. In the first of these, a 1983 exhibition review for *Fine Woodworking*, Arthur Espenet Carpenter articulated the concerns of his peers and labeled the new work "artiture." He distrusted the emphasis on play, pun, or farce; sensed there was little concern for technique; and based his judgment largely on common notions of utility. To him, "most artiture pieces had little to do with wood and less to do with craftsmanship." Revealing a bias for quiet practicality, Carpenter felt that ego and a desire for higher prices had driven this work. Ironically, most of the work was well made, using wood as the primary material. What distinguished it from the work that Carpenter admired was the attempt of the makers to use wood and traditional techniques in a different context. They sought to explore more varied and challenging avenues, to make the pieces "useful, fun, individual, and visually pleasing." Wendy Maruyama could have been speaking for this group of makers when she explained how she was merely building on her predecessors: "Although I feel an obligation to teach the traditions of woodworking, I also hold strong to the ideas of experimentation with concepts rather than falling back on what's been done before."[39]

In 1984, the maker and writer Anthony Chastain-Chapman published a review of several studio furniture exhibitions in *American Craft*. With a historian's eye, he contrasted the coherent approach and style of the "Early Craft Revival" of the 1950s with the diffuse work of the 1980s. Chastain-Chapman sensed a concern with "design" that led not to full understanding and internalization of techniques, materials, and historical styles but rather to the vagaries of fashion: "Not interested in looking inward to the slowly evolving modes of an autarkic movement, they look instead to an outer world where fashion seems to rule. Here they find uncertainty and confusion, quirks and fads, tastemakers without author-

ity." In his opinion, the work of the 1980s represented a visual cacophony that privileged the trendy, the flashy, and the individual.[40]

The fact that Carpenter and Chastain-Chapman were commissioned to make gallery visits also attests to the increased visibility of the field and the rise of galleries. The emergence of the studio furniture market can be seen not only in the growth of a Taunton Press publishing house, which expanded beyond *Fine Woodworking* and a series of occasional design books to a number of books and video tapes about various techniques, but also in the emergence of new venues for shows and sales. In the 1960s and 1970s, most makers worked on commission and relied on word of mouth to reach new clients. Studio furniture makers who wanted to show their work were restricted to small craft shops, American Craft Council fairs (which emphasized sales to retailers), and regional museums or craft centers. Galleries, which fill an essential role in educating the public and nurturing the consumer or collector, played only a small part. Craft galleries, such as The Elements Gallery in New York and Greenwich,

■ Cat. 54. Michael Fortune, chair, Toronto, Ontario, Canada, late 1980s. Walnut, holly; h. 34 in., w. 25 in., d. 25 in. Collection of Audrey Mackenzie.

■ Fig. 9. Richard Kagan, chest of drawers, Philadelphia, Pennsylvania, 1981. Walnut; h. 36 in., w. 44 in., d. 20 in. Photo, courtesy of the artist.

Connecticut, and The Works Gallery in Philadelphia, carried some wooden objects.[41]

The exception to this rule was the Richard Kagan Gallery in Philadelphia, the first devoted exclusively to wood and furniture. Opened in 1973 by the furniture maker in a space adjoining his shop, the gallery exhibited a wide variety of work, from the conservative older approaches of the turner Bob Stocksdale to the organic work of Wendell Castle and further to the newer refined works of Dan Jackson, Jere Osgood, Edward Zucca, Alphonse Mattia, and other emerging students. The gallery grew out of Kagan's knowledge as a maker and his commitment to the field (fig. 9). He subsidized the gallery with his workshop budget, used it as a way to increase visibility for his own work, and showed only the work of makers he knew and respected. Kagan mounted about three shows a year, eschewed flashy publicity, and paid little attention to sales. The real impact of the gallery was on the makers themselves. Students and younger woodworkers without com-

missions had something to aim for, while established makers could examine new developments firsthand. The gallery offered peer recognition and review, but as the commercial landscape shifted in the 1980s, Kagan found his approach anachronistic and closed the gallery in 1983.[42]

The greater visibility and market health of the studio furniture field in the 1980s was evident in an increasing number of craft and art galleries, more professional national exhibitions, the active participation of larger museums, and an expansion of direct sales. Bernice Wollman and Judy Coady at Workbench Gallery in New York developed theme shows that charted the consolidation of the field. Beginning with a Garry Knox Bennett show in 1980, Workbench Gallery sustained a program that included a show of works by PIA faculty and students, another for the works of women only, and one in which the makers were required to work in more than wood. In 1981, the Society of Arts and Crafts in Boston also began to show PIA furniture. Other important galleries of this period included Pritam and Eames, established by Warren and Bebe Johnson in East Hampton, New York, in 1980, and Snyderman Gallery, established in Philadelphia in 1983 by Rick and Ruth Snyderman. These two galleries assembled stables of makers, mounted special exhibitions, produced colorful announcements and publicity materials, and stimulated interest in commissions. Pritam and Eames as well as Snyderman strove to show the work of both established and new talent.[43]

The dramatic commercial turning point, however, occurred in 1983, when Wendell Castle, whose 1978 exhibition of illusionistic work at Carl Solway Gallery in New York received little public attention, recognized a new interest in historically inspired work. With the encouragement of his later New York gallery representative, Alexander Milliken, Castle devoted his considerable energies and resources from 1981 until 1983 to the production of contemporary interpretations of Biedermeier and Art Deco furniture with exquisite woods and refined techniques. In direct opposition to modernism and in accordance with postmodern theory, he proclaimed "more is more." Although the pieces were well designed and celebrated workmanship as a form of art, their importance was more in the impact upon the marketplace. Milliken marketed the work aggressively and sold a lady's writing desk with two chairs (see chapter 3, fig. 13) by Castle for the incredible price of seventy-five thousand dollars, far exceeding any previous price for studio furniture. Milliken's effective promotion and the prices he established sent shock waves throughout the craft and art worlds. Castle set the agenda for the new professional studio furniture maker by undertaking speculative work, emphasizing technical skill as an art form, and deploring the low prices typical of mere craftwork.[44]

In direct response to the 1983 Milliken show and the growth of practitioners, interest in studio furniture greatly expanded to a national audience. The cumulative effect of gallery education and the exhibition of consistently good work led to an expansion of the market. Galleries that had formerly shown only fine arts, such as Henoch in New York and Clark and NAGA in the Boston area, began to show studio furniture consistently. Interest was wide and not restricted to the East Coast: Gallery Fair in Mendocino, California, began to mount successful furniture exhibitions, and Hokin Kaufman Gallery in Chicago hosted an annual furniture show entitled "Furniture of the Eighties," beginning in 1983. Another Chicago event, "New Art Forms," began in 1986 and placed furniture within a mainstream context of twentieth-century decorative arts, including glass, ceramics, and fiber.[45] (Now called "SOFA"— for "sculpture, objects, and functional art"—this exposition is currently held on a biannual basis in Chicago and New York.)

With furniture's increased exposure and a growing competition among galleries, publicity assumed an important role in the presentation of material. Many galleries began to rely on color slides and photographs to showcase their offerings. Even *Fine Woodworking*, initially founded as a black-and-white magazine along the lines of *Scientific American*,

began to feature a color cover in 1984. It is no coincidence that painted surfaces, richly colored woods, and strong graphic design elements dominated the field during the 1980s. These types of furniture, rather than quiet refined work or complex asymmetrical work, were easily translated as photographic images. The difficulty of showing the full range of one maker's work, as well as the problems inherent in gathering, shipping, and displaying a sizable number of pieces for a single show, reinforced the importance of good photography. Even the graphic design of invitations and advertisements for *American Craft* and other magazines became noticeably more professional during this period.[46]

Three publications and several traveling exhibitions also served to broaden the public's awareness of studio furniture. In *Contemporary American Woodworkers*, Michael Stone chronicled the personal histories of ten of the field's founders: Esherick, Maloof, Stocksdale, Castle, Osgood, Bennett, and several others. This well-researched volume provided an essential historical foundation for furniture makers, gallery owners, and the interested public. Patricia Conway and Robert Jensen's *Ornamentalism: The New Decoration in Architecture and Design* linked the studio work of Bennett, Castle, McKie, Zucca, and others to a broader movement in architecture and design. During an era in which leading architects such as Robert Venturi and Michael Graves were deified and commodified, such linkage bestowed great legitimacy on the growing field of furniture. A third book, Denise Domergue's *Artists Design Furniture*, linked studio furniture makers like Castle, Maruyama, and McKie to a more functional art that she believed was able "to liberate us from our habitual responses, to broaden our expectations of functional forms, and to offer us a means of reclaiming our humanity."[47]

Conway and Jensen were indebted to the educational outreach of Workbench Gallery. In 1985, Workbench and Formica together organized the traveling exhibition "Material Evidence: New Color Techniques in Handmade Furniture," in which nineteen studio furniture makers used the plastic laminate ColorCore to construct furniture. With a wide variety of styles and ideas, the show served as the American version of Memphis-designed furniture. It demonstrated to a U.S. audience that studio furniture transcended wood and was not necessarily all about serious design. A touring exhibition of Castle's clocks, "Masterpieces of Time," which opened at the Taft Museum in Cincinnati, also attracted national attention, but less for the concepts of the clocks than for their scale, ostentation, and six-figure prices.[48]

The 1986 exhibition "Craft Today: Poetry of the Physical," at the American Craft Museum in New York, served as an announcement that studio furniture was now fully accepted within the crafts world. In both quality and quantity, furniture dominated the show, eclipsing the well-established media of ceramics and glass. Large color photographs in a slickly produced coffee-table catalogue made the objects all the more alluring, and a national tour presented both the objects and catalogue to a wider audience. Such visibility helped raise awareness of a field that had been burdened by limited exposure, the result of the time-consuming and relatively slow processes and the tendency for commissioned work. Soon after "Poetry of the Physical," *House and Garden*, *Metropolitan Home*, *Metropolis*, and other interior-design magazines began to publish features on studio furniture and included interiors complete with examples of recent work. Hard on the heels of the two exhibitions came Patricia Conway's *Art for Everyday: The New Craft Movement*, a profusely illustrated book demonstrating that collecting and practical use of studio furniture could coexist.[49]

Broader exposure led to the emergence of new markets. Previously, most work was purchased spontaneously or commissioned for a specific purpose, but, in the 1980s, young professionals in their thirties and forties, especially those in venture capital and investment companies, began to buy studio furniture for their own use. Most buyers purchased just a few pieces, either all from the same maker or a small number from several. A new exceptional group of buyers emerged at this time as collectors. Ronald and Anne Abramson, Virginia and Andrew

Lewis, and Peter Joseph began to broadly acquire from numerous makers. The surge of interest in collecting helped fuel the work of first-generation maker Sam Maloof. In the 1960s and early 1970s, Maloof had not been able to sell many rockers, but over the course of the 1980s and early 1990s he began to devote half of his work time to them, which gained popularity from such prominent buyers as the Museum of Fine Arts, Boston, U.S. Vice President Walter Mondale, and U.S. President Ronald Reagan. The new collectors followed these trends, and buyers clamored for the well-publicized Maloof form. He also began to substitute curly maple, a more decorative wood that appealed to the new clients, for his traditional, subtler walnut. The fetishizing of the craft object thus triggered the emergence of a well-understood Maloof style, creating a recognizable fashion out of what had once been a decidedly antifashion pursuit, seemingly without style. As the number of collectors began to increase, museums, ranging in size from the Brockton Art Museum/Fuller Memorial to the Detroit Institute of Art, began to purchase and acquire the work.[50]

Publications, exhibitions, and noticeable purchasing patterns reflect a heightened public awareness of and involvement in the field, but many furniture makers continued to play a major role in their own professionalization. Two smaller but highly influential shows developed by makers had more of an impact on the universe of the maker than on the market or collector: the 1983 "Color/Wood" at the Brookfield Craft Center in Connecticut and the 1986 "Furniture in the Aluminum Vein" at the Kaiser Center Art Gallery in Oakland, California. The former, organized by James Schriber, a PIA graduate who was another trailblazer in painted furniture (fig. 10), emphasized the ability of paint and color to free up and reenergize the field. Norman Petersen curated the aluminum show, further encouraging furniture makers to incorporate other media.[51]

At the end of 1989, two museum exhibitions triggered an explosion of public interest in studio furniture: "Furniture by Wendell Castle" at the Detroit Institute of Arts and "New American

Furniture" at the Museum of Fine Arts, Boston. These shows provided historical analysis, legitimized the field with institutional support, and educated a wider audience about studio furniture's roots and dynamic heterogeneity. The success of this outreach was the catalyst for nationally prominent critics to write about the field: John Updike contributed a review article to *Art and Antiques*, and Arthur Danto published his commentary in *The Nation*. *Newsweek*, *USA Today*, and other national publications also drew popular attention to the exhibitions.[52]

The success of professionalization in the 1980s was readily apparent, but the process also raised the question of what was left behind. The cultural critic Edward Said wrote about the downside of professionalization, pointing out that it brought with it certain pressures. He warned about specialization and the accompanying cult of the "certified expert," which, in the case of studio furniture, placed emphasis on school-educated makers who aspired to gallery representation as a means of acquiring credentials. He also warned about the tendency of professionals to gravitate toward power and authority—in this case, the marketplace. To correct this potentially dangerous shift, Said encouraged the reinstatement of the amateur, someone not beholden to a particular power system but instead willing to fight trends and fashion. Much of the work of the 1980s demonstrates the evolution of professionalization, but the writings of Carpenter and Chastain-Chapman and the work of committed self-taught or amateur makers provided an excellent counterbalance to the shift. Future historians of American studio furniture will chart how these tensions play out into the twenty-first century.[53]

■ Fig. 10. James Schriber, painted cabinet, New Milford, Connecticut, 1985. Painted poplar; h. 84 in., w. 36 in., d. 18 in. Private collection.

NOTES

1. The catalogue of the 1979 exhibition provides valuable insight into the state of the field in the late 1970s: American Craft Museum, *New Handmade Furniture: American Furniture Makers Working in Hardwood*, exh. cat. (New York: American Craft Museum, 1979). For reviews of this exhibition, see "Working Wonders with Wood: American Furnituremakers Working in Hardwood," *American Craft* 39, no. 3 (June–July 1979): 10–15; and John Kelsey, "Editor's Notebook," *Fine Woodworking*, no. 18 (September–October 1979): 89.

2. The term "negotiation of cognitive exclusiveness" is borrowed from Magali Sarfatti Larson, *The Rise of Professionalism: A Sociological Analysis* (Berkeley: University of California Press, 1977). For an insightful and suggestive application of market professionalization to American material culture, see Dell Upton, "Pattern Books and Professionalism: Aspects of the Transformation of Domestic Architecture in America, 1800–1860," *Winterthur Portfolio* 19, nos. 2–3 (summer–autumn 1984): 107–50.

3. For a review that reveals this split, see Glenn Gordon, "Current Work," *Fine Woodworking*, no. 68 (January–February 1988): 81–85. Lewis Buchner also differentiates between self-taught makers (who work in a "more intuitive, nonverbalized, and less intellectual way") and schooled makers (who are "more likely to be more comfortable with verbal concepts and reasoned attempts at solving aesthetic and philosophical issues") in his "Ideas Go Further Than Technique," *Fine Woodworking*, no. 46 (May–June 1984): 76–81.

4. Kaufman is quoted in Barbara Jepson, "Art Furniture," *American Craft* 45, no. 5 (October–November 1985): 10. The view of the 1980s as "the decade of the object" is drawn from Joseph Giovannini's helpful essay "Wendell Castle: Occupying the Blur," in Davira S. Taragin, Edward S. Cooke, Jr., and Joseph Giovannini, *Furniture by Wendell Castle*, exh. cat. (New York: Hudson Hills Press in association with the Founders Society, Detroit Institute of Arts, 1989), 101–15. See also Brian Wallis, ed., *Art after Modernism: Rethinking Representation*, exh. cat. (New York: New York Museum of Contemporary Art, 1984); and Judith Fox, *Furniture, Furnishings: Subject and Object*, exh. cat. (Providence: Rhode School of Design Museum of Art, 1984).

5. A helpful discussion of this terrain is Jepson, "Art Furniture," 10–17.

6. Robert Venturi, *Complexity and Contradiction in Architecture* (New York: Museum of Modern Art, 1966); and Venturi et al., *Learning from Las Vegas* (Cambridge: MIT Press, 1972).

7. Margolin develops this distinction in "Consumers and Users: Two Publics for Design," in *Phoenix: New Attitudes in Design* (Toronto: Queen's Quay Terminal, 1984): 48–55.

8. The best summary of Memphis is Barbara Radice, *Memphis: Research, Experiences, Results, Failure and Successes of New Design* (New York: Rizzoli, 1984). For a recent reassessment of Memphis, see Horacio Silva, "Memphis Has Left the Building," *New York Times Magazine: Home Design* (spring 2002): 42–48.

9. On the structure of the Italian furniture industry, see Josh Markel, "Furnituremaking in Italy: Competition and Cooperation," *Fine Woodworking*, no. 58 (May–June 1986): 50–53. On the connection of 1950s Good Design and 1960s pop, see Nigel Whiteley, "'Semi-Works of Art': Consumerism, Youth Culture and Chair Design in the 1960s," *Furniture History* 23 (1987): 108–26.

10. Smith wrote this in a letter to the editor that responded to Arthur Espenet Carpenter's "Artiture": *Fine Woodworking*, no. 40 (May–June 1983): 4. See also Buchner, "Ideas Go Further Than Technique," 76–81.

11. On Loeser's indebtedness to Memphis, see Edward S. Cooke, Jr., *New American Furniture: The Second Generation of Studio Furnituremakers*, exh. cat. (Boston: Museum of Fine Arts, 1989), 64. For Maruyama's views, see Cooke, *New American Furniture*, 74; and Denise Domergue, *Artists Design Furniture* (New York: Harry N. Abrams, 1984), 117.

12. For an in-depth analysis of Bennett's career and influence, see Ursula Ilse-Neuman et al., *Made in Oakland: The Furniture of Garry Knox Bennett*, exh. cat. (New York: American Craft Museum, 2001).

13. *Material Evidence: New Color Techniques in Handmade Furniture*, exh. cat. (Washington, D.C.: Smithsonian Institution, 1985).

14. John Marlowe, "California Crossover," *Fine Woodworking*, no. 61 (November–December 1986): 60–64.

15. On Whittlesey, see *Woodwork*, no. 9 (spring 1991): 32–36.

16. See Cooke, *New American Furniture*, 100–3.

17. Ibid., 128–31.

18. Ibid., 80–83; and Carl Belz, *McKie: Todd McKie and Judy Kensley McKie*, exh. cat. (Waltham, Mass.: Rose Art Museum of Brandeis University, 1990).

19. Cooke, *New American Furniture*, 60–63; and Kari Main, *Please Be Seated: Contemporary Studio Seating Furniture*, exh. cat. (New Haven: Yale University Art Gallery, 1999), 24–25.

20. Cooke, *New American Furniture*, 64–67; and Main, *Please Be Seated*, 14.

21. Folklorist Henry Glassie explains bricolage in a craftsperson's conceptual stage in "Folk Art," in Richard Dorson, ed., *Folklore and Folklife* (Chicago: University of Chicago Press, 1972), esp. 259–60.

22. Cooke, *New American Furniture*, 92–95.

23. Ibid., 84–87.

24. Ibid., 48–51.

25. Ibid., 56–59.

26. Ibid., 68–71; and Andrea Olsen, "Kristina Madsen: Textures with a Touch of Class," *Woodwork*, no. 10 (summer 1991): 38–42.

27. Cooke, *New American Furniture*, 116–19.

28. Ibid., 40–43.

29. Quotation is from *Interiors*, April 1946, as quoted in Arthur Pulos, *The American Design Adventure, 1940–1975* (Cambridge, Mass.: MIT Press, 1988), 170. On the evolution of the School for American Craftsmen, see *Craft Horizons* 4, no. 8 (February 1945): 1; *Craft Horizons* 4, no. 10 (August 1945): 4–9; *Craft Horizons* 5, no. 13 (May 1946): 5; *Craft Horizons* 8, no. 21 (May 1948): 14; Harold Brennan, "The School for American Craftsmen," *Craft Horizons* 20, no. 36 (May–June 1960): 21–24; and *SAC: Twenty-fifth Anniversary* (Rochester: Rochester Institute of Technology, 1975), 2–3.

30. There is no in-depth study of either the field of academic furniture making or any of these individual programs. For a brief introduction, refer to the bibliography and the "Selected Schools and Programs" section in this book as well as Cooke, *New American Furniture*, 13, 17–23; and Taragin, Cooke, and Giovannini, *Furniture by Wendell Castle*, 24 and 36–37. An article that points out the widespread interest in woodworking instruction in the 1970s is "Woodworking Schools: Where They Are, What They Offer," *Fine Woodworking*, no. 6 (spring 1977): 62–63. Most of the schools tend to offer vocational education in the broadest sense of woodworking.

31. On the increased concentration in academic furniture making and the importance of graduate schools, see "Woodworking Education," *Fine Woodworking*, no. 26 (January–February 1981): 88–95. See also Taragin, Cooke, and Giovannini, *Furniture by Wendell Castle*, 59–60.

32. Cooke, *New American Furniture*, 76–79.

33. Ibid., 72–75.

34. See Edward Cooke, Jr., "Garry Knox Bennett: The Urban Cowboy as Furniture Maker," in Ilse-Neuman et al., *Made in Oakland: The Furniture of Garry Knox Bennett*, 32–35; and Cooke, "Women Furniture Makers: From Decorative Designers to Studio Makers," in Pat Kirkham, ed., *Women Designers in the USA: 1900–2000*, exh. cat. (New Haven and London: Bard Graduate Center for Studies in the Decorative Arts, New York, for the Yale University Press, 2000), 301–2.

35. Cooke, *New American Furniture*, 52–55.

36. Jonathan Binzen, "William Walker's Furniture-Balancing Act," *Home Furniture*, no. 11 (June–July 1997): 56–61.

37. Brian Gladwell, "Putting It Together," in *Furniture Studio: The Heart of the Functional Arts*, ed. John Kelsey and Rick Mastelli (Free Union, Va.: Furniture Society, 1999), 119–25.

38. On "Wood '79," see *Fine Woodworking*, no. 20 (January–February 1980): 80. Quotations from Rick Mastelli, "Sam Maloof," *Fine Woodworking*, no. 25 (November–December 1980): 54; and John Kelsey, "George Nakashima," *Fine Woodworking*, no. 14 (January–February 1979): 46.

39. Arthur Espenet Carpenter, "The Rise of Artiture," *Fine Woodworking*, no. 38 (January–February 1983): 98–103. Unattributed quotation is from studio furniture maker Jim Fawcett to the editor, as published in *Fine Woodworking*, no. 40 (May–June 1983): 4. Maruyama quotation is from Terrie Noll, "Finding Your Own Voice," *Woodwork*, no. 1 (spring 1989): 39.

40. A. U. Chastain-Chapman, "Fine Furnituremaking," *American Craft* 44, no. 6 (December 1984–January 1985): 10–17. Quotation is from page 17.

41. Edward Cooke, Jr., "Wood in the 1980s: Expansion or Commodification?" in Davira Taragin et al., *Contemporary Crafts and the Saxe Collection*, exh. cat. (New York: Hudson Hills Press, 1993), 150.

42. John Kelsey, "Craftsman's Gallery," *Fine Woodworking*, no. 3 (summer 1976): 44–45.

43. Cooke, "Wood in the 1980s," 150–51; and Leslie Cochran, "To Market, to Market: The Growing Interest in Handmade Furniture," *Craft International* 5, no. 2 (October–November 1985): 13–15.

44. Taragin, Cooke, and Giovannini, *Furniture by Wendell Castle*, 60–65.

45. Cooke, *New American Furniture*, 27.

46. The first color cover of *Fine Woodworking* appeared on no. 48 (September–October 1984). See also Cooke, "Wood in the 1980s," 152.

47. Michael Stone, *Contemporary American Woodworkers* (Salt Lake City, Utah: Gibbs M. Smith, 1986); Patricia Conway and Robert Jensen, *Ornamentalism: The New Decoration in Architecture and Design* (New York: Clarkson Potter, 1982); and Denise Domergue, *Artists Design Furniture*.

48. *Material Evidence*; and Taragin, Cooke, and Giovannini, *Furniture by Wendell Castle*, 74–79.

49. Paul J. Smith and Edward Lucie-Smith, *Craft Today: Poetry of the Physical*, exh. cat. (New York: Weidenfeld and Nicolson in association with the American Craft Museum, 1986); and Patricia Conway, *Art for Everyday: The New Craft Movement* (New York: Clarkson Potter, 1990).

50. Cooke, "Wood in the 1980s," 154.

51. Roger Holmes, "Color and Wood," *Fine Woodworking*, no. 41 (July–August 1983): 70–73; and John Marlowe, "California Crossover," *Fine Woodworking*, no. 61 (November–December 1986): 60–64.

52. Cooke, "Wood in the 1980s," 156.

53. Edward Said, *Representations of the Intellectual* (New York: Pantheon, 1994), 73–83. For a recent look at the past decade, see Glenn Adamson, "Studio Furniture: The Last Ten Years," in *Contemporary Studio Case Furniture: The Inside Story*, exh. cat. (Madison, Wis.: Elvehjem Museum of Art, 2002), 12–22.

AFTERWORD

■ Details of John Dunnigan's desk, West Kingston, Rhode Island, 1988. Cherry, curly maple, patinated bronze; h. 29½ in., w. 58 in., d. 28½ in. Museum of Fine Arts, Boston; Gift of Anne and Ronald Abramson 1989.30.

The heady success of the late 1980s suggested great promise for the studio furniture movement. However, the prosperity of the early 1990s brought success and vitality to only a small group of makers, as studio furniture increasingly became an art commodity. As part of the commodification of the movement, many buyers were investment-driven collectors who purchased works more for the fashionable buzz than for a personal connection to the maker. Similarly, many sellers viewed furniture as merely the most recent trendy genre, and they therefore dramatically increased prices and deployed sophisticated marketing and sales techniques, developments that paralleled those seen in the studio glass and ceramics fields. Because of the professionalization and academic control of those media, specialized galleries pushed the work of selected "artists," and collectors eagerly snatched up the latest objects from those approved stables.[1]

In furniture, this phenomenon can be seen most clearly in the activity of the Peter Joseph Gallery in New York. Joseph, a successful businessman and collector of studio furniture, believed there was an opportunity to incorporate furniture into the commercial art world of New York. Opening an upscale gallery in midtown Manhattan in 1991, he provided funding to a select group of artists (most of whom had been canonized by the "New American Furniture" exhibition at the Museum of Fine Arts, Boston) so that they would have the time and resources to undertake ambitious bodies of work.

In addition, he published illustrated catalogues with essays commissioned from leading writers in the art and design fields, and produced slick advertising that appeared in the *New York Times* and other New York periodicals as well as in craft magazines. To justify this expenditure and draw attention to the importance of the furniture he showed, Joseph also raised prices significantly. In the early 1990s, the Peter Joseph Gallery chose to participate in the international exposition called "New Art Forms," a retail show held in Chicago that was dominated by glass and ceramics. Joseph's presence there signaled his belief that furniture had arrived and, further, deserved to be taken seriously as an art form.[2]

While the Peter Joseph Gallery was the most prominent, other galleries regularly exhibited studio furniture. In fact, art and furniture galleries became the main venue for the field in the 1990s. This trend heightened latent fissures within the movement. Ironically, the rise of art gallery activity took place at the same time as a decline in the number of juried regional shows and exhibitions in the small or university museums that had dominated the field from the 1960s through much of the 1980s. Federal and state funding for such "academic" exhibitions began to dry up during the eighties; this development removed an important entry point for "undiscovered" furniture makers and an essential forum for those whose work fell outside the stylistic mainstream. Instead, the emphasis of the galleries was often on an elite group of established makers (who

could be relied on for sales) or perhaps a fashionable new talent. Since the late 1980s, there has been
a noticeable trend toward major retrospective exhibitions and monographs devoted to the furniture of
Wendell Castle, Garry Knox Bennett, John Cederquist,
and Sam Maloof, among others. Such market-driven
hegemony has often buried the quiet work of self-
taught, more traditionally oriented craftsmen or
those who work in less popular modes.[3]

The goal of gallery representation in the eighties
and early nineties proved seductive to many. Some
of the established academic makers finally earned a
decent income, but that success came with a trade-
off. The prosperous elite continued to explore individual pieces in which personality or expressiveness
eclipsed function, but the work thus became more
difficult to present as furniture. A tension arose
between the personal narrative envisioned by the
maker and the functional needs and aesthetic tastes
of the viewer/collector. This shift toward expressive
avant-garde work restricted the potential pool of
customers. At the same time, those graduating from
academic programs harbored unreal expectations
and felt driven to land a gallery show or representation as soon as possible. Less frequently did emerging makers develop expertise, confidence, and range
by dividing time and effort between commissions
and speculative work; instead, there was immense
pressure to develop a signature style that would
attract attention. The buzz around academia and the
galleries also left nonacademic craftspeople isolated,
to be considered lesser talents because they were
restricted to functionality and the commission market. Rather than embracing a plurality of expression,
the field became balkanized due to market forces.[4]

In the mid-1990s, the nonacademic voice
regained some of its visibility and helped restore
balance to the field. Critical to this resurrection was
the launch of the West Coast magazine *Woodwork*
in 1989, and the brief appearance of a new journal,
Home Furniture. The former responded to a void left
by *Fine Woodworking*'s increased focus during the
1980s on plans, techniques, and projects for the
hobbyist. The articles in *Woodwork* ran the gamut
from discussions of tools to features on a variety of
makers, wood turners, and galleries of current work.
The sheer diversity of furniture illustrated, including
antique reproductions, fine wood furniture, painted
objects, and mixed-media constructions, fairly
reflected the plurality of the field. *Home Furniture*,
established by Taunton Press in 1994 and published
until 1998, focused on the whys of design (in articles
on sketchbooks, historical inspirations, and construction options for certain details such as drawers
and doors and how these options relate to overall
composition) and the presence of studio furniture
within the home environment. In this new journal,
quiet refined work in wood gained new value.

Just as these new magazines helped to develop
coherence within the field, the establishment of
The Furniture Society in 1996 provided the commu-
nicative glue for an inclusive, ecumenical field that
embraces makers, collectors, dealers, curators, students, and many others. Through its annual conferences and publications, the Society has taken the
lead in bringing diverse perspectives together, building a helpful history that locates furniture at the
heart of the creative endeavor, and establishing a
common language. The World Wide Web has given
this organization a virtual presence and also allowed
individual makers to gain visibility for their work. In
some ways, the Web has replaced regional exhibitions and nongallery shows as a means of maintaining diversity in the furniture realm and keeping the
general public aware of studio furniture.

The society's journal, *Furniture Studio*, reflects
the variety within the movement. The first volume,
published in 1999 and subtitled *The Heart of the
Functional Arts*, contains articles that encapsulate
the broad areas embraced by the studio furniture
movement: the history of art and design, the meaning of material culture, the development of techniques and craft practices, and the commercial
nexus of the marketplace, with its makers, dealers,
and collectors. A second volume—*Tradition in
Contemporary Furniture*, issued in 2001—presents a
similar "smorgasbord" (to quote the coeditors) of
images and text. As the series moves on, it likely will

continue to define the parameters of the movement, to assess its direction and qualities, and to provide the participants—makers, dealers, critics, curators, collectors, students, and others—an established forum for sharing information and concerns that will also be of interest to a wide public.[5]

The dawn of the new century finds the movement in a period of seemingly broad growth, although the uncertainties of a recession economy might challenge that health. The continued vitality of the field rests upon the centrality of furniture as a domestic artifact and the long-standing American fondness for working with wood and later with other materials to produce three-dimensional objects. There has been much change since Wharton Esherick exhibited his furniture at the World's Fair in 1940, but in many respects the current movement still strongly reflects its origins. In particular, the "reverence for wood" attitude of the early designer-craftsmen is still blended with the emphasis on furniture as artistic sculpture and personal expression that was added to the mix in the 1960s. Our modern respect for pluralism has made both attitudes acceptable and softened the criticism of either approach within the field; it also has allowed for a renewed interest in contract furniture, as the movement has reawakened old relationships with larger-scale production.

As George Hepplewhite observed in the late eighteenth century, "to unite elegance and utility, and blend the useful with the agreeable, has ever been considered a difficult, but an honourable task."[6] It is within those parameters, perhaps, that the most successful new objects will find honorable expression. How people achieve and express this alchemy of art and craft—of creating sculptural, functional objects—will determine the nature of the studio furniture movement in the coming years.

NOTES

1. Edward S. Cooke, Jr., "Wood in the 1980s: Expansion or Commodification?" in Davira Taragin et al., *Contemporary Crafts and the Saxe Collection*, exh. cat. (New York: Hudson Hills, 1993), 148–61. See also Susanne Frantz, "The Evolution of Studio Glass Collect-ing and Documentation in the United States," and Martha Drexler Lynn, "Clay Leads the Studio Crafts into the Art World," in the same volume, 21–89 and 90–131.

2. The best assessment of the Peter Joseph Gallery appears in Glenn Adamson, "Studio Furniture: The Last Ten Years," in *Contemporary Studio Case Furniture: The Inside Story*, exh. cat. (Madison, Wis.: Elvehjem Museum of Art, 2002), 14–16. The gallery closed after Joseph's death in 1998.

3. For period commentary on this, see Edward S. Cooke, Jr., "Juror's Statement," in *American Contemporary Works in Wood*, exh. cat. (Athens: Dairy Barn, Southeastern Ohio Cultural Arts Center, 1989).

4. In a 1996 talk, Wendell Castle, one of the elite makers, sought to distinguish between art furniture and studio furniture, viewing the latter as straightforward quiet or functional work; see Lita Solis-Cohen, "Making a Market for Wharton Esherick's Work," *Maine Antique Digest* (July 1996): 44D–46D.

5. Kelsey, John, and Rick Mastelli, eds., *Furniture Studio: The Heart of the Functional Arts* (Free Union, Va.: Furniture Society, 1999); and Rick Mastelli and and John Kelsey, eds., *Furniture Studio: Tradition in Contemporary Furniture* (Free Union, Va.: Furniture Society, 2001).

6. From the preface to George Hepplewhite, *The Cabinet-Maker and Upholsterer's Guide*, 3rd ed. (London, 1794; reprint, New York: Dover Publications, 1969).

Makers' Biographies

Note to the Reader

Select references are listed in chronological order for each artist. In addition to the works cited below, other sources consulted include material in the research files of the Art of the Americas Department, Museum of Fine Arts, Boston (MFA files). These files include artists' resumes, biographical questionnaires, press releases, gallery announcements, exhibition brochures, correspondence, and miscellaneous papers, as well as notes from telephone interviews with the artists.

Extensive use has been made of the following published sources, for which shortened references are used:

COOKE 1989
Edward S. Cooke, Jr., *New American Furniture: The Second Generation of Studio Furniture-makers*, exh. cat. (Boston: Museum of Fine Arts, 1989).

NORDNESS 1970
Lee Nordness, *Objects: USA*, exh. cat. (New York: Viking Press, 1970).

STONE 1986
Michael A. Stone, *Contemporary American Woodworkers* (Salt Lake City, Utah: Gibbs M. Smith, 1986).

■ Fig. 1. Bruce Beeken.
■ Fig. 2. (opposite page) Walker T. Weed.

Bruce Beeken

Born 1953, Hanover, New Hampshire

Beeken grew up hiking and canoeing in the New Hampshire woodlands and first tried his hand at woodworking when he apprenticed with Vermont canoe maker Carl Bausch. As he became fascinated by the process of building things, he decided that making furniture offered more creative possibilities than canoe building. He entered into an apprenticeship with furniture maker Simon Watts in Putney, Vermont, in 1974, where he learned the fundamentals of woodworking, such as traditional joinery, lathe work, and bending techniques.

After a school friend introduced him to the field of studio furniture, Beeken enrolled in 1976 in the Program in Artisanry (PIA) at Boston University. There, Dan Jackson encouraged him to pursue innovation rather than familiar tradition, and Jere Osgood became a mentor who showed Beeken how to develop a personal relationship with his work. Fellow students James Schriber, Timothy Philbrick, and many others enriched Beeken's experience at PIA. After graduation in 1978, he established his own shop in Burlington, Vermont. His earliest work in these years reflected his interest in "lyrical" and "graceful" qualities of hand-shaped wood, as seen in his tea cart (cat. no. 25).

In 1980, Beeken moved to a studio in a large barn at Shelburne Museum in Vermont. Inspired by the scale of the barn and by his collaborations with

local architects, he began to produce heavily massed pieces of furniture, which he thought of as small buildings. In 1983, Depot Woodworking, a production company in nearby Burlington, asked Beeken to design a piece of furniture for a new line; he agreed on the condition that Jeff Parsons, then employed at Depot, would help build the prototype. Having met him at PIA, Beeken knew that Parsons could bridge the gap between production and studio furniture making.

After collaborating on the prototype, they formed a partnership that continues to this day: Beeken contributes an intuitive design sense, while Parsons connects form and construction methods. In the early

years of their partnership, they took on a wide range of woodworking projects, from creating kitchen interiors to redesigning traditional Adirondack chairs for a commercial manufacturer. Their work has included subcontracting for other shops and designers, further allowing them to explore alternative technical and conceptual approaches and to acquire new shop equipment. Beeken and Parsons have continued to construct limited-production furniture from their own designs, using wood procured from sustainable harvests.

EDUCATION
Apprenticeship with Carl Bausch, canoe maker, Charlotte, Vt., 1972.

Apprenticeship with Simon Watts, furniture maker, Putney, Vt., 1974.

Boston University, Program in Artisanry, certificate of mastery 1978.

TEACHING
Boston University, Program in Artisanry, visiting professor, 1985.

SELECT REFERENCES
John Kelsey, "A Portfolio of Recent Work," *Fine Woodworking*, no. 14 (January 1979): 82.

Tanya Barter, John Dunnigan, and Seth Stem, *Bentwood*, exh. cat. (Providence: Rhode Island School of Design, 1984), 20–21.

Bruce Beeken and Jeff Parsons, "Adirondack Chair," *Fine Woodworking*, no. 52 (May–June 1985): 46–49.

Cooke 1989, 32–35.

Scott Landis, "Furniture with a Sense of Place," in *Furniture Studio: Tradition in Contemporary Furniture*, ed. Rick Mastelli and John Kelsey (Free Union, Va.: Furniture Society, 2001), 128–39.

GARRY KNOX BENNETT

Born 1934, Alameda, California

Bennett came to furniture making from a background in metalworking, sculpture, and the California counterculture of the 1960s. Interested in art since childhood, he enrolled from 1958/59 to 1962 at the California College of Arts and Crafts in Oakland, where he studied metal sculpture, but left before graduating. In 1963, while living near Sacramento, Bennett began using his metalworking skills to create jewelry and roach clips. By 1966, he returned to Oakland to start an electroplating company called Squirkenworks; later, Bennett began to experiment with artistic metalworking in lamps and clocks.

He enjoyed the immediacy of developing new design ideas in clocks, which he could make in a day or two. In the early 1970s, his clocks, made of brass and aluminum in cartoonlike forms with colorful surfaces, were sold at galleries in San Francisco, New York, Illinois, and Arizona. Making clocks prompted Bennett to explore other functional objects such as light fixtures and chests of drawers, which led him to working in wood.

In the late 1970s, Bennett refined his woodworking techniques but soon became frustrated with the reverence for wood and fine joinery prevalent in the furniture field. In 1979, he produced a technically sophisticated cabinet in exotic padauk wood and then drove a bent nail into the fine surface (cat. no. 34). When

this provoked uproar among furniture makers, he commented, "I wanted to make a statement that I thought people were getting a little too goddamn precious with their technique. I think tricky joinery is just to show, in most instances, you can do tricky joinery."

In the 1980s, Bennett established his characteristic work method with benches, trestle tables, and desks made in series. More interested in the final product than the rituals of handwork, he used large machines such as band saws, drill presses, milling machines, and even a chain saw to make large pieces of furniture that could be created in a single week. Bennett made no drawings, preferring instead to transfer his ideas directly to the materials as the designs took shape in his mind.

At the same time, he began to combine wood with aluminum, brass, glass, and plastic in exuberant designs. His 1984 ColorCore desk (cat. no. 35) won recognition at the exhibition "Material Evidence: New Techniques in Handmade Furniture." By the mid-1980s, Bennett's work was included in major national exhibitions, such as the 1986 "Craft Today: Poetry of the Physical," as well as shows at important galleries on both the East and West Coasts. A recent retrospective of his thirty-year career demonstrates the impact of Bennett's unconventional approach in the field.

EDUCATION

Attended California College of Arts and Crafts, 1958/59–1962.

SELECT REFERENCES

"Decoration vs. Desecration," *Fine Woodworking*, no. 24 (September–October 1980): 92.

Oakland Museum of Art. *California Woodworking: An Exhibition of Contemporary Handcrafted Furniture*, exh. cat. (Oakland, Calif.: Oakland Museum of Art Special Gallery, [1980]), 8.

John Kelsey, "Portfolio: Garry Knox Bennett," *Fine Woodworking*, no. 45 (March–April 1984): 79–81.

Stone 1986, 130–43.

Cooke 1989, 36–39.

Ursula Ilse-Neuman et al., *Made in Oakland: The Furniture of Garry Knox Bennett*, exh. cat. (New York: American Craft Museum, 2000).

J. B. BLUNK

Born 1926, Ottawa, Kansas; died 2002

A master of the chain saw, J. B. Blunk used massive redwood trunks, burled stumps, and other enormous pieces of wood to create some of the most distinctive furniture, installations, and "environments" representative of the California counterculture in the 1960s and later.

Born in the Midwest, Blunk attended UCLA, where he studied with the ceramist Laura Andreson (1902–1999). After graduation in 1949, he entered the army and served in the Korean War. At the conclusion of his service, he was discharged to Japan, where he met the sculptor Isamu Noguchi (1904–1988), an encounter that led to apprenticeships with the famous Japanese potters Rosanjin Kitaoji (1883–1959) and Toyo Kaneshige (1896–1967).

After returning to America in 1954, Blunk spent his career in northern California, living for much of his life in a home he built on private land in a state forest near Inverness in Marin County. Although he is best known for furniture, his work included ceramics, jewelry, weavings, and large sculptures in bronze and stone.

Early in his career, Blunk worked as a carpenter, and his efforts on the large roof of a house designed by the architect Warren Callister for Gordon Onslow Ford, a surrealist painter, played a crucial role in his interest in woodworking. Patronage from individuals and universities followed in the 1960s, including an important commission from the University of California, Santa Cruz, in 1968 for a large public seating sculpture, a genre for which he became well known. In 1969, the Oakland Museum commissioned *Planet*, an enormous sculpture carved from a single redwood burl some twelve feet in diameter that serves as a meeting place at the entrance to the museum. The next year, a redwood bench (twelve feet long and three feet wide) was chosen for the "Objects: USA" exhibition in Washington, D.C., which praised the piece's wandering, organic form and vigorous presence. David Holzapfel, in a 1985 article on several subtractive woodworkers, noted that

Blunk had "the most spectacular wood collection" of them all, consisting of some forty tons of redwood and cypress logs and burls.

In the 1970s, Blunk turned his attention to joined furniture and began to take a greater interest in ergonomics. Later, by about 1980, he began to concentrate on large sculptures of various materials.

In 1999, Blunk explained his lifelong focus on evoking "the soul of the piece." "In carving wood," he wrote, "it is a matter of revealing the theme and is achieved by removing material. Since I principally use a chainsaw to do this, it is a process that moves quickly. At times the cutting away and forming happen so fast it is almost unconscious....Often, as I uncover more of the form, I encounter unexpected qualities, faults or voids in the wood which may change my intention, and sometimes the theme itself." Thus, his goal was that of modifying and en-hancing the natural properties of wood, rather than subjugating the timbers to his will. As Noguchi observed, Blunk took great trees and roused "them from their long sleep to become part of our own life and times, sharing with us the afterglow of a land that was once here."

EDUCATION
University of California at Los Angeles, BA 1949.

TEACHING
Palo Verde College, 1954–55.

SELECT REFERENCES
Dona Z. Meilach, *Contemporary Art with Wood: Creative Techniques and Appreciation* (New York: Crown Publishers, 1968), 176.

Nordness 1970, 268.

Exhibition review, *Craft Horizons* 38, no. 2 (April 1978): 67.

David Holzapfel, "Subtractive Woodworking," *Fine Woodworking*, no. 54 (September–October 1985): 88–91.

Glenn Adamson, "California Dreaming," in *Furniture Studio: The Heart of the Functional Arts*, ed. John Kelsey and Rick Mastelli (Free Union, Va.: Furniture Society, 1999), 32–42.

Glenn Adamson, "California Spirit: Rediscovering the Furniture of J. B. Blunk," *Woodwork*, no. 59 (October 1999): 22–29.

J. B. Blunk, "Work and Home: A Visit with J. B. Blunk," *Woodwork*, no. 59 (October 1999): 30.

JON BROOKS

Born 1944, Manchester, New Hampshire

Once introduced as the maker of "Flintstone furniture," Jon Brooks entered the field of studio furniture as a "subtractive woodworker" in the late 1960s. Along with J. B. Blunk, Erik Gronberg, Heather Hilton, David Van Nostrand, Howard Werner, and others, Brooks began with a whole log or tree section and carved portions away to generate a form best described as sculptural furniture. In the 1960s, he was recognized as an important member of the new generation of artist-craftsmen for his expressive work.

Brooks participated in the children's art program at the Currier Gallery of Art (now the Currier Museum of Art) in Manchester, New Hampshire, and, at an early age, demonstrated a facility for woodworking in his family's basement shop. He was encouraged by his parents, who gave him a book on Brancusi's sculpture that cemented his interest in art.

Attracted by the contemporary orientation of professors Wendell Castle and William Keyser, Brooks enrolled at the Rochester Institute of Technology in New York, where he earned both his bachelor's and master's degrees. Castle, in particular, exerted a strong influence on him, and they have had an enduring friendship and relationship. Castle's favorable review of Brooks's first solo exhibition at the Shop

One gallery in Rochester helped establish the young artist's reputation.

During his career, Brooks has taught at St. Anselm's College, the Penland School of Crafts, Haystack Mountain School of Crafts, and other institutions. After a year-long residency in Australia at the University of Tasmania in 1983, Brooks's work shifted from "solid subtractive carving to construction." He was "exposed to aboriginal Australian art and began to work with construction, paint, and figurative pieces." He has maintained a small shop in New Boston, New Hampshire, since 1972. Like Wharton Esherick, Sam Maloof, and others, Brooks also created his own home. Inspired by the architecture of Antonio Gaudi and the experimental work he observed during a four-year stay in California, he began building his extraordinary home in the early 1970s, ultimately fashioning an unconventional structure that, as described by Christine Hamm, "looks as organic as a toadstool that somehow stepped out of the nearby woods."

A member of the New Hampshire Furniture Masters Association, Brooks is widely known today for his innovative and poetic furniture that always explores the intersection of function and art. In a recent statement, he observed: "I enjoy making furniture and sculpture that you can dance with, that is participatory, playful, and suggestive.... For me working with wood is a subtractive process, removing all that is unnecessary. It's like eating an artichoke, peeling the outer leaves to get to the heart."

EDUCATION
School for American Craftsmen, Rochester
Institute of Technology, BFA 1966, MFA 1967.

TEACHING
St. Anselm's College, Manchester, N.H.,
1970–78.

SELECT REFERENCES
Wendell Castle, exhibition review, *Craft Horizons*
29, no. 2 (March–April 1969): 42.

David Holzapfel, "Subtractive Woodworking:
Furniture from Logs and Limbs," *Fine Woodworking*, no. 54 (September–October 1985):
88–93.

Christine Hamm, "Storybook Style," *New
Hampshire Home* (March–April 1995): 33–35.

ARTHUR ESPENET CARPENTER

Born 1920, New York City

Carpenter was among the first generation
of self-taught woodworkers and is associated with the organic, experimental style
of West Coast furniture making. He
earned a BA in economics at Dartmouth
College in New Hampshire at his father's
urging but was more interested in his
visual arts courses. Graduating in 1942,
he joined the navy and served for four
years. After the war, Carpenter returned
to New York to work for his father's Asian
art wholesale business. In the late 1940s,
he attended Edgar Kaufman's "Good
Design" exhibitions at the Museum of
Modern Art (MOMA), which inspired him
to pursue a career making beautiful, useful objects.

In 1948, Carpenter drove to San
Francisco, bought a lathe, taught himself
to turn wooden bowls, and began to sell
his work. From 1950 to 1954, his bowls
were included in the MOMA "Good
Design" exhibitions that had initially
inspired him. Through trial and error, and
with advice from older cabinetmakers in
the Bay Area, Carpenter taught himself
to make simple furniture such as coffee
tables. Using his mother's maiden name,
Espenet, as a business name, he expanded his small manufacturing firm to a
staff of seven. However, he soon sought
greater independence as a designer-
craftsman, and he bought a farm in 1957
in Bolinas, a coastal town north of San
Francisco. In Bolinas, he built a circular
home of his own design and began to
focus on making furniture full-time.

While his early furniture was influenced by the hard-edged industrial design
of the 1950s, work by Wharton Esherick
and Sam Maloof influenced Carpenter to
make furniture that was more sculptural.
By the 1960s, he developed his characteristic style of curved lines and rounded
edges, later known as "California
Roundover." Seeking to reduce the labor
of making drawers, Carpenter developed
his much-imitated "band-saw boxes,"
which he used to make drawers and
pigeonholes in desks and small cabinets.
His furniture, mostly one-of-a-kind pieces
built on commission and sold directly
through his shop, was designed with
an emphasis on utility, simplicity, and
sensuousness.

By the late 1960s, Carpenter was
recognized as a leader in the studio furniture movement. His work was shown at
Galeria del Sol in Santa Barbara. He was
also represented in several national exhibitions, including "Objects: USA," and the
"California Design" shows (8–11), as well
as at the Renwick Gallery's inaugural exhibition, "Woodenworks." A successful furniture maker, Carpenter turned his attention to teaching in the early 1970s, helping to found what is now the Baulines
Craft Guild to place apprentices with master craftsmen in the Bay Area. Believing
that "it's very important to be an independent producer of some kind,"
Carpenter says he is "actually aggressive
about bringing people into the fold. The
more free spirits there are in society the
better."

EDUCATION
Dartmouth College, Hanover, N.H., BA 1942.

SELECT REFERENCES
Nordness 1970, 264.

Renwick Gallery, *Woodenworks: Furniture Objects
by Five Contemporary Craftsmen*, exh. cat. (St.
Paul: Minnesota Museum of Art and
Smithsonian Institution, 1972), 30–33.

Oakland Museum of Art, *California Woodwork-
ing: An Exhibition of Contemporary Handcrafted
Furniture*, exh. cat. (Oakland, Calif.: Oakland
Museum of Art Special Gallery, [1980]), 8.

Rick Mastelli, "Art Carpenter: The Independent
Spirit of the Baulines Craftsmen's Guild," *Fine
Woodworking*, no. 37 (November–December
1982): 62–68.

Arthur Espenet Carpenter, "The Rise of
Artiture," *Fine Woodworking*, no. 38 (January–
February 1983): 98–103.

Stone 1986, 82–99.

Glenn Adamson, "California Dreaming," in
*Furniture Studio: The Heart of the Functional
Arts*, ed. John Kelsey and Rick Mastelli (Free
Union, Va.: Furniture Society, 1999), 32–42.

Arthur Espenet Carpenter, "Memoir," in
*Furniture Studio: The Heart of the Functional
Arts*, ed. John Kelsey and Rick Mastelli (Free
Union, Va.: Furniture Society, 1999), 43–49.

WENDELL CASTLE

Born 1932, Emporia, Kansas

Throughout his four decades in furniture
making, Wendell Castle has blurred
boundaries between furniture and sculpture. Trained in industrial design and
sculpture at the University of Kansas, he
first began to make furniture after seeing
the work of Wharton Esherick in 1958. For
Castle, Esherick's work revealed how furniture could be a form of sculpture and
an expressive art.

After some of Castle's early works
won prizes in juried craft exhibitions, he
moved to New York in 1961 and assumed
a teaching position at the Rochester Institute of Technology (RIT) in 1963. At RIT,
Castle expanded his technical abilities and
used the machinery of the school's woodshop. Seeking a way to create organic,
expressive forms in wood, he experimented with stack lamination, which had been
widely used by wood sculptors in the
1950s and 1960s. As the first artist to use
stack lamination regularly in furniture
making, Castle emphasized aesthetic concerns over function in works that defied
traditional furniture forms.

Throughout the 1960s and 1970s, Castle continued to make stack-laminated wood furniture but also experimented with new forms such as "environments," lamps, and outdoor sculpture. In 1969, he left RIT, accepted a teaching position at SUNY, Brockport, and began to explore nonwood materials such as fiberglass, Styrofoam, neon, and plastic. From his studio in Scottsville, New York, he began a line of limited-edition and quantity-production furniture with the help of his assistants. He gained increasing national recognition when his work was exhibited in both craft and fine arts galleries, as well as in major museum exhibitions. His shows, lectures, and writings, particularly his book on wood lamination, inspired a host of imitators.

In 1978, Castle, seeking a new direction, began to produce trompe l'oeil wood sculptures resembling historical furniture with carved still-life arrangements of everyday objects resting on them. These pieces led him to reverse his earlier, ahistorical approach to design. In 1981, he began to produce "fine" furniture using costly materials and employing masterful workmanship, inspired by the Art Deco furniture of Jacques-Emile Ruhlmann. Castle and gallery owner Alexander Milliken promoted the work in order to raise the price ceiling for studio furniture; their success helped inaugurate the flourishing market of the 1980s.

During that decade, Castle used historical and Classical motifs, brightly colored surfaces, metal embellishments, and the whimsical style of the Italian design group Memphis Milano. The cooperation of highly skilled staff in his workshop allowed him to take on ambitious projects, such as a series of thirteen tall clocks exploring the theme of time. He sold his work primarily to private collectors through galleries, although he also received notable public commissions. His work has been shown in dozens of significant studio furniture exhibitions and acquired by many important museums. Since the late 1980s, Castle has returned to making furniture that is nearly nonfunctional, emphasizing sculptural qualities.

EDUCATION

University of Kansas, Lawrence, BFA (industrial design) 1958; MFA (sculpture) 1961.

TEACHING

University of Kansas, Lawrence, 1959–61.

School for American Crafts, Rochester Institute of Technology, Rochester, N.Y., 1963–69.

State University of New York, Brockport, 1969–80.

Wendell Castle School of Woodworking, Scottsville, N.Y., 1980–88

SELECT REFERENCES

Nordness 1970, 256–57.

Renwick Gallery, *Woodenworks: Furniture Objects by Five Contemporary Craftsmen*, exh. cat. (St. Paul: Minnesota Museum of Art and Smithsonian Institution, 1972), 38–46.

Wendell Castle and David Edman, *The Wendell Castle Book of Wood Lamination* (New York: Van Nostrand Reinhold, 1980).

Stone 1986, 114–29.

Davira S. Taragin, Edward S. Cooke, Jr., and Joseph Giovannini, *Furniture by Wendell Castle*, exh. cat. (New York: Hudson Hills Press in association with the Founders Society, Detroit Institute of Arts, 1989).

JOHN CEDERQUIST

Born 1946, Altadena, California

A native of southern California, John Cederquist graduated from Long Beach State College with a BA in art and an MA in craft. In the early 1970s, his sculptural wall cabinets and storage units were shown at Galeria del Sol, the Fairtree Gallery, and the Renwick Gallery's 1976 exhibition "Craft Multiples." Inspired by the organic forms of Wendell Castle and by the industrial landscape of Long Beach's refineries, these early works included curving and tubular forms made of leather and wood. He also used steam bending and bent lamination to create rockers and chairs inspired by Art Nouveau furniture.

In 1973, he moved with his family to Costa Mesa and began teaching three-dimensional design at various campuses of California State University. Through work on his "Michelin Man" series, he discovered ways of creating illusionistic images using leather and wood veneers. After moving to Capistrano Beach and accepting a teaching position at Saddleback Community College in Mission Viejo

in 1976, he continued to participate in important craft exhibitions, including the "California Design" series. However, by the late 1970s, Cederquist's interest in wood and leather waned.

Through teaching courses in two- and three-dimensional design at Saddleback, he became increasingly interested in the problematic relationship between the images of objects and the actual objects themselves. Influenced by the spatial qualities of Japanese woodblock prints and *Popeye* cartoons, he began to explore pictorial imagery through veneer and inlay, airbrushed surfaces, and perspective drawings. He sought to depict the fixed point of view of a two-dimensional drawing on three-dimensional pieces of furniture.

In the early 1980s, Cederquist began

making furniture-inspired objects that look convincingly three-dimensional when viewed from a single, "correct" point of view. As the viewer moves around the object, distortions in perspective appear. The tension between reality and illusion in these pieces echoes the work of surrealists in the 1920s and 1930s, particularly René Magritte, but Cederquist added a layer of ambiguity by making his objects semifunctional pieces of furniture.

In 1983, he took a sabbatical from teaching to develop new work for a solo exhibition, "John Cederquist: Deceptions," at the Craft and Folk Art Museum in Los Angeles. His 1989 piece, *Le Fleuron Manquant*, created for "New American Furniture" at the Museum of Fine Arts, Boston, has been praised for its illusionistic deconstruction of a classic Newport high chest (cat. no. 48). Throughout the 1980s, his work was included in major exhibitions, including "Material Evidence" in 1984, "Craft Today: Poetry of the Physical" in 1986, and "The Eloquent Object" in 1987. Since 1990, Cederquist has been represented by Franklin Parrasch Gallery; he has continued to create trompe l'oeil furniture incorporating images of shipping crates, tubes with steam puffs, and breaking waves reminiscent of Hokusai's prints and southern California surfing.

EDUCATION

Long Beach State College (now California State University, Long Beach), BA 1969, MA 1971.

TEACHING

California State University, Long Beach and Los Angeles campuses, 1972.

California State University, Fullerton, 1973.

Saddleback Community College, Mission Viejo, Calif., 1976–86.

SELECT REFERENCES

Pasadena Art Museum, *California Design Eleven*, exh. cat. (Pasadena, Calif.: California Design, 1971), 25.

Oakland Museum of Art, *California Woodworking: An Exhibition of Contemporary Handcrafted Furniture*, exh. cat. (Oakland, Calif.: Oakland Museum of Art Special Gallery, [1980]), 9.

Sharon K. Emanuelli, *John Cederquist: Deceptions*, exh. cat. (Los Angeles: Craft and Folk Art Museum, 1983).

Cooke 1989, 40–43.

Arthur C. Danto and Nancy Princenthal, *The Art of John Cederquist: Reality of Illusion*, exh. cat. (Oakland: Oakland Museum of California, 1997).

Pamela Blotner, "The Wizardry of John Cederquist," *Woodwork*, no. 50 (April 1998): 20–29.

FRANK E. CUMMINGS III

Born 1938, Los Angeles, California

During his long career in California, Frank Cummings has become well known as both a teacher and a maker of furniture, jewelry, turned wooden vessels, and clocks. After receiving his master's degree in crafts at California State University, Fullerton, he attended a symposium in 1974 entitled "Chairs in Motion," with sessions chaired by Sam Maloof and the sculptor Harry Bertoia, and this meeting had a powerful impact on his career.

Known for the high quality of his work, Cummings often includes such exotica as Japanese pheasant feathers, zebra fur, ebony, ivory, African goatskins, lignum vitae, and other precious materials in his objects. His philosophical stance embraces the Shaker ethic of good, honest craftsmanship and includes a spiritual respect for nature and natural materials. Central to his art is his appreciation of the ceremonial significance of everyday objects, derived from African traditions. Although Cummings has extensive teaching experience, both in this country and in Africa, he works alone and has not taken apprentices. His work was first exhibited in "California Design Eleven" in 1971, and a one-person traveling exhibition of his work was seen at seven venues in Africa in 1981. A highlight of his career was the "Ornamental Turning: New Works" exhibition held at the National Museum of American History, Smithsonian Institution, Washington, D.C., in 1989.

Cummings created his tall ebony clock of 1979–80 (cat. no. 32) without a door, leaving the works and weights exposed. The gears of hand-carved ivory and an African hardwood "were developed from an original paper design of snowflakes and seapods. The paper was glued to the ivory and then all ivory parts carved." The result is an almost Mannerist exercise in "kinetic sculpture."

EDUCATION

Los Angeles Harbor College, 1958–60.

California State College, Long Beach, BA (art) 1968.

California State University, Fullerton, MA (crafts) 1971.

TEACHING

California State College, Long Beach, 1969–82.

California State University, Fullerton, 1982–present.

SELECT REFERENCES

Dona Z. Meilach, *Creating Modern Furniture: Trends, Techniques, Appreciation* (New York: Crown Publishers, 1975), 286.

Dona Z. Meilach, *Woodworking: The New Wave* (New York: Crown Publishers, 1980), 32, 33, 111, 114–15, 126, 128, 231.

Woodturning in North America since 1930 (New Haven: Wood Turning Center and Yale University Art Gallery, 2001), 52, 165.

PETER DANKO

Born 1949, Washington, D.C.

Peter Danko made a transition from studio furniture to industrial design because of his desire to retain autonomy in the design process; one of the problems he encountered in doing commission work was that "you kind of end up doing what the customer wants to do. That's business, but it may not be what you want to do." By having his furniture produced in quantity, he has found he can make a living while retaining creative control.

After graduating with a fine arts degree from the University of Maryland in 1971, Danko came upon woodworking by chance. While working in a store in the Georgetown neighborhood of Washington, D.C., he was enticed by the smell of wood being sawn in the woodshop next door. He was hired as a carver because of his experience carving marble and immediately became "addicted to woodworking." Danko began his own studio in Georgetown making sculptural furniture, much of it stack laminated or carved in organic shapes. Finding it difficult to make a living with his one-off work, he turned to production, accepting his first commission from a large local restaurant. He moved his shop to Alexandria, Virginia, where Danko hired architecture students from the local annex of Virginia Polytechnic Institute to help build his furniture.

In the late 1970s, his career as a production designer took off when he developed the prototype for his "Danko chair," made from a single piece of plywood. With the help of his father, formerly a pattern maker for the navy, Danko invented the machinery to laminate, cut, and mold the chair. Although manufacturers initially rejected the design, he got the chair into the permanent collection of the Museum of Modern Art in New York as well as the 1979 "New Handmade Furniture" exhibition at the American Craft Museum. In 1980, the company Thonet contracted with Danko to produce and market the chair.

In 1981, he established Peter Danko and Associates to design and produce molded plywood seating furniture. He introduced his first catalogue of designs and subcontracted with Sauder Manufacturing of Stryker, Ohio, to produce some of the chairs. Beginning in the late 1980s, Danko successfully marketed his designs to architects, interior designers, and corporate clients nationwide. Eventually, his shop made all the furniture, and his staff comprised about twenty-five full-time

employees including shop crew, sales, and administration. The shop produced and sold about a thousand chairs each year. In 1995, after the effects of the recession of the early 1990s forced Danko to declare bankruptcy, his business was purchased by and became a division of Persing Enterprises in Red Lion, Pennsylvania, where he continues to develop new designs.

EDUCATION
University of Maryland, College Park, Md., BFA (art and art history) 1971.

SELECT REFERENCES
J. K., "A One-Piece Chair: They Said It Couldn't Be Done," *Fine Woodworking*, no. 20 (January 1980): 46–47.

Iris Krasnow, "Chairman of the Board: 'Go On, Sit on It,'" *Museum and Arts Washington* 5, no. 2 (March–April 1989): 78–80, 91, 105.

Dick Burrows, "Peter Danko: Props in the Play of Life," *American Craft* 53, no. 2 (April–May 1993): 54–57.

Tod Riggio, "Danko Molds His Life around Unique Chairs," *Woodshop News* (September 1999): T3.

ALEJANDRO DE LA CRUZ

Born about 1924, Madrid, Spain; died 1990

A member of the first generation of studio furniture makers, Alejandro de la Cruz was born in Spain and trained with a master cabinetmaker in Madrid. While still a young man, he was severely injured in the Spanish civil war, when an artillery shell shattered his jaw. He fled Spain in 1942 at the age of eighteen to avoid being drafted into Francisco Franco's Fascist army, traveling first to South America. In 1949, seeking medical attention for his jaw, he went to New York City. During his period of recuperation, with his funds dwindling, he was befriended by Walter Comee and his family of Canterbury, New Hampshire. He stayed with the Comee family for five years, undergoing additional surgery and earning his keep through undertaking woodworking projects for them and others. Soon he established his own home and shop in Canterbury across from the Shaker Village there.

Colorful and opinionated, de la Cruz became known for his high-quality furniture echoing eighteenth-century Georgian

and nineteenth-century Shaker designs, and he soon established both a local and an international clientele. One of his earliest commissions involved five large benches of Peruvian mahogany made for the Currier Gallery of Art (now the Currier Museum of Art) in Manchester, New Hampshire; one of these, along with a museum reception desk, were lent to the landmark 1957 "Furniture by Craftsmen" exhibition at the Museum of Contemporary Crafts. Their design was credited to the influential architect David R. Campbell of Concord, the director of what later became the League of New Hampshire Craftsmen; de la Cruz used his considerable traditional skills to fashion these modernist designs.

Among de la Cruz's students was the young David Lamb, today a noted New Hampshire cabinetmaker in the Early American tradition who eventually bought de la Cruz's home and shop. De la Cruz retired to Spain about 1986 and died there in 1990.

EDUCATION
Cabinetmaking school, Madrid, Spain, late 1930s–early 1940s.

SELECT REFERENCES
Nyleen Morrison, "Refugee Artist," *New Hampshire Profiles* 4, no. 8 (August 1955): 30–31.

Roger Tulin, "Tradition in the Crafts," *Yankee Magazine* (December 1977).

David Lamb, telephone conversation with Pat Warner, September 19, 2002.

■ Fig. 12. John Dunnigan.
■ Fig. 13. Wharton Esherick.
■ Fig. 14. Michael Fortune.

JOHN DUNNIGAN

Born 1950, Providence, Rhode Island

Initially self-taught in woodworking, John Dunnigan joined the second generation of studio furniture makers who trained at university and explored cultural and conceptual meanings in furniture. Dunnigan had virtually no exposure to art or furniture making before college, although he had held summer jobs in construction and carpentry throughout high school. In college, he majored in English, edited two literary magazines, and wanted to become a poet, but during his junior year he taught himself woodworking as an alternative lifestyle. Renting his own small shop and using borrowed tools, he soon found that furniture making replaced writing as his primary creative endeavor.

In the early 1970s, Dunnigan supported himself by woodworking in his own shop and in other production woodshops. The recession of 1974 and the loss of his shop forced him to take a job with a Swedish company in Newport, Rhode Island, where he built boats and boat interiors for a year while continuing to do commissions in borrowed shop space. By 1975, he was able to set up his own shop, work on commissions, and have his first gallery show.

During the years from 1974 to 1976, Dunnigan considered going back to school and visited Boston University's Program in Artisanry and the Rhode Island School of Design (RISD). Tage Frid, then teaching at RISD, discouraged Dunnigan from attending graduate school because he believed it would be an unnecessary expense, since Dunnigan was already making a successful living run-

ning his own shop. Dunnigan decided, however, that he needed school in order to further develop as a furniture maker. He enrolled in RISD's furniture design program in 1978. While a student, he was hired as furniture shop manager and part-time teacher; since 1980 he has been on the program's full-time faculty. While studying and teaching, Dunnigan has participated in numerous gallery shows and built commissions for his own clients.

He found that graduate school validated his self-taught skills and also helped him fill in gaps in his training. In the 1970s, his work demonstrated complex technical skills, especially lamination and steam bending, but in the 1980s he sought ways to make his work both technically simple and conceptually challenging. He explored historical forms, particularly influences from Classical and Egyptian architecture, and used a variety of materials as subtle complements to wood. He became especially interested in upholstered furniture as a way to enhance sensual and tactile qualities and collaborated with textile designer Wendy Wahl to develop custom upholstery fabrics. In the 1980 and 1990s, while Dunnigan continued to teach at RISD as well as at craft centers like Penland, Haystack, and the Appalachian Center for Crafts, his work achieved wide recognition and was represented by several important galleries.

EDUCATION
University of Rhode Island, Kingston, BA (English) 1972.

Rhode Island School of Design, Providence, MFA (furniture design) 1980.

TEACHING
Rhode Island School of Design, Providence, 1980–present.

SELECT REFERENCES
John Dunnigan, "Upholstered Furniture: Filling Out the Frame," *Fine Woodworking*, no. 68 (January–February 1988): 52–55.

Cooke 1989, 48–51.

Peter Joseph Gallery, *John Dunnigan: Furniture Maker*, exh. cat. (New York: Peter Joseph Gallery, 1991).

Christine Temin, "Poet in Wood: John Dunnigan," *American Craft* 55, no. 6 (December 1995–January 1996): 50–53.

John Dunnigan, "Understanding Furniture," in *Furniture Studio: The Heart of the Functional Arts*, ed. John Kelsey and Rick Mastelli (Free Union, Va.: Furniture Society, 1999), 12–23.

WHARTON ESHERICK

Born 1887, Philadelphia, Pennsylvania; died 1970

Wharton Esherick was a seminal figure in the development of American studio furniture; his sculptural furniture and independent lifestyle helped define the field for later generations of woodworkers. Inclined toward art from early childhood, Esherick defied the wishes of his parents and attended a manual-training high school. He went on to study painting at the Pennsylvania Museum and School of Industrial Art and the Pennsylvania Academy of the Fine Arts. However, he became frustrated with formal art education and left school six weeks before graduation.

In 1913, he moved with his wife to a farmhouse in Paoli, Pennsylvania, where he built a painting studio. During the 1920s, Esherick pursued a career in painting but met with little success. At the same time, he explored wood carving, woodblock prints, sculpture, and theater design. In 1926, considering himself a sculptor, he built a studio for sculpture that would later become his home. However, he made some furniture and interior installations for himself, including a twisting red oak staircase. At the urging of friends, he began to make furniture to sell; his early pieces reflected Art Deco and Cubist influences.

From the late 1920s through the 1950s, Esherick made furniture by collaborating with the local cabinetmaker John Schmidt. Esherick designed and hand-shaped the furniture but had little interest in the technical aspects of furniture making. He relied on Schmidt and other assistants to join and finish his pieces. He worked primarily in the woods native to southeastern Pennsylvania, including walnut, black cherry, cottonwood, and hickory; his wood supplier, Ed Ray, provided logs with unusual grain patterns. By the 1940s, Esherick had developed his own "free-form" style, using flowing lines and "tree angles and tree forms" following the natural shapes of the wood grain. In 1956, he collaborated with the architect Louis I. Kahn (1901–1974) to design and build a furniture workshop at his home studio.

Esherick made furniture and interior installations primarily for local private commissions, the best-known being the

Curtis and Nellie Bok home in Gulph Mills, Pennsylvania. However, his work was exhibited nationally and internationally, beginning in 1940 at the New York World's Fair. Throughout the 1950s and 1960s, Esherick's furniture appeared in the American Pavilion at the 1958 Brussels World's Fair, the Tate Gallery in London, the Worcester Art Museum in Massachusetts, the Brooklyn Museum, and the following Manhattan venues: the Bertha Schaefer Gallery, the Metropolitan Museum of Art, the Museum of Modern Art, the Museum of Contemporary Crafts, and the Whitney Museum Annuals. Several first-generation studio furniture makers, including Sam Maloof, Wendell Castle, and Arthur Espenet Carpenter, have recalled Esherick's work as a powerful influence in their own careers. Following his death in 1970, Esherick's Pennsylvania home and studio were opened to the public as the Wharton Esherick Museum.

EDUCATION

Central Manual Training High School, Philadelphia, Pa., 1903.

Studied painting at Philadelphia Museum and School of Industrial Art of the Pennsylvania Museum of Art, 1907–8.

Studied painting at Pennsylvania Academy of the Fine Arts, Philadelphia, 1909–10.

SELECT REFERENCES

Gertrude Benson, "Wharton Esherick," *Craft Horizons* 19, no. 1 (January–February 1959): 32–37.

Nordness 1970, 252–54.

Renwick Gallery, *Woodenworks: Furniture Objects by Five Contemporary Craftsmen*, exh. cat. (St. Paul: Minnesota Museum of Art and Smithsonian Institution, 1972), 22–29.

Mansfield Bascom, "Wharton Esherick: Dean of American Woodworking," *Craft International* (October–November–December 1985): 22.

Stone 1986, 2–17.

Wharton Esherick Museum, *Half a Century in Wood: 1920–1970, The Woodenworks of Wharton Esherick*, exh. cat. (Paoli, Pa.: Wharton Esherick Museum, 1988).

Robert Edwards and Robert Aibel, *Wharton Esherick, 1887–1970: American Woodworker*, exh. cat. (Philadelphia: Moderne Gallery, 1996).

MICHAEL FORTUNE

Born 1951, Toronto, Ontario, Canada

Michael Fortune believes that studio furniture makers have an important role to play in linking the aesthetic and creative values of studio furniture with mainstream furniture production and economic development. His career has included one-off pieces for private commissions, speculative work, design for production, and consulting projects worldwide, as well as lectures and teaching throughout North America.

Fortune was encouraged to pursue woodworking by his relatives, who gave him woodworking tools as gifts and supported his decision to enroll in the furniture design program at Sheridan College in Mississauga, Ontario. At Sheridan, Fortune studied with department head Donald McKinley, who taught product design and established Fortune's interest in working with the furniture industry. Other faculty introduced him to historical furniture and suggested various career possibilities, while at the same time he gained practical experience working as the on-site manager for designer David Lamb. After graduation, a travel/study scholarship allowed Fortune to spend time in Europe. While abroad, Fortune apprenticed in the studio of English furniture maker Alan Peters and studied at the Stenebyskolen in Sweden; through these experiences he became familiar with the European model of the designer-maker.

In 1980, an early commission from Judith and Michael John inspired Fortune to explore chairs in series throughout his career. Working in series or multiples allowed Fortune to explore aesthetic issues and to resolve technical problems economically. He is particularly well known for his innovative steam bending techniques, which adapted an industrial process for studio work. These techniques allowed him to achieve, in his words, "design flexibility, a reasonable rate of productivity, quick set-up time and easy operation by one person, and low capital investment."

Fortune's broad experience has included consulting projects for large furniture manufacturers, including Craftwood Industries, a specialty maker in Toronto. He has also offered consulting services to economic development projects in the Caribbean and Central America, where he assisted with the initiatives for furniture manufacturing and woodworking facilities. In addition, he has taught and lectured at a wide variety of institutions and craft centers, while maintaining his own studio and preparing new works for exhibitions and private clients.

EDUCATION

Sheridan College, School of Crafts and Design, Mississauga, Ontario, Dip. (furniture design) 1971–74.

Evening studies in architectural design and drawing, Ryerson Polytechnic Institute, 1972–74.

TEACHING

Sheridan College, School of Crafts and Design, Mississauga, Ontario, Canada, 1980–88.

Kootenay School of the Arts, Nelson, British Columbia, Canada, wood products design program, department head, 1996–98.

SELECT REFERENCES

J. K., "Out of the Woods: Touring Show Features Designer-Craftsmen of Ontario," *Fine Woodworking*, no. 17 (July–August 1979): 76–77.

Michael C. Fortune, "Fixtures for Steambending," *Fine Woodworking*, no. 30 (September–October 1981): 84–86.

Stephen Hogbin, "Design Processes; Four Canadians," *The Workshop* (fall 1983).

Tom Hurley, "Furniture-Making in Toronto: Style and Success in Canada's Largest Art Market," *Fine Woodworking*, no. 73 (November–December 1988): 42–47.

Brian Gladwell, "Putting it Together," in *Furniture Studio: The Heart of the Functional Arts*, ed. John Kelsey and Rick Mastelli (Free Union, Va.: Furniture Society, 1999), 119–25.

Michael Fortune, "The Elements of Inlay," *Woodwork*, no. 73 (February 2002): 44–54.

TAGE FRID

Born 1915, Copenhagen, Denmark

The son of a silversmith, Tage Frid underwent a rigorous period of training and apprenticeship and experienced a brief sojourn in Iceland before coming to the United States in 1948 at the request of the American Craft Council to head the program in woodworking at the School for American Craftsmen in Alfred and then Rochester, New York. He remained at the Rochester Institute of Technology until 1962, when he accepted a similar position at the Rhode Island School of Design in Providence, where he would remain until his retirement in 1985. For more than thirty years, Frid exerted an influence on the studio furniture movement through his teaching; energetic and lively, he was a memorable instructor to such furniture makers as Hank Gilpin, Jere Osgood, Alphonse Mattia, William Keyser, John Dunnigan, and Rosanne Somerson. He is also renowned for his numerous articles in *Fine Woodworking*, beginning in 1975, and his three-volume series, *Tage Frid Teaches Woodworking* (published by the Taunton Press in 1979, 1981, 1985, and republished in 1993). He is regarded by Michael A. Stone as "the single greatest influence on American woodworking education."

In his teaching and writing, Frid consistently emphasized that students should understand the nature of wood as a material and the importance of learning traditional techniques: furniture makers "should automatically design around the construction, and not construct around the design." This principle is reflected in his own unpretentious yet superbly constructed furniture, such as the 1953 liquor cabinet (cat. no. 6) included here, with its book-matched rosewood veneers. In 1979, the Museum of Fine Arts, Boston, commissioned eight pieces from Frid for use in the museum's ancient art galleries. Among his most famous designs is a three-legged stool that is an essay in the economy of means and in sturdiness. Throughout his career, Frid accepted religious, commercial, and business commissions; he has fabricated kitchens and other domestic interiors as well.

EDUCATION

Apprenticeship with Gronlund Jensen, woodworking and furniture design, Copenhagen, Denmark, 1929–34.

Copenhagen Technical School, Denmark, 1934.

Vedins School, Copenhagen, Denmark, 1940.

School of Interior Design, Copenhagen, Denmark, 1944.

TEACHING

School for American Craftsmen, Rochester Institute of Technology, Rochester, N.Y., 1948–62.

Rhode Island School of Design, Providence, 1962–85.

SELECT REFERENCES

Tage Frid, *Joinery*, vol. 1, and *Shaping, Veneering, Finishing*, vol. 2, *Tage Frid Teaches Woodworking* (1979–81; reprint, two volumes in one, Newtown, Conn.: Taunton Press, 1993).

Tage Frid, *Furnituremaking*, vol. 3, *Tage Frid Teaches Woodworking* (Newtown, Conn.: Taunton Press, 1985).

John Kelsey, "Tage Frid: A Talk with the Old Master," *Fine Woodworking*, no. 52 (May–June 1985): 66–67.

Stone 1986, 48–63.

Hank Gilpin, "Professor Frid," *Fine Woodworking*, no. 146 (winter 2000–2001): 80–85.

HANK GILPIN

Born 1946, Stamford, Connecticut

Since 1974, Hank Gilpin has produced unpretentious, functional, and meticulously crafted furniture in his independent shop. After earning a bachelor's degree in photojournalism at Boston University in 1968, he served as a photojournalist with the U.S. Army in Vietnam until 1970. He returned to enroll in graduate studies in photography at the Rhode Island School of Design, where he took woodworking as an elective course and soon switched to furniture as his major. Gilpin studied with instructor Tage Frid while earning his MFA, and continued as Frid's apprentice for six months after graduation. Frid instilled in Gilpin essential technical skills, an emphasis on efficient work, and a design sense that responds to clients' practical needs. Gilpin credits Frid with teaching him how to become self-sufficient as a furniture maker.

After establishing his own shop in Lincoln, Rhode Island, in 1974, Gilpin began to develop his own approach to furniture making by studying and synthesizing historical styles. Having focused on the use of veneers in his last year of graduate work, Gilpin intensively studied historical furniture in London and Paris in the summer of 1976 and collected hundreds of books on furniture design. These

studies gave Gilpin a broad range of visual ideas that have inspired his own designs.

He also worked on a variety of woodworking jobs to support himself while trying to establish a business making commissioned furniture. In the late 1970s, Gilpin abandoned veneers in favor of working in hardwood, which he found more durable and pleasing to use. Beginning in 1981, his work was represented by Pritam and Eames Gallery, and he gave up other types of woodworking to focus on furniture in the early 1980s. With the help of two or three assistants, Gilpin ran an efficient shop in which he minimized paperwork in order to spend time building furniture.

In the 1990s, after many years of using only a few types of hardwood, Gilpin began to use rare and unusual woods salvaged by lumber dealers; he enjoyed the design challenges of making beautiful and useful furniture from underrated local species of wood. He also expressed his interests in functional design and the practical aspects of furniture making in articles he contributed to *Fine Woodworking* and *Home Furniture* magazines. Over the years, he has cultivated a large base of clients in the New England area, and his work has been shown in several galleries in New York and Providence, Rhode Island.

EDUCATION

Boston University, BS (journalism) 1968.

Rhode Island School of Design, Providence, MFA (industrial design/furniture) 1973.

Study in the furniture collections of the Victoria and Albert Museum, London, and the Museum of Decorative Arts, Paris, summer 1976.

TEACHING

Rhode Island School of Design, Providence, 1977.

SELECT REFERENCES

Roger Holmes, "Survivors," *Fine Woodworking*, no. 55 (November–December 1985): 91–97.

Hank Gilpin, "Stepped Sideboard in White Oak," *Home Furniture* 5 (winter 1995): 42–43.

Hank Gilpin, "Raising the Lot of the Lowly Bench: A Designer Explains Why He Builds Benches," *Home Furniture* 9 (January 1997): 22–25.

Hank Gilpin, "Not Your Father's Pegboard," *Fine Woodworking*, no. 130 (June 1998): 64–65.

Hank Gilpin, "Master Class: Great Shapes—without a Shaper," *Fine Woodworking*, no. 134 (February 1999): 114–18.

MARY GREGORY

Born 1914, Woodmere, New York

Mary Gregory, one of the first female members of the studio furniture movement, pursued her pioneering career in an independent, strong-minded, and thoughtful fashion. Exposed to the rudiments of woodworking while growing up on her family farm, Gregory, after graduating from Bennington College, then a new women's school in Vermont, taught sculpture for several years at the private Cambridge School in Weston, Massachusetts. Alfred Hulst, the shop teacher at the Cambridge School, furthered her woodworking skills, and Gregory accepted a position at Black Mountain College in North Carolina in 1941. While there, she ran the woodshop and became an apprentice woodworking teacher with the distinguished artist and painter Josef Albers (1888–1976). She quickly joined the full-time faculty and taught at Black Mountain until 1947.

Albers, she recalls, "didn't teach painting, but seeing; not art, but the psychology or philosophy of art.... We had to be alert, disciplined, and neat." Albers, for example, "made us look at an auger bit till we could see just how it pulls itself into the wood and as it goes pushes the chips out behind it. That's exciting. Then we drew it." Gregory learned a respect for the art of the past from Albers, but he also encouraged her individual perspective. Thus, as she notes, "the work one subsequently produces is a measure of your respect and understanding plus that which is given to you to contribute yourself." Under her direction, the woodshop produced a variety of objects. Mary Emma Harris notes that Gregory's teaching emphasized "good craftsmanship, traditional methods of joining...and inventive solutions to problems....She possessed a rare combination of pragmatism and idealism," and was a valuable member of the Black Mountain community in many ways.

In 1947, Gregory moved to Woodstock, Vermont, where she ran Woodstock Enterprises, a custom furniture shop that made objects for Hans Knoll and Josef Albers, and managed several house-building crews. Eager to be on her own, she left Vermont in 1954 for Lexington,

Massachusetts, and then moved to nearby Lincoln, where she established her own shop. Several male employees, including Bob Lloyd and Ted Dodd, assisted her in the production of objects that reflect her own unique blend of construction and ornamental details taken from Scandinavian, Asian, and Shaker furniture. She "wants to do every job myself, all of it, savoring the appropriateness or uniqueness of each assignment."

Raised as an Episcopalian, Gregory became a Quaker "primarily because I wanted to affirm the responsibility for my own inner leadings and the requirement that I make a life that reflects that light." Since she served only a local clientele, Gregory's work remained largely unknown until recent years, when her achievements as a studio furniture maker have begun to be recognized.

EDUCATION

Bennington College, Bennington, Vt., BA 1936.

TEACHING

Black Mountain College, N.C., 1941–47.

SELECT REFERENCES

Mary Emma Harris, *The Arts at Black Mountain College* (Cambridge: MIT Press, 1987).

Edward S. Cooke, Jr., "Furniture," in *Women Designers in the USA, 1900–2000: Diversity and Difference*, ed. Pat Kirkham, exh. cat. (New Haven and London: Yale University Press, for the Bard Graduate Center for Studies in the Decorative Arts, New York, 2000), 296–98.

"Selected List of Teachers and Students," Black Mountain College Museum and Arts Center, http://blackmountaincollege.org/bmcref/teachers.html, accessed September 2002.

STEPHEN HARRIS

*Born 1939, Toronto, Ontario, Canada;
died 1991*

Stephen Harris arrived at studio furniture
making after spending his youth rebelling
against conventional education and working as a theater-set builder. After one year
at the University of New Brunswick in
Canada, he moved to Toronto and built
sets for a repertory theater company.
Starting in 1963, Harris spent five years
in London, where he enjoyed the stimulating counterculture flourishing in that city
and again built sets, this time for several
major theaters. Returning to Canada in
1968, Harris began working for the drama
department at the University of Alberta in
Edmonton, where he met a number of
furniture makers. In 1969, he turned to a
new career designing and building furniture in a small shop in Toronto.

With his limited set of woodworking
skills, Harris initially built simple and
utilitarian cabinetry and furniture. As he
began to meet other artists and craftspeople in the city, however, he was exposed to
new work in the studio craft movement,
including that of Wendell Castle. Fellow
woodworkers Paul Epp and Stephen
Hogbin imparted technical expertise,
design ideas, and intellectual stimulation.
In the early 1970s, Harris, Epp, Hogbin,
and American woodworker Bill Hayes

moved to a large shared studio at 86
Nelson Street. Gradually, Harris developed his drawing and design skills;
between 1971 and 1976, he showed work
in several exhibitions and received commissions from new clients.

As Harris developed his own style, he
moved away from his earlier hard-edged
work and explored increasingly organic
forms with subtle Art Nouveau, biomorphic, and Scandinavian influences. Using
technically complex inlaying and joinery,
he strove for graceful curves and light,
sensual shapes. Although it had sculptural attributes, his work was always clearly
domestic, revealing its function in answer
to specific needs. Harris employed at
least one assistant at all times, demand-
ing high standards and expecting employees to solve complex technical challenges
on their own. During the 1970s and
1980s, his workshop was a focal point
and gathering place for the craft scene in
Toronto.

In the mid-1980s, Harris moved to
his own shop space at 35 Booth Avenue,
where he completed the largest and most
important commission of his career, the
Alexander Wandich penthouse. This group
of furnishings, built from 1984 to 1991,
represented some of Harris's most
refined work in its use of exotic woods
and inlays. In 1991, he was killed in a bicy-
cle accident at the age of fifty-two.

EDUCATION
Upper Canada College, Toronto, Ontario,
through grade thirteen, 1955–58.

University of New Brunswick, Fredericton, general arts, 1961–62.

TEACHING
Sheridan College, School of Crafts and Design,
Oakville, Ontario, part-time instructor, 1977,
1980–81.

SELECT REFERENCES
Stephen Hogbin, "Design Processes; Four
Canadians," *The Workshop* (fall 1983).

Tom Hurley, "Furniture-Making in Toronto: Style
and Success in Canada's Largest Art Market,"
Fine Woodworking, no. 73 (November–
December 1988): 42–47.

Hart Massey, *Stephen Harris:
Designer/Craftsman* (Toronto, Ontario, Canada:
Boston Mills Press, 1994).

STEPHEN HOGBIN

Born 1942, Tolworth, Surrey, England

A wood turner since 1971 and a major figure in the revival of that craft, Stephen
Hogbin has also produced innovative
turned furniture forms. Born and educated in England, he emigrated to Canada
in 1968 and currently resides in Wiarton,
Ontario. His distinguished academic
career includes teaching positions at
Sheridan College and Georgian College
in Canada, and a number of residencies
in the United States and Australia.

In the twentieth century, the development of the craft of wood turning has paralleled the history of furniture making.
While most turners made small bowls
and other vessels, a few experimented
with larger forms, including Hogbin.
His "unique approach" (see chapter 3)
opened "new horizons" by "stretching the
potential of laminated woods," as noted
by Dona Z. Meilach, who in 1975 illustrated his huge lathe in line drawings and
photographs.

EDUCATION
Rycotewood College, Thame, Oxfordshire,
England, 1957–58.

Kingston College of Art, Kingston upon
Thames, Surrey, England, NDD 1961.

Royal College of Art, London, Des. RCA 1965.

TEACHING
Sheridan College School of Design, Toronto,
Ontario, 1968–72.

College of Education, University of Toronto,
Ontario, 1971–72.

Sheridan College/Creative Arts, Toronto, Ontario, 1973.

Sheridan College, School of Crafts and Design, Toronto, Ontario, 1978–80.

Georgian College, design and visual arts department, Owen Sound, Ontario, 1980–82.

Georgian College, design and visual arts, Barrie, Ontario, 1985–87.

SELECT REFERENCES

Donald Lloyd McKinley, "The Wood-Turned Forms of Stephen Hogbin," *Craft Horizons* 34, no. 2 (April 1974): 28–31, 64.

Dona Z. Meilach, *Creating Modern Furniture: Trends, Techniques, Appreciation* (New York: Crown Publishers, 1975), 168–69.

J. K., "Out of the Woods: Touring Show Features Designer-Craftsmen of Ontario," *Fine Woodworking*, no. 17 (July–August 1979): 76–77.

Stephen Hogbin, *Wood Turning: The Purpose of the Object* (Sydney: John Ferguson Proprietary and Crafts Council of Australia, 1980).

Wood Turning Center and Yale University Art Gallery, *Woodturning in North America since 1930*, exh. cat. (New Haven: Wood Turning Center and Yale University Art Gallery, 2001), 167.

Jack Rogers Hopkins

Born 1920, Modesto, California

Jack Rogers Hopkins, a master of sculptural laminated furniture, is one of the early members of the California branch of the studio furniture movement. Educated there, he taught for more than a decade at Bakersfield High School and Junior College. He moved to San Diego State University in 1961 and was a professor of art there for the next thirty years, until retiring in 1991.

With a lifelong interest in art, Hopkins came under the influence of Millard Sheets (1907–1989), a master artist at the Claremont Colleges who also affected the career of Sam Maloof. He became dissatisfied with his initial goal of becoming "the best watercolorist in the world"—it wasn't physical enough to be rewarding—so he tried his hand at other forms of art.

During his long career, in addition to his teaching, Hopkins created "sculpture in wood, clay, and metal," and his furniture, ceramics, and jewelry were exhibited widely. Regarding himself as a "designer-craftsman," Hopkins advertised that he made "one of a kind and limited edition personal statements in natural materials. . . employing the lamination tech-

nique." His laminated work, related to and even more expressive than that of Wendell Castle, included chairs, tables, clocks, and other forms with strongly curved arms and legs, and all with dramatic, flowing contours. Many of his objects incorporate hidden compartments for sound or office equipment, carefully concealed within the outlines of the object. One of numerous craftsmen working with lamination, including Al Lockwood, Jocko Johnson, Milon Hutchinson, John Snidecor, James Nash, John Bauer, Bob Falwell, and Castle, Hopkins was praised in the mid-1970s by Dona Z. Meilach for his "organically conceived, flowing sculptural laminated forms. . . carried to exciting new heights." She chose his chair-table as the first illustration in her survey of modern furniture published in 1975 and illustrated a dozen of his pieces, the most by any artist whose work was included in this early survey of the field.

Perhaps Hopkins's most expressive object was his environmental piece (which unfortunately doesn't survive) known as the *Womb Room* (see chapter 2, fig. 6). Conceived and made in just three months, this enormous sectional object included a chair, footstool, coffee table, reading light, library space, and stereo with twenty-three speakers. Perhaps no other single object represents the heights (literally and figuratively) that laminated furniture could achieve.

EDUCATION

California College of Arts and Crafts, Oakland, Calif., BA 1950.

Scripps Art Department, Claremont Colleges, Claremont, Calif., MFA 1958.

TEACHING

California College of Arts and Crafts, Oakland, 1948–50.

Bakersfield High School and Junior College, Bakersfield, Calif., 1950–61.

San Diego State University, San Diego, Calif., 1961–91.

SELECT REFERENCES

Pasadena Art Museum, *California Design Eleven*, exh. cat. (Pasadena, Calif.: California Design, 1971), 38–39.

Dona Z. Meilach, *Creating Modern Furniture: Trends, Techniques, Appreciation* (New York: Crown Publishers, 1975).

Thomas Hucker

Born 1955, Bryn Mawr, Pennsylvania

Thomas Hucker's career has spanned work in studio furniture, industrial production, and interior design. Hucker was inspired to become a furniture maker when he saw the work of Wendell Castle, Sam Maloof, William Keyser, and Jere Osgood in the "Objects: USA" exhibition, in Philadelphia in 1973. He had been interested in art while in high school but found the standards for fine arts in the 1970s "too wide-open." Furniture making appealed to him because it offered the parameters of function and technical mastery.

Hucker pursued hands-on training in woodworking throughout the 1970s. In 1973, he worked with Daniel Jackson and studied at Penland School in North Carolina with Sam Maloof. In 1974, he began a two-year apprenticeship with Lenord Hilgner, a fifth-generation German cabinetmaker who offered Hucker both traditional training and a sense of self-respect as a craftsman. After entering Boston University's Program in Artisanry in 1976, Hucker studied with Alphonse Mattia and Jere Osgood; he graduated with a certificate of mastery in 1980. His early works, exhibited in "New Handmade Furniture" in 1979 in New York and "Bentwood" in 1984 in Providence, Rhode Island, emphasized proportion and structure and revealed the design influence of Osgood.

While in Boston, Hucker also studied at the Urasenke School of Tea Ceremony and became fascinated by Japanese aesthetics. In 1982, he was an artist-in-resi-

dence at Tokyo National University of Fine Arts. His interest in both Japanese architecture and Chinese furniture was reflected in the balance, spareness, and restraint of his work in the 1980s, yet Hucker also incorporated Western influences, such as Queen Anne and William and Mary furniture. He began to explore transparency, lighting, lacquered finishes, and materials such as bronze, steel, and stone.

In the late 1980s, Hucker continued making one-off furniture but also pursued industrial design, collaborating with woodworker Tim Wells, who produced his designs from drawings. In 1986 and 1988 he designed tablewares for Dansk International, and his designs for furniture and lighting won recognition from *I.D. Magazine of International Design*. A Fulbright-Hays fellowship enabled him to study at the Domus Academy in Milan in 1989, where he became interested in the conceptual elements of furniture and interiors. Hucker began to seek ways in which furniture could interact with its environment and engage multiple senses, including sound and smell. In the early 1990s, he received a grant from the Fragrance Foundation to apply scents to what he called "ambental furniture," which he exhibited at Franklin Parrasch Gallery. His work is represented in several museums, including the American Museum of Arts and Design, the Museum of Fine Arts, Boston, and the Renwick Gallery of the Smithsonian Institution.

EDUCATION

Apprenticeship with furniture maker Daniel Jackson, Philadelphia, Pa., 1973.

Apprenticeship with cabinetmaker Lenord Hilgner, Philadelphia, Pa., 1974–76.

Urasenke School of Tea Ceremony, Boston chapter, 1977–80.

Boston University, Program in Artisanry, certificate of mastery, 1980.

Domus Academy, Milan, Italy, 1989.

TEACHING

Appalachian Center for Crafts, Smithville, Tenn., department head, furniture design and fabrication, 1980–82.

Parsons School of Art and Design, New York, N.Y., 1990.

SELECT REFERENCES

American Craft Museum, *New Handmade Furniture: American Furniture Makers Working in Hardwood*, exh. cat. (New York: American Craft Museum, 1979).

Tanya Barter, John Dunnigan, and Seth Stem, *Bentwood*, exh. cat. (Providence: Rhode Island School of Design, 1984), 32–33.

Cooke 1989, 56–59.

Peter Joseph Gallery, *Thomas Hucker*, exh. cat. (New York: Peter Joseph Gallery, 1992).

Rose Slivka, "Thomas Hucker: Counting Angels," *American Craft* 52, no. 3 (June–July 1992): 46–49.

Amy Forsyth, "Jere Osgood and Thomas Hucker: A Tale of Shared Inspiration and a Study in Opposites," *Woodwork*, no. 69 (June 2001): 24–33.

MICHAEL HURWITZ

Born 1955, Miami, Florida

While in high school, Hurwitz was introduced to studio furniture and to the work of independent craftsmen such as Sam Maloof and George Nakashima, through the Renwick Gallery's 1972 exhibition "Woodenworks." Encouraged by his parents to pursue his interests in art and music, he unsuccessfully sought an apprenticeship in guitar making. In 1974, Hurwitz enrolled at the Massachusetts College of Art in Boston as a metals major. In the following year, he transferred to the newly formed Program in Artisanry (PIA) at Boston University, where he intended to study with Don Warnoch, a highly respected instrument maker. Through furniture courses with Jere Osgood, Daniel Jackson, and Alphonse Mattia, as well as the camaraderie of the other PIA students, Hurwitz became drawn to furniture making.

After graduating from PIA in 1979, he joined the Cambridgeport Cooperative Workshops, in Cambridge, Massachusetts, where low overhead costs allowed him to experiment with furniture designs. A tall side chair that he exhibited in the American Craft Museum's 1979 exhibition "New Handmade Furniture," widely cited in articles about the exhibition, reflected the predominant characteristics of Hurwitz's early work: simple forms constructed of solid wood with exposed joinery. In 1983, he began to investigate painted and textured surfaces to suggest the passage of time. A 1985 fellowship in the Dominican Republic allowed Hurwitz to explore ideas of self-expression, "primitive" art, and traditional joinery.

Moving from the Boston area that same year, he headed the wood department and taught at the Philadelphia College of Art (now the University of the Arts) until 1990. He then embarked on a six-month fellowship for study in Kyoto, awarded by the Japan–U.S. Friendship Commission and the National Endowment for the Arts. While in Japan, Hurwitz met and studied with several native master craftsmen, reexamined his perspectives on craftwork, and developed Japanese-influenced designs.

During the 1990s, he continued to explore refined design incorporating a variety of influences. The *Rocking Chaise* he created for the 1989 exhibition "New American Furniture" at the Museum of Fine Arts, Boston, the first in a series of chaises, revealed Hurwitz's interest in lines and curves, the relationship between positive and negative space, and the reinterpretation of historic furniture forms. In 1994, he began to make labor-intensive installations and pieces of furniture incorporating inlaid marble mosaics. Another Japan fellowship in 1997 allowed Hurwitz to pursue further study with local artists. He continues to work as an independent furniture maker from his studio in Philadelphia.

EDUCATION

Massachusetts College of Art, Boston, 1974–75.

Boston University, Program in Artisanry, BFA 1979.

TEACHING

Boston University, Program in Artisanry, 1982.

Appalachian Center for Crafts, Smithville, Tenn., 1981, 1982, 1984.

Altos de Chavon School of Design, Dominican Republic, 1985, 1989.

University of the Arts, Philadelphia, Pa., associate professor and program head, wood department, 1985–90.

SELECT REFERENCES

American Craft Museum, *New Handmade Furniture: American Furniture Makers Working in Hardwood*, exh. cat. (New York: American Craft Museum, 1979).

Brockton Art Museum/Fuller Memorial, *Woodforms: Contemporary Hand-Crafted Furniture of Original Design*, exh. cat. (Brockton, Mass.: Brockton Art Museum/Fuller Memorial, 1981), 9.

"New Furniture: In Search of a Contemporary Style," *Fine Woodworking*, no. 30 (September–October 1981): 94–97.

"Portfolio: Michael Hurwitz," *American Craft* 46, no. 1 (February–March 1986): 41.

Cooke 1989, 60–63.

Peter Joseph Gallery, *Michael Hurwitz*, exh. cat. (New York: Peter Joseph Gallery, 1992).

Michael Rush, "Michael Hurwitz," *American Craft* 57, no. 2 (April–May 1997): 62–66.

DANIEL JACKSON

Born 1938, Milwaukee, Wisconsin; died 1995

Daniel Jackson's career as a furniture maker and teacher, although tragically cut short by illness, had a significant impact on the field. Jackson's childhood surroundings inspired him to work with wood; he was raised in a house that had been in his family for five generations and was filled with antiques. By age ten, he was carving wooden objects and utensils; by age thirteen, he was buying, restoring, and selling antique furniture.

After attending the College of William and Mary in Williamsburg, Virginia, for two years, Jackson transferred to the School for American Crafts (SAC) at the Rochester Institute of Technology in New York in 1958. At SAC, he studied furniture making with Danish-born master craftsman Tage Frid and began a lifelong friendship with fellow student Jere Osgood. In 1960, he left SAC to study in Denmark, then the source of much modern furniture design. His instructor, Peder Moos, imparted to Jackson a respect for wood as a material, a concern for traditional construction, and a willingness to experiment with sculptural expression.

In 1964, Jackson accepted an offer to found the woodworking and furniture design program at the Philadelphia College of Art (PCA). Jackson soon became a vital part of the emerging craft scene in Philadelphia. His students, including second-generation furniture makers Thomas Hucker, Ed Zucca, and Alphonse Mattia, recalled Jackson's contagious enthusiasm as a teacher. In 1967, Jackson joined with other Philadelphia-area craftspeople to found the Philadelphia Council of Professional Craftsmen (PCPC), which sponsored Triannual Philadelphia Crafts-man shows and attracted other craft exhibitions to the area.

In the late 1960s and early 1970s, Jackson's work appeared frequently in national and regional exhibitions, including the Museum of Contemporary Craft's "Craftsmen USA '66," and several of the PCPC Craftsman shows, as well as at the newly founded Richard Kagan Gallery. His furniture was characterized by organic, sensual shapes with references to plant, animal, or human forms; the mixing of different types of wood for colorful effect; and an emphasis on visible structure through decorative joinery.

As Jackson was reaching the height of his career, the sudden onset of debilitating illness in 1974 forced him to stop teaching at PCA. His friend Jere Osgood persuaded him to help start the new furniture program at Boston University's Program in Artisanry in 1975, but Jackson's failing health did not permit him to continue. After a brief attempt to return to teaching at PCA in 1976, Jackson was forced to retire from furniture making as well. At his death in 1995, his colleagues remembered him as a seminal force in furniture making, who, along with Osgood, provided a link between the first and second generations of studio furniture makers.

EDUCATION

College of William and Mary, Williamsburg, Va., about 1956–58.

School for American Crafts, Rochester Institute of Technology, Rochester, N.Y., 1958–60.

Scandinavian Seminar Program, Denmark, apprenticeship with Peder Moos, 1960–62.

TEACHING

University of Illinois, Urbana-Champaign, 1963.

Philadelphia College of Art, founded woodworking program, 1964–74, 1976.

Boston University, Program in Artisanry, 1975.

SELECT REFERENCES

"Daniel Jackson," *Craft Horizons* 30, no. 3 (May–June 1970): 61.

Daniel Jackson, "Hand Shaping: A Simple Approach to Sculpturing Wood," *Fine Woodworking* 1, no. 3 (summer 1976): 24–25.

Franklin Parrasch Galleries, *A Tribute to Daniel Jackson*, exh. cat. (Washington, D.C.: Franklin Parrasch Galleries, 1989).

Nancy A. Corwin, "Vital Connections: The Furniture of Daniel Jackson," *American Craft* 50, no. 3 (June–July 1990): 50–55, 74–75.

"Daniel Jackson 1938–1995," *American Craft* 55, no. 5 (October–November 1995): 23.

VLADIMIR KAGAN

Born 1927, Worms am Rhein, Germany

Kagan came from a woodworking and artistic family; his father, Illi, made furniture in czarist Russia before emigrating to Germany after the First World War. The family, in turn, came to the United States in 1938. After studying architecture for a time at Columbia University, Kagan joined his father's New York City cabinetmaking shop in 1947, where he began to learn all aspects of the trade: "My schooling was architecture, my training woodwork." He established his own shop in 1949 and soon was successful in marketing his wares to many famous personalities and institutions. The shop expanded over time from a staff of about six craftsmen to a dozen and later peaked at approximately thirty, under the direction of master craftsman and foreman Victor Medina. The shop issued its products in small batches, usually about a dozen examples at a time. Kagan took a very hands-on role in production, dividing his time between the workshop and his salesroom, first located on East Sixty-fifth Street and, by 1950, on Fifty-seventh Street.

Initially influenced by Bauhaus principles and Scandinavian furniture, he quickly moved to a less austere, less linear, and more sculptural approach that "emphasizes the interplay of wood and structure; of space, and light, simplicity and function." Kagan's shop produced a wide range of office and domestic furniture, including upholstered work, such as his "barrel" chair designed in 1947. His most successful designs from the 1950s, perhaps, are his "sculptured" and "contoured" forms of seating furniture and tables, including armchairs, rocking chairs, footstools, dining tables, and tea carts. Large "free-form" and "wide-angle" sofas and biomorphic coffee tables by Kagan also date to the 1950s and are in harmony with other furniture of the period, designed, for example, by Isamu Noguchi (1904–1988).

Some of his more innovative objects of the 1960s are chairs and tables supported by V-shaped aluminum pedestals strongly resembling automobile hood ornaments of the same time, as well as other forms incorporating Lucite, glass, and steel elements. He has been credited with introducing polyurethane foam for use in furniture and for designing case pieces at an early date that incorporated sound systems for audio and video entertainment. In the 1960s, for example, Kagan created a "Sound Room" for the General Electric Company; in the same decade, he redesigned Disneyland's Plastic House of the Future. Later in his career, he became noted for his composite furniture groupings that incorporated multiple functions, creating "environments" suitable for smaller apartment and domestic spaces.

Kagan began to focus on contract design for industry after 1987, but his early career reflects the difficulties inherent in creating strict separations between "designers" and "craftsmen."

EDUCATION
Columbia University, New York City.

TEACHING
Parsons School of Design, New York City.

SELECT REFERENCES
Twenty Years of Vladimir Kagan Designs: Furniture Classics for the Connoisseur (New York: Vladimir Kagan Designs, 1967).

Kagan: Three Decades of Design, exh. cat. (New York: Galleries at FIT, 1980), introduction by Christian Rohlfing.

Mel Byars, *The Design Encyclopedia* (New York: John Wiley and Sons, 1994), s.v. "Kagan, Vladimir."

Vladimir Kagan: Classic Design Collection (New York: Vladimir Kagan Design Group, 1998).

WILLIAM A. KEYSER, JR.

Born 1936, Pittsburgh, Pennsylvania

Throughout his career, William Keyser simultaneously taught furniture design and produced custom work for public and private commissions. After earning a degree in mechanical engineering at Carnegie-Mellon University, he studied furniture making with Tage Frid at the School for American Crafts (SAC) in Rochester, New York, and was awarded an MFA there in 1961. Keyser taught for a year in Ohio, then returned to Rochester to teach furniture design at SAC for thirty-five years before retiring in 1997.

At the same time, he maintained an active studio for both commission and speculative work. He executed works for a number of schools and businesses but was best known for his ecclesiastical commissions. Beginning in 1962, when he was asked to make a set of candlesticks for St. Bernard's Seminary in Rochester, Keyser designed and built custom liturgical furniture for churches of various denominations. He enjoyed the design challenges of accommodating the liturgical practices of different faiths, working within the architectural contexts of specific sites, and conveying abstract spiritual ideas through furniture forms. His engineering training also enabled him to collaborate with architects and designers, manage large-scale installations, and design artworks for safety and durability.

Like other early studio furniture mak-

ers, Keyser worked primarily in wood. He found wood particularly suited to public art because it "invites participation.... People are compelled to touch, caress, lean against, sit on, or grasp wood." While he held a traditionalist's respect for wood, Keyser enjoyed exploring innovative ways to manipulate the material, including steam bending and coopering. He was particularly interested in boatbuilding techniques such as lapstrake and "cold molding" and early aircraft techniques using a plywood "skin" applied over a curved frame.

Keyser's furniture, including private works and speculative pieces, was shown in important galleries and museum exhibitions from the 1960s through the 1980s, including the Richard Kagan Gallery, "Young Americans 1962," "Objects: USA" (1969), "New Handmade Furniture" (1979), and "Bentwood" (1984).

EDUCATION

Carnegie-Mellon University, Pittsburgh, Pa., BS (mechanical engineering) 1958.

School of American Crafts, Rochester Institute of Technology, Rochester, N.Y., MFA 1961.

TEACHING

Ohio University, 1961–62.

School of American Crafts, Rochester Institute of Technology, Rochester, N.Y., 1962–97.

SELECT REFERENCES

"Young Americans 1962," *Craft Horizons* 22, no. 4 (July–August 1962): 10–21.

Nordness 1970, 260.

William A. Keyser, Jr., "Steam Bending," *Fine Woodworking* 2, no. 2 (fall 1977): 40–45.

Bevier Gallery, College of Fine and Applied Arts, Rochester Institute of Technology, *Keyser: Wood Furniture, Sculpture, and Ecclesiastical Objects,* exh. cat. (Rochester, N.Y.: Rochester Institute of Technology, 1978).

"Portfolio: W. A. Keyser," *Fine Woodworking,* no. 15 (March–April 1979): 52–55.

Tanya Barter, John Dunnigan, and Seth Stem, *Bentwood,* exh. cat. (Providence: Rhode Island School of Design, 1984), 38–39.

JAMES KRENOV

Born 1920, Siberia

James Krenov has offered an alternative voice in the field of studio furniture, advocating "quiet craftsmanship" and a personal relationship with wood, as opposed to what he views as a market-driven quest for novel forms and contrived styles. Through his many publications, lectures, and teaching, Krenov has inspired a dedicated group of students who share his approach to furniture making.

Krenov's aristocratic Russian parents lived in Siberia in the wake of the Russian Revolution. The family emigrated in 1923 to China and then to Seattle, Washington; they spent some years in Alaska before Krenov and his mother returned to Seattle about 1932. After working in Seattle's shipyards as a young man, he went to Europe in 1947 and settled in Sweden. There, he happened upon the showroom of leading furniture designer Carl Malmsten and enrolled in Malmsten's cabinetmaking school. After graduation, Krenov established his own shop in a suburb of Stockholm, where he began to make small cabinets and showcases of his own design.

In 1968, he was invited to teach at the School for American Crafts (SAC) in Rochester, New York, during William Keyser's one-year sabbatical. Krenov gave lectures and seminars throughout the United States and Europe during the 1970s, including summer sessions at the SAC in 1973 and 1974. He also published several influential books and articles in the United States, including his widely read first book, *A Cabinetmaker's Notebook* (1976). Krenov's writings express his love for wood, his personal pleasure in the woodworking process, and his devotion to "sensitive," refined craftsmanship. Despite his growing American following, he maintained his residence in Bromma, Sweden, for many years. However, after an especially successful series of workshops for the Mendocino Woodworkers Association in California from 1978 to 1980, Krenov moved with his family to nearby Fort Bragg in 1981 to help found a formal woodworking program at the College of the Redwoods.

He has continued to produce a few pieces each year in addition to teaching and occasionally exhibits his work in group shows with his students. Krenov uses few drawings, preferring to allow designs to evolve as he works the wood slowly and patiently. He uses machinery with restraint and favors hand tools, such as the planes he makes himself. Although his work has appeared at Pritam and

Eames Gallery and in museum exhibitions such as "Craft Today: Poetry of the Physical" (1986), Krenov prefers to retain his outsider identity, proudly declaring that he "never became a member of the club of super-star craftsmen."

EDUCATION

Carl Malmsten cabinetmaking school, Stockholm, Sweden, late 1950s.

TEACHING

School for American Crafts, Rochester Institute of Technology, Rochester, N.Y., 1968, 1973, 1974.

College of the Redwoods, Fort Bragg, Calif., 1981–present.

SELECT REFERENCES

James Krenov, "Wood: 'The Friendly Mystery,'" *Craft Horizons* 27, no. 2 (March–April 1967): 28–29.

James Krenov, *A Cabinetmaker's Notebook* (New York: Van Nostrand Reinhold, 1976). [For other books by Krenov, see the bibliography.]

Paul Bertorelli, "Two Schools: Castle and Krenov—Different Ideas about How to Teach," *Fine Woodworking,* no. 39 (March–April 1983): 103–4.

Glenn Gordon, "James Krenov: Reflections on the Risks of Pure Craft," *Fine Woodworking,* no. 55 (November–December 1985): 42–49.

Stone 1986, 100–113.

Ross Day, "A Krenov Student's Notebook," *Fine Woodworking,* no. 146 (winter 2000–2001): 98–103.

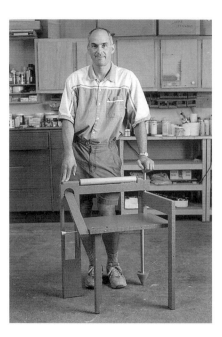

Tom Loeser

Born 1956, Boston, Massachusetts

Tom Loeser is best known for his skillful use of color to define and decorate furniture forms. His earliest exposure to craft was in a high school ceramics studio and a year of work as a thrower in a production ceramics shop. After high school, he worked at the New England Craftsmanship Center in Watertown, Massachusetts, where he was increasingly drawn to the woodworking shop. During his four years of college, Loeser held summer jobs in construction but otherwise did not pursue crafts or woodworking.

After graduation, he visited his childhood friend, Mitch Ryerson, who was enrolled at the Program in Artisanry (PIA) at Boston University, then thriving under the direction of Jere Osgood and Alphonse Mattia. Loeser soon enrolled, too. While at the PIA in the early 1980s, he found contact with the other students especially stimulating; he was also influenced by exposure to historical furniture through the teaching of decorative arts scholar John T. Kirk, as well as by reading contemporary architecture magazines such as Domus and Abitare. The Memphis furniture movement was important to Loeser "not because I like the stuff, but more because it opened up the field, and made more things possible and accepted."

Inspired by both traditional furniture and the new possibilities of avante-garde design, he began using color in his work during his last year at PIA. An assignment to design a chair produced in series led Loeser to design his wall-hung folding chair (cat. no. 41), cut from a single sheet of plywood and brightly painted. The chair caught the eye of Bernice Wollman and Judy Coady of the Workbench Gallery in New York, beginning his affiliation with the gallery and helping him launch a career as a studio furniture maker. In 1983, he spent a summer as an artist-in-residence at the Appalachian Center for Crafts in Smithville, Tennessee, where he began to produce more relaxed designs under the influence of program head Wendy Maruyama. In the same year, he joined the Emily Street cooperative in Cambridge, Massachusetts, where he established his shop in the company of other PIA graduates.

In the late 1980s, Loeser began teaching in woodworking programs; he joined the wood program at the University of Wisconsin–Madison in 1991. Along with teaching and commission work, he has continued to produce speculative pieces for shows and galleries. While drawing on historical forms such as blanket chests, Loeser has refined his use of color and surface decoration to articulate form by exploring chip-carved and gouged surfaces enhanced with milk paints. Recent work has included kinetic pieces introducing a playful element. Throughout the 1990s, Loeser brought a conceptual approach to traditional furniture forms, forcing viewers to rethink their expectations about how furniture is used.

EDUCATION

Haverford College, Haverford, Pa., BA (sociology and anthropology) 1979.

Boston University, Program in Artisanry, BFA 1982.

University of Massachusetts, Program in Artisanry, North Dartmouth, MFA 1992.

TEACHING

Swain School of Design, Program of Artisanry, New Bedford, Mass., 1987.

Rhode Island School of Design, Providence, 1987–88.

California College of Arts and Crafts, Oakland, 1989–90.

University of Wisconsin–Madison, 1991–present.

SELECT REFERENCES

"Portfolio: Tom Loeser," *American Craft* 44, no. 1 (February–March 1984): 32.

Gallery at Workbench and Formica Corporation, *Material Evidence: New Color Techniques in Handmade Furniture*, exh. cat. (Washington, D.C: Smithsonian Institution, 1985), 13–15.

Cooke 1989, 64–67.

Peter Joseph Gallery, *Tom Loeser: Sixty-five Drawers, Eleven Doors, and Four Lids*, exh. cat. (New York: Peter Joseph Gallery, 1992).

Jody Clowes, "Romancing the Surface," *American Craft* 54, no. 4 (August–September 1994): 54–57, 68.

Glenn Adamson, "More Than Meets the Eye: Tom Loeser's Kinetic Furniture," *Woodwork*, no. 72 (December 2001): 26–34.

KRISTINA MADSEN

Born 1955, Northampton, Massachusetts

Kristina Madsen's work is characterized by refined, simple forms embellished with intricately carved surfaces. Although she did not begin woodworking until 1975, she developed hand skills and an eye for complex patterns by learning quilting, lace making, and sewing from her female relatives. After briefly studying at the University of Maine in Orono, Madsen met furniture maker David Powell by chance. She immediately decided she wanted to be a craftsperson and left college to begin an internship with Powell at his recently formed Leeds Design Workshops.

Madsen learned expert technical skills in furniture making from the English-trained Powell, though she had no formal

design training. Instead, she evolved her own intuitive sense of design. In 1979, after completing four years of study, she began teaching at the Leeds Design Workshops, initiated her own furniture business, and started to exhibit her work in group shows at museums and galleries.

While Madsen's early work tended to be refined and traditional, based on her training with Powell, she took a new direction in 1982 after encountering examples of carving in a museum catalogue of Pacific artifacts. Intrigued by the "richness and power" of the carved objects, she began to experiment with textured surfaces using familiar tools such the router to create gouged and patterned surfaces on her furniture. She also chose to use more fabric and upholstery, along with textured surfaces, to make her work inviting and tactile.

In 1988, Madsen secured an artist-in-residence position at the School of Art at the University of Tasmania in Australia, during which time she also briefly visited Fiji and New Zealand. She observed for herself the freehand carving techniques employed by local carvers; the Fijian master carver Makiti Koto also demonstrated his freehand low-relief gouge carving. In the same year, Madsen concluded that she had reached a "technical plateau" and was being "stigmatized by the description 'traditional.'" Seeking greater depth in her work, she applied for and received a Fulbright grant to return to Fiji to study with Koto. For nine months from 1991 into 1992, Madsen lived with Koto's family, studied carving with him, and immersed herself in the local Fijian culture.

Although she learned traditional carving and finishing techniques and practiced creating Fijian patterns during her travels, upon her return to New England Madsen worked to incorporate these new influences without directly appropriating Fijian images. Instead, she began to adapt the techniques to create carved patterns of original design based on elements from her own culture, such as lace, calligraphy, or typography. During the 1990s, Madsen reached a new level of maturity as her work increasingly concerned itself with "self-development and expression."

EDUCATION
University of Maine, Orono, January–June 1975.

Leeds Design Workshops, Easthampton, Mass., June 1975–June 1979.

TEACHING
Leeds Design Workshops, Easthampton, Mass., part-time instructor, 1979–84.

SELECT REFERENCES
Cooke 1989, 68–71.

"Portfolio: Kristina Madsen," American Craft 49, no. 5 (October–November 1989): 64–65.

Andrea J. Olsen, "Kristina Madsen: Textures with a Touch of Class," Woodwork, no. 10 (summer 1991): 38–42.

Norbert Nelson, "Pacific Transfer," American Craft 53, no. 6 (December 1993–January 1994): 50–51.

Laura J. MacKay, "Fiji Reconfigured," Design Times 8, no. 1 (February–March 1996): 52–53.

Terrie Noll, "Return of the Native: Kristina Madsen Revisited," Woodwork, no. 51 (June 1998): 20–27.

SAM MALOOF

Born 1916, Chino, California

Sam Maloof's fifty-year career has earned him a reputation as one of America's preeminent living woodworkers. The son of Lebanese immigrants, he demonstrated an aptitude for art during his childhood. After high school, he worked as an architectural draftsman, a graphic artist, and an assistant to industrial designer Harold Graham, in whose shop he first worked with wood. After serving in the U.S. Army during World War II, Maloof moved to Los Angeles and worked as a graphic artist and a studio assistant to artist Millard Sheets. He began to consider a career in industrial design after building furniture for his own apartment.

While working for Sheets, Maloof met his wife and lifelong business partner Alfreda; the two married in 1948. With Freda's support and a few commissions from friends, he quit his job and took up furniture making full-time. A breakthrough occurred when the famous industrial designer Henry Dreyfuss asked Maloof to design and build furniture for his home and office. Dreyfuss encouraged him to pursue industrial design, but Maloof decided in 1952 that he preferred making custom furniture and set up his workshop in Alta Loma, California, that same year.

During the 1950s and 1960s, with Freda acting as his business manager, he increased production and built a larger workshop to keep up with the flow of orders from West Coast clients. He also developed many new designs, including seating pieces with innovative "sculptured" armrests. Although he used templates, Maloof freely shaped each piece; he explained that "design does not exist just on paper. It pervades every step in the creation of a piece of furniture." His work gained exposure in the "California Design" shows and in magazines before appearing in the 1957 "Furniture by Craftsmen" exhibition in New York. Maloof's active participation in craft conferences and organizations connected him to the emerging community of independent craftspeople.

In the 1970s and 1980s, many came to see him as heir to Wharton Esherick's role as the "dean of American woodworking." While he continued to make furniture for private clients, Maloof devoted more time to travel, lectures, and workshops. His furniture evolved gradually, and his pieces became sought-after acquisitions for art collectors and museums. Maloof has been granted an honorary doctorate from the Rhode Island School of Design as well as numerous prestigious awards from the American Craft Council.

■ Fig. 30. Wendy Maruyama.
■ Fig. 31. Alphonse Mattia.
■ Fig. 32. Judy Kensley McKie.

TEACHING

California State University, Northridge, 1970.

Penland School of Crafts, Penland, N.C., summer workshops, 1970–75.

Anderson Ranch Arts Center, Aspen, Colo., summer workshops, about 1975–90.

SELECT REFERENCES

Shirley Ashton, "Maloof...Designer, Craftsman of Furniture," *Craft Horizons* 14, no. 3 (May–June 1954): 15–19.

Renwick Gallery, *Woodenworks: Furniture Objects by Five Contemporary Craftsmen*, exh. cat. (St. Paul: Minnesota Museum of Art and Smithsonian Institution, 1972), 12–21.

Sam Maloof, *Sam Maloof: Woodworker* (Tokyo, New York, and San Francisco: Kodansha International, 1983).

Stone 1986, 64–81.

Jeremy Adamson, *The Furniture of Sam Maloof*, exh. cat. (Washington, D.C.: Smithsonian American Art Museum, 2001).

WENDY MARUYAMA

Born 1952, La Junta, California

Wendy Maruyama challenged accepted notions of furniture by using sculptural forms, colored surfaces, social commentary, and humor in her work. She first became attracted to woodworking while taking a multimedia crafts class at a junior college in San Diego. After enrolling in San Diego State University, Maruyama studied woodworking under Larry Hunter, who taught stack lamination methods and showed books and slides of contemporary furniture to his students. During these years, she became aware of the work of Wendell Castle and Tommy Simpson, which suggested to her the possibilities of furniture as an art form.

Realizing that woodworking was very different on the two U.S. coasts, Maruyama enrolled in graduate school at Virginia Commonwealth University in Richmond. However, in her first semester, she found that her technical skills were inadequate, and she transferred to Boston University's Program in Artisanry. There, instructors Alphonse Mattia and Jere Osgood, as well as talented students, helped Maruyama master traditional techniques and develop a commitment to the field. She went on to become one of the first women to complete an MFA at the Rochester Institute of Technology's School for American Crafts in New York. Her reaction to the school's conservative culture strengthened her sense of individuality and inspired her to try unconventional approaches. At the same time, she was influenced by Wendell Castle, who set high standards for the quality of "art furniture," and the Memphis Group, who—in Maruyama's opinion—"had an eye-opening effect on furniture design, and...eliminated the fear of doing timely or trendy work simply for the fun and need to express something."

Throughout the 1980s, her work reflected aesthetic experimentation. In the early 1980s, she used decorative colored surfaces, angular forms, and a variety of media, including neon tubes and glass. In 1984, tiring of the trend toward surface colors, Maruyama entered her "white period." Calling the style "post-nuclear primitive"—an objection to nuclear testing—she made bleached or white-painted forms to suggest the pale, stark furniture that she imagined would exist after a nuclear holocaust. About 1986, Maruyama began a new phase of work, in which she explored organic images, especially pod- or fin-shaped forms, returned to color to express emotions, and integrated function with decoration.

Maruyama has combined teaching with making furniture for commissions and gallery shows. Her works have been shown in several exhibitions, including "Material Evidence" (1984) and "Craft Today USA" (1989), and at important galleries. Grants from the National Endowment for the Arts have allowed her to study abroad and take time to develop new designs, while her teaching and her role as a board member of the Furniture Society have helped her stay in touch with new currents in the field.

EDUCATION

San Diego State University, BA 1975.

Virginia Commonwealth University, Richmond, Va., 1975.

Boston University, Program in Artisanry, 1976–78.

School for American Crafts, Rochester Institute of Technology, Rochester, N.Y., MFA 1980.

TEACHING

Appalachian Center for Crafts, Smithville, Tenn., 1980–85; head of woodworking and furniture design program, 1982–85.

California College of Arts and Crafts, Oakland, Calif., head of woodworking and furniture design program, 1985–89.

San Diego State University, head of woodworking and furniture design program, 1989–present.

SELECT REFERENCES

"Wendy Maruyama," *Women Artists News* 12 (fall–winter 1987): 18–19.

Cooke 1989, 72–75.

Edward S. Cooke, Jr., *Wendy Maruyama: Form and Function* (Boston: Gallery NAGA, 1991).

Nina Stritzler, "Wendy Maruyama," in *Explorations II: The New Furniture*, exh. cat. (New York: American Craft Museum, 1991), 38–41.

Lisa Hammel, "Wendy's World," *American Craft* 53, no. 1 (February–March 1993): 8–31.

Brian Caldwell, "The Colorful World of Wendy Maruyama," *Woodshop News* (February 2002): T35–T36.

ALPHONSE MATTIA

Born 1947, Philadelphia, Pennsylvania

Alphonse Mattia began his career in Philadelphia woodworking in the late 1960s and early 1970s; he later studied and taught at several other major furniture programs. Although he had no formal art training before college, during high school he constructed displays for a local hobby store and built model cars with his father, a carpenter who learned woodworking in Italy. With the support of his parents and his employers at the hobby shop, Mattia chose to study art at the Philadelphia College of Art (PCA).

He had intended to concentrate in industrial design, but, in his second year, he moved to PCA's woodworking program led by Daniel Jackson. Mattia and the other students were encouraged to create original, contemporary designs inspired by a range of sources, including antique, Art Nouveau, and Scandinavian Modern furniture. After earning his BFA in 1969, he stayed in Philadelphia for two years while renting studio space from Jackson and his assistant Bob Worth. Seeking to continue his education outside Philadelphia, Mattia joined other PCA graduates in the furniture program at the Rhode Island School of Design (RISD), studying under Tage Frid. He found that Frid's gregarious personality and devotion to traditional furniture making techniques helped him build on his experience at PCA and refine his own approach to design.

Immediately after graduation from RISD in 1973, Mattia began teaching woodworking at Virginia Commonwealth University. When positions opened at the new Program in Artisanry (PIA) at Boston University, he and Jere Osgood were hired to teach. He remained a professor with PIA when it first moved to the Swain School of Design in 1985 and when it was later absorbed by Southeastern Massachusetts University. In 1991, Mattia began teaching at RISD in the furniture department, which was headed by his wife, Rosanne Somerson.

Although he was trained in the 1970s approach to woodworking, which emphasized technical mastery and the organic character of wood, he became frustrated with furniture makers' reluctance to explore color and expressive content by 1979. Mattia took a hiatus from making furniture and created a series of mirrors and a wall sculpture; this work allowed him to investigate decorative techniques such as painting, carving, and even sandblasting. After this experimentation reenergized his work, he pursued two tracks: formally designed, one-of-a-kind pieces using severe geometry, and whimsical, spontaneous works, such as his well-known valet series. The valets, inspired by those designed by Hans Wegner in the 1950s, were high-backed chairs incorporating humorous and often anthropomorphic imagery (cat. no. 49). They related to function but also provided a format in which Mattia could create playful, expressive designs using shaping and decoration. He continues to teach full-time and also makes furniture at his home and studio in Westport, Massachusetts.

EDUCATION

Philadelphia College of Art, BFA (dimensional design) 1969.

Rhode Island School of Design, Providence, MFA (industrial design) 1973.

TEACHING

Virginia Commonwealth University, Richmond, Va., head of furniture design department, 1973–76.

Boston University, Program in Artisanry, 1976–85.

San Diego State University, visiting professor, 1979.

Swain School of Design, New Bedford, Mass., Program in Artisanry, head of woodworking and furniture design, 1985–88.

Southeastern Massachusetts University, College of Fine and Performing Arts, Dartmouth, head of wood/furniture design studio, 1988–91.

Rhode Island School of Design, Providence, associate professor, 1991–present.

SELECT REFERENCES

Brockton Art Museum/Fuller Memorial, *Woodforms: Contemporary Hand-Crafted Furniture of Original Design*, exh. cat. (Brockton, Mass.: Brockton Art Museum/Fuller Memorial, 1981), 14.

Joy Cattanach Smith, "Furniture: A Sculptural Medium," *Art New England* 7 (December–January 1986): 4–5.

Cooke 1989, 76–79.

Joan Jeffri, ed., *The Craftsperson Speaks: Artists in Varied Media Discuss Their Crafts* (New York: Greenwood Press, 1992), 98–116.

Peter Joseph Gallery, *Alphonse Mattia: Bookshelves Any Size*, exh. cat. (New York: Peter Joseph Gallery, 1993).

Mary Frakes, "Alphonse Mattia, Rosanne Somerson," *American Craft* 53, no. 6 (December 1993–January 1994): 38–43, 64–65.

JUDY KENSLEY McKIE

Born 1944, Boston, Massachusetts

Judy Kensley McKie was trained in painting but taught herself woodworking to make expressive furniture. She first experienced practical woodworking as a teenager while helping her family convert an old boathouse into a winter cabin. Her BFA in painting at the Rhode Island School of Design (RISD) helped McKie learn to develop visual ideas through drawing, although she found painting unfulfilling as a career. After earning her degree, she married another RISD graduate, painter Todd McKie. While the two supported themselves by making fabric wall hangings, she began creating simple furniture for their apartment and also for friends.

In 1971, McKie joined the New Hamburger Cabinetworks cooperative in Roxbury, Massachusetts (later in Cambridgeport), where she had access to better equipment and learned woodworking by trial and error. Her early furniture was unadorned and utilitarian, but she became dissatisfied with this work, finding it "cold and impersonal" by 1975. Seeking greater personal expression in furniture, she began to look at Native American, pre-Columbian, African, Greek, and Egyptian art for inspiration.

Beginning with sketches of stylized animals, McKie first transferred her new ideas to wood by decorating boxes with low-relief carvings. As she grew more confident with hand tools, she began shaping structural members into animal forms. In

1979, she received national attention when her work was included in the "New Handmade Furniture" show at the American Craft Museum in New York, and she received a commission from the Museum of Fine Arts, Boston. Grants from the National Endowment for the Arts allowed her to purchase new equipment and explore new designs. As a result of this recognition, her commissions increased, and her work was widely published and shown in museums and galleries.

By the early 1980s, McKie had a clear vision for her work; she sought to make "inanimate objects that are animated" by integrating animal forms with "a formal vocabulary of furniture-making." She began each work with drawings of plants and animals, later adapting these images to furniture, whether as structural members or surface decoration. She then selected the simplest joinery needed and used plain-figured woods such as poplar and limewood, which would not compete with her imagery.

McKie has often experimented with finishing techniques, such as bleaching, lacquer, and gold leaf, and she began to explore new media in the late 1980s when she had some of her designs cast in bronze. Most recently, she has collaborated with jeweler Tim McClelland to produce jewelry based on her animal designs. Throughout her career, she has limited her teaching to occasional workshops, preferring to devote her time to producing new work.

EDUCATION
Rhode Island School of Design, Providence, BFA (painting) 1966.

SELECT REFERENCES
Alphonse Mattia, "Judy Kensley McKie," *Workshop* (summer 1983): 10–12.

Joy Cattanach Smith, "Judy Kensley McKie," *American Craft* 43, no. 1 (December 1983–January 1984): 2–6.

Judy Kensley McKie, "Portfolio: Judy Kensley McKie," *Fine Woodworking*, no. 44 (January–February 1984): 76–81.

Cooke 1989, 80–83.

Gallery NAGA, *Judy Kensley McKie*, exh. cat. (Boston: Gallery NAGA, 1995).

Akiko Busch, "Judy McKie: Connecting to the World," *American Craft* 54, no. 6 (December 1994–January 1995): 32–35.

DONALD LLOYD MCKINLEY

Born 1932, Bartlesville, Oklahoma; died 1998

Like many studio furniture makers, McKinley was born in the Midwest but spent his life elsewhere. After studying at Alfred University in New York and working for several years, he spent a year abroad in Finland as a Fulbright fellow and then earned his master's degree from Syracuse University. The defining step in McKinley's career came in 1967, when he began to teach as the first director and "furniture master" at Sheridan College's School of Crafts and Design in Mississauga (and later Oakville), Ontario, Canada. With the exception of several sabbaticals and guest teaching assignments, he would remain at Sheridan until his retirement in 1995, establishing a reputation as a superb teacher. In addition, he was always active in many professional organizations, including the World Crafts Council, the Tasmanian Woodworkers Association in Australia, and the Ontario Woodworkers Association. Although he did not publish widely or have a large clientele, his long teaching career made McKinley an influential figure.

At the beginning of his career, he was impressed by the attitudes and abilities of the early studio furniture woodworkers, including Sam Maloof, George Nakashima, and Tage Frid. However, his open mind and inquisitive nature led him to the more adventurous work of the artist-craftsmen coming to the fore in the 1960s. As his biographer, Karen R. White, notes, "it was

McKinley's great contribution to open up and occupy the liminal area between these zones."

His interest in experimentation led him to the use of plastics in the mid-1960s, and his PVC chaise and ottoman was selected for the "Objects: USA" exhibition in 1969. His modular-tube forms, including side tables, storage units, and floor lamps made with found materials, earned him a reputation as a *bricoleur* and member of the Pop art phenomenon.

In the 1970s and 1980s, McKinley returned to woodworking, producing angular, cantilevered, often geometric forms. Some of his objects, such as a liquor cabinet made in 1983 that features surfaces with the cambium layer of the wood exposed, evoke Nakashima's rustic work, while others express humor and wit in their playful surface decoration.

EDUCATION
Wichita State University, Wichita, Kans., 1950–52.

State University of New York College of Ceramics, Alfred University, Alfred, BFA 1955.

Taideteollinen Oppilaitos, Helsinki, Finland, 1962–63.

Syracuse University, Syracuse, N.Y., master's degree (industrial design) 1965.

TEACHING
State University of New York College of Ceramics, Alfred University, Alfred, 1964.

Sheridan College, School of Crafts and Design, Mississauga and Oakville, Canada, 1967–95.

SELECT REFERENCES
"The New American Craftsman: First Generation," *Craft Horizons* 26, no. 3 (June 1966): 15–34.

Nordness 1970, 236.

Joan Murray, "Joinings: Furniture and Other Useful Objects," *American Craft* 41, no. 2 (April–May 1981): 36–39.

Stephen Hogbin and John Kelsey, "The McKinley Connection: A Craftsman Wrestles with the Demons of Industrial Design," *Fine Woodworking*, no. 31 (November–December 1981): 50–55.

Karen R. White, *Donald Lloyd McKinley: A Studio Practice in Furniture* (Oakville, Ontario, Canada: Oakville Galleries, 2000).

GEORGE NAKASHIMA

Born 1905, Spokane, Washington; died 1990

Trained as an architect but dissatisfied with modern architecture, George Nakashima turned to furniture making to pursue his philosophy of integrity in design and craftsmanship. After earning degrees in architecture at the University of Washington and Massachusetts Institute of Technology, he traveled and worked in France, India, and Japan. In Tokyo, he worked in the architectural firm of Antonin Raymond during the 1930s. Following a 1937 commission to design a dormitory for an Indian spiritual community led by Sri Aurobindo, Nakashima remained as a disciple until 1939. He later traced his philosophy of craft to Aurobindo's teachings.

Nakashima met his wife, Marion Okajiima, in Tokyo in 1939, and the two returned to the United States in 1940, settling in Seattle. After comparing the work of modern West Coast architects with traditional Japanese artisanry, he abandoned architecture to pursue woodworking, "something that [he] could coordinate from beginning to end." After completing furniture commissions for a few clients, his career was interrupted in 1942 when he, his wife, and their newborn daughter were sent to an internment camp for Japanese-Americans in Idaho. While there, Nakashima met a carpenter trained in Japan who taught him that country's traditional woodworking skills. In 1943, when the family was released, they settled in rural New Hope, Pennsylvania.

Over the years, Nakashima built a home and studio in New Hope. Although he entered into two short-lived design contracts with large firms, Knoll Associates and Widdicomb-Mueller, he preferred to design and build furniture in his independent shop. In the 1940s, Nakashima himself made each piece, but he took on the role of the master craftsman, supervising the work of up to a dozen woodworkers as demand grew. In 1951, he began to issue catalogues of his designs; by the 1980s, his shop produced about seventy-five standard designs developed by Nakashima over many decades. His wife and two children managed the shop's business affairs.

Like many designers of the 1940s and 1950s, Nakashima derived design inspiration from vernacular forms such as early American Windsor chairs, which were associated with anonymity and simplicity. Yet unlike many industrial designers, he preferred the "honesty" of solid wood to veneer, incorporating unusual burls and free edges to emphasize the natural configurations of the wood. In the 1960s, Nakashima began to complicate his simple designs by using increasingly expressive specimens of exotic woods. His growing interest in dramatic forms was evident in the Conoid Studio (1957) and the Minguren Museum (1969), which he designed and built on the New Hope property.

An outspoken critic of modern architecture, design, and craftsmanship, Nakashima set out his philosophy of woodworking in his 1981 book, *The Soul of a Tree*. As one of the pioneers of American studio furniture, his career was covered for decades in a variety of art and design publications, and his work was shown in major galleries and museums. After Nakashima's death in 1990, his daughter Mira Nakashima-Yarnall continued the family business with the help of her mother and brother.

EDUCATION

Ecole Americaine des Beaux-Arts, Fontainbleau, Dip. 1928.

University of Washington, Seattle, B. Arch. 1929.

Massachusetts Institute of Technology, Cambridge, M. Arch. 1930.

SELECT REFERENCES

George Nakashima, "Craftsmanship in Architecture," *Craft Horizons* 16, no. 3 (May–June 1956): 26–31.

Renwick Gallery, *Woodenworks: Furniture Objects by Five Contemporary Craftsmen*, exh. cat. (St. Paul: Minnesota Museum of Art and Smithsonian Institution, 1972), 4–11.

John Kelsey, "George Nakashima: For Each Plank There's One Perfect Use," *Fine Woodworking*, no. 14 (January–February 1979): 40–46.

George Nakashima, *The Soul of a Tree: A Woodworker's Reflections* (Tokyo, New York, and San Francisco: Kodansha International, 1981).

Stone 1986, 18–33.

Derek E. Ostergard, *George Nakashima: Full Circle*, exh. cat. (New York: Weidenfeld and Nicolson in association with American Craft Council, 1989).

RICHARD SCOTT NEWMAN

Born 1946, New York, New York

Although Richard Scott Newman trained in woodworking in the "free-wheeling" 1960s and began his career making the sculptural, ahistorical furniture prevalent in those years, his style matured when he began to make neoclassically inspired furniture in the early 1980s. He had enjoyed "making things" since childhood and was fascinated by tools, scientific instruments, and work requiring technical precision. While at Cornell University, where he studied engineering, Newman became more interested in building musical instruments and took a leave of absence to work in a piano factory. During this time, he became aware of the discipline and technical skill required of master arti-

sans and also encountered an exhibition of studio furniture featuring the work of Wendell Castle, Tommy Simpson, and Sam Maloof. After a brief return to Cornell, where he tried unsuccessfully to transfer from engineering to the art school, he enrolled in the woodworking program at the School for American Craftsmen at the Rochester Institute of Technology (RIT) in 1966, then the only four-year degree-granting program in wood and furniture design.

At RIT, Newman studied under Bill Keyser and Wendell Castle, teachers who offered vastly different approaches to woodworking. After a year, he quit school, began to work for Castle, and opened a studio to develop his own commission work. During the late 1960s and early 1970s, his work blended conventional furniture making techniques with swelling, sculptural forms. When Castle left the faculty at RIT, Newman returned to the program to study under James Krenov, whose reverence for wood he found inspiring; he finished his degree learning sophisticated technical skills from Jere Osgood, who joined the faculty in the early 1970s.

After graduation, Newman acted upon his original interest in instrument making and began to build traditional banjos, to which he brought a concern for perfection. Though the venture was financially unsuccessful, he found intense satisfaction in building objects connected to a historical tradition. A commission from his mother-in-law for a dining table to match her reproduction Louis XVI chairs led Newman to research French historical furniture and interpret it in his own terms. The success of the table launched his strongest body of work, in which he explored the technical and aesthetic elements of refined Neoclassical furniture. Countering the initially negative reaction to his new work and rejecting the modernist assumptions behind the criticism, Newman explained, "I definitely consider myself a contemporary furniture maker, but I am drawing my inspiration from the great furniture of the past rather than the sculpture and architecture of the twentieth century. I'm not reproducing anything, but I feel free to use whatever elements and techniques appeal to me."

EDUCATION
Studied engineering physics at Cornell University, Ithaca, N.Y., , 1962–65.

School for American Craftsmen, Rochester Institute of Technology, Rochester, N.Y., BFA (woodworking and furniture design) 1974.

TEACHING
School for American Craftsmen, Rochester Institute of Technology, Rochester, N.Y., 1977, 1979.

Wendell Castle Workshop, 1982–84.

SELECT REFERENCES
Rick Mastelli, "New Furniture…in Rochester, N.Y.," *Fine Woodworking*, no. 31 (November–December 1981): 97.

Dick Lignum, "Interview: Richard Scott Newman," *The Workshop* (spring 1984): 10–11.

Cooke 1989, 84–87.

JERE OSGOOD

Born 1936, Staten Island, New York

Jere Osgood, who bridged the first and second generation of studio furniture makers, was known for his technically innovative furniture as well as his profoundly influential teaching. He began woodworking in his father's basement workshop. While enrolled in the architecture program at the University of Illinois, he learned design and drafting skills that would later serve him in furniture design. However, Osgood left after two years because he wanted to work with the smaller scale of furniture; he preferred the notion that he could both visualize the object and make it. To become a designer-craftsman, he enrolled in 1959 in the School for American Craftsmen (SAC) at the Rochester Institute of Technology (RIT), where he studied under Tage Frid.

Shortly before entering RIT, Osgood encountered the work of Wharton Esherick at America House in Manhattan and was impressed by its sensitivity and personal expression. Of Esherick, he recalled, "What he did was make me see that it was all right to design things your own way." At SAC, Osgood learned technical skills from Frid but diverged from his teacher's emphasis on using established techniques and "design around construction." Instead, the student pre-

ferred experimenting with design and inventing his own joinery. His natural aptitude for working with his hands allowed him to complete the four-year program in two years and begin his graduate degree. While at RIT, Osgood also exhibited work in numerous shows and produced small wooden objects, which he sold at America House to support himself.

After graduation, Osgood studied at the Scandinavian Seminar Program in Denmark in 1960 and 1961, where he learned new techniques for making refined, graceful furniture. Returning to the United States, he established his own shop in New Milford, Connecticut, and supported himself with occasional teaching and the sale of small objects at America House. In the late 1960s, Osgood began to make larger pieces of furniture and devised the technique of compound stave lamination to create sensual shaping without the wastefulness of stack lamination. He first used tapered lamination to create curved legs for his elliptical shell desk (see chapter 3, fig. 3) in 1970 because he found lamination an economical way to make curved members without risking short-grain weakness. Osgood published a series of articles on his complex lamination and bending techniques in *Fine Woodworking* magazine in 1977 and 1979.

In the early 1970s, after briefly teaching at the Philadelphia College of Art, he returned to RIT, where he taught for three years before being asked to help start the Program in Artisanry (PIA) at Boston University after James Krenov's departure in 1975. At PIA, Osgood collaborated with Dan Jackson and, later, Alphonse Mattia to develop a program that went on to become one of the most influential in the field of studio furniture. He remained with the program until it closed in 1985, at which time he retired from teaching and focused on his own work. His furniture has continued to evolve over the years, as is evident in pieces created for commissions and speculative show work.

EDUCATION

Studied architecture at University of Illinois, Urbana-Champaign, 1955–57.

School for American Craftsmen, Rochester Institute of Technology, Rochester, N.Y., BFA (furniture design) 1959–60.

Scandinavian Seminar Program, Denmark, 1960–61.

TEACHING

Philadelphia College of Art, woodworking and furniture design, 1970–72.

School for American Craftsmen, Rochester Institute of Technology, Rochester, N.Y., woodworking and furniture design, 1972–75.

Boston University, Program in Artisanry, associate professor, 1975–85; acting director, 1980–81.

SELECT REFERENCES

Nordness 1970, 265.

Jere Osgood, "Tapered Lamination," *Fine Woodworking*, no. 14 (January–February 1979): 48–51.

Rosanne Somerson, "Perfect Sweep," *American Craft* 45, no. 3 (June–July 1985): 30–34.

Stone 1986, 144–59.

Cooke 1989, 88–91.

Jere Osgood, "A Meditation on the Desk," in *Furniture Studio: Tradition in Contemporary Furniture*, ed. Rick Mastelli and John Kelsey (Free Union, Va.: Furniture Society, 2001), 72–83.

TIMOTHY PHILBRICK

Born 1952, Providence, Rhode Island

Unlike John Dunnigan and Richard Scott Newman, who arrived at making historically inspired furniture after working in contemporary styles, Timothy Philbrick began his career reproducing and restoring American period furniture. He discovered his love of woodworking as a child, when he and his father built a kayak. Encouraged to pursue his interest in wood by his father, Philbrick became an apprentice to cabinetmaker and restorer John C. Northrup in Narragansett, Rhode Island, after finishing high school. In this work, he learned the nuances of design and construction in eighteenth-century furniture and interiors. Nevertheless, he disagreed with Northrup's view that "if it was early, it was good; if it was late it was bad, and there was nothing built after 1815 that was worth saving."

In order to broaden his understanding of furniture design, Philbrick sought out John Kirk, a furniture historian and family acquaintance who had recently begun teaching at Boston University. On Kirk's advice, he applied to BU's Program in Artisanry (PIA), where he was accepted into the certificate of mastery program on

the strength of his prior experience with Northrup.

While at PIA, Philbrick took graduate courses in furniture history with Kirk and felt a sense of exhilaration in learning about post-1815 furniture design and construction. Instructors Dan Jackson, Jere Osgood, and Alphonse Mattia encouraged him to enlarge his repertoire of techniques and helped him (in his own words) "loosen up" and make his work more sculptural. At the same time, Philbrick helped his fellow students gain a better understanding of historical styles and published an important article on proportions in eighteenth-century furniture.

After graduation, he started his own furniture making shop, which has succeeded largely through commission work but also through sales at galleries such as Richard Kagan's and Pritam and Eames. His work begins with carefully planned designs based on mathematical relationships and Classical proportions. From sketches, he makes a pattern, such as a sample leg, to work out the full-size form before proceeding to build the final object. On the subject of proportion, he has emphasized that mathematical expressions for the relationship of parts to the whole can be only rough guidelines and that design must be guided by an intuitive sense of grace. Philbrick's work of the 1980s and 1990s reflected the growing importance of historicism in contemporary studio furniture.

EDUCATION

Apprenticeship with John C. Northrup, Jr., Narragansett, R.I., 1971–75.

Boston University, Program in Artisanry, wood design program, certificate of mastery 1975–78.

SELECT REFERENCES

Timothy Philbrick, "Tall Chests: The Art of Proportioning," *Fine Woodworking*, no. 9 (winter 1977): 39–43.

"Portfolio: Timothy Philbrick," *American Craft* 46, no. 6 (December 1986–January 1987): 56–57.

Cooke 1989, 92–95.

Peter Joseph Gallery, *Timothy Philbrick: New Furniture*, exh. cat. (New York: Peter Joseph Gallery, 1992).

■ Fig. 38. Martha Rising.
■ Fig. 39. Mitch Ryerson.
■ Fig. 40. Tommy Simpson.

MARTHA RISING

Born 1954, North Hollywood, California

Martha Rising (now Martha Rising Rosson) enjoyed an active career in studio furniture making from the late 1970s through the mid-1980s. She first experienced woodworking with her father, an aerospace engineer who used his home workshop to teach her how to develop designs, make measured drawings, and execute the work. Rising entered California State University, Northridge, intending to major in math or science, but she soon found that she enjoyed the "technical and aesthetic problem solving [and] the creative process" in classes in three-dimensional art. Deciding to pursue the art department's specialty major in "Design in Wood," Rising was encouraged by her instructor Ralph Evans to try more challenging techniques and assignments, and Tom Trammel helped her learn to be "a producing woodworker and artist." During her woodworking classes, visits to the studios of Sam Maloof, Jan DeSwart, J. B. Blunk, Art Carpenter, and Larry Hunter offered inspiration as well as practical models for making a living. While an undergraduate, Rising began to exhibit her work at the Women's Art Center in San Francisco, and her work was shown at more than twenty exhibitions throughout California between 1975 and 1980.

After graduating from college, she apprenticed with sculptor and furniture maker Michael Jean Cooper. He had worked with Robert Strini and developed a style of sculptural furniture using complex bent laminations and influenced by California's "hot rod" imagery and kinetic sculpture. From Cooper, Rising learned three-dimensional bending skills and "fell in love with the use of various colors of wood." His influence on her work may be seen in her rocking chair *Delight* (cat. no. 26), with its slender laminated members, curved joinery, contrasting woods, and sense of energetic movement. As Rising explained in 1984, "the dynamic vitality and rhythm I seek to give each piece allows a relationship to the piece beyond its utilitarian function—it portrays a moment of motion captured or portrayed in the piece."

She furthered her studies at California State University, Northridge, with woodworker Tom Trammel, earning her MFA in 1981. Rising exhibited her work widely until 1984, after which time she began to scale back. She continued teaching workshops on bent lamination techniques through the mid-1980s and produced commission work until 1988. In 1989, as her two children grew older, she stopped making furniture.

EDUCATION

Apprenticeship with Michael Jean Cooper, 1977.

California State University, Northridge, BA 1976; MFA 1981.

SELECT REFERENCES

Oakland Museum of Art, *California Woodworking: An Exhibition of Contemporary Handcrafted Furniture*, exh. cat. (Oakland, Calif.: Oakland Museum of Art Special Gallery, [1980]), 11.

Tanya Barter, John Dunnigan, and Seth Stem, *Bentwood*, exh. cat. (Providence: Rhode Island School of Design, 1984), 44–45.

Glenn Adamson, "California Dreaming," in *Furniture Studio: The Heart of the Functional Arts*, ed. John Kelsey and Rick Mastelli (Free Union, Va.: Furniture Society, 1999), 32–42.

MITCH RYERSON

Born 1955, Boston, Massachusetts

Mitch Ryerson's work plays with themes of personal narrative, change over time, and whimsy. His interest in woodworking began in childhood, when he enjoyed the hands-on processes taught in shop and art classes. After high school, Ryerson studied traditional boatbuilding in Lubec, Maine, where he learned sophisticated joinery and three-dimensional design and gained a pragmatic approach to earning a living by making functional objects. From 1974 to 1978, he worked at various boat shops in Brooklin, Maine, and in Boston, including the Waterfront Workshop cooperative. Also while in Boston, Ryerson experimented with furniture design and construction and enrolled in a summer course at Boston University's Program in Artisanry (PIA). Since he already knew other students at PIA and found the atmosphere at the school "unique and exciting," he decided to enter the program as a full-time student.

Ryerson's early furniture borrowed techniques from boatbuilding, such as steam bending and wood riveting. However, by the early 1980s, he began to move toward more geometric, hard-edged forms in which bright colors distinguished the various parts of each object. Ryerson became interested in expressing personal narrative that would invite viewer interaction and sought to incorporate found objects in his furniture. As he explained in 1986, "I am especially drawn to certain old pieces that have been used for years and that reflect the lives and personalities of their users as well as their makers. When I create a new piece…I use color, playful arrangement, historical references, and anything else I can think of to make furniture that I hope is irresistibly inviting and reasonably functional."

During the 1980s, Ryerson's work matured through his association with other Boston-area studio furniture makers at the Emily Street cooperative in Cambridge, Massachusetts. Working alongside Judy Kensley McKie, John Everdell, Tom Loeser, and others in an environment that balanced cooperation and individualism, Ryerson was inspired to develop new work. During his time at Emily Street, he avoided overdesigned and overworked furniture and learned to "approach pieces more loosely and as part of an ongoing process of experimentation."

After the Emily Street cooperative closed, Ryerson moved to the Powderhouse Woodworking studios in Medford, Massachusetts, in the early 1990s. He began a series of outdoor public seating projects in the Boston area in 1994, sometimes incorporating the stumps of large dead trees at the site. He continues to produce studio furniture that makes use of color, painted surfaces, and found objects.

EDUCATION
Washington County Vocational Technical Institute, boatbuilding technology program, Lubec, Maine, 1973–74.

Boston University, Program in Artisanry, BAA 1982.

TEACHING
Penland School of Crafts, Penland, N.C., 1987, 1997, 2002.

Swain School of Design, Program in Artisanry, New Bedford, Mass., 1988.

Haystack Mountain School of Crafts, Deer Isle, Maine, 1997–98, 2001–2.

Peters Valley Craft Education Center, Layton, N.J., 1999.

SELECT REFERENCES
"Portfolio: Mitch Ryerson," *American Craft* 46, no. 3 (June–July 1986): 48–49.

Cooke 1989, 100–103.

Edward S. Cooke, "Coming of Age in Boston," *Art New England* (December–January 1990): 10–13, 49.

Paul Parcellin, "Wit and Widgets: The Furniture of Mitch Ryerson," *American Craft* 60, no. 1 (February–March 2000): 70–73.

TOMMY SIMPSON

Born 1939, Elgin, Illinois

A seminal figure in the artist-craftsman mode of studio furniture making, Tommy Simpson's well-documented and publicized career as an artist began in his childhood years in Dundee, Illinois. His formal training in art came in painting and printmaking, but he began to experiment with furniture in the early 1960s while pursuing a graduate degree at Cranbrook Academy of Art in Michigan. Using simply constructed pine furniture as his canvas, he produced brightly colored and lively objects, often in striking, organic forms

and frequently tinged with wit and satire. These objects, likened by critics to the ceramics of Peter Voulkos, earned him a place in exhibitions at the Museum of Contemporary Crafts in New York that emphasized such new developments. "Whimsy," "fantasy," "playful," "joyful," and "fun," are the most commonly used words to describe Simpson's work. In one of the great understatements in the literature, one curator noted in 1996, that "Tommy Simpson is not motivated by the functional aspect of furniture." While Sam Maloof and Simpson might be thought of as standing at opposite ends of the spectrum of styles in studio furniture, Maloof was quoted in 1989 as saying, "If I were to select a piece of contemporary furniture, it would be one of Tommy Simpson's."

After several shifts in his artistic career, Simpson's furniture making in the mid-1970s began to express more narrative concerns, involving historical references and humorous social commentary in chairs, pie safes, and other forms. His *Boston Throne* of 1989, for example, included in "New American Furniture," is a slightly asymmetrical Windsor chair, principally decorated with symbolic ornaments derived from more than a dozen works of art in the collection of the Museum of Fine Arts, Boston. Pam Koob has chronicled the multiple sources that Simpson has drawn upon for his imagery and allusions, including the paintings of Fra Angelico, Raphael, Botticelli, Picasso, Calder, Chagall, Kandinsky, and others; Indian Mughal miniatures; folk art from the Northwest Coast, Africa, and the South Seas; and early American decorative arts.

Throughout his career, he has taught both formally and informally at many institutions and has participated in symposia and workshops at many venues. Through this sharing and teaching, as well as through his furniture, paintings, and other objects, Simpson has established himself, in his words, as "an individual expressing his own joyful response to life through the act of creating."

EDUCATION
University of Illinois, Urbana-Champaign, 1957–58.

Elgin Community College, Elgin, Ill., 1960.

University of London, England, 1961.

Northern Illinois University, DeKalb, BS 1962.

University of Iowa, Iowa City, 1962–63.

Cranbrook Academy of Art, Bloomfield Hills, Mich., MFA 1964.

Illinois Institute of Technology, Chicago, 1969.

TEACHING
Cranbrook Academy of Art, Bloomfield Hills, Mich., 1965.

Elgin Academy, Elgin, Ill., 1967–68.

University of Illinois, Chicago, 1969.

Wadsworth Atheneum School, Hartford, Conn., 1970.

University of Hartford, Hartford, Conn., 1970–71.

Program in Artisanry, Boston University, 1979.

Rhode Island School of Design, Providence, 1979–90.

SELECT REFERENCES
Nordness 1970, 269.

Marshall Davidson, "Wooden Wiles of Tommy Simpson," *Craft Horizons* 38, no. 1 (February 1978): 45–47, 67.

Perspectives: Tommy Simpson, exh. cat. (Sheboygan, Wis.: John Michael Kohler Arts Center, 1982).

Cooke 1989, 112–15.

Peter Barnet, "Snakes and Ladders," in *Tommy Simpson* (New York: Leo Kaplan Modern, 1996), 4–5.

Tommy Simpson, with an introduction by Pam Koob, *Two Looks to Home: The Art of Tommy Simpson* (Boston: Bulfinch Press, Little, Brown, and Company, 1999).

EVERT SODERGREN

Born 1920, Seattle, Washington

A fourth-generation woodworker in his family, Evert Sodergren was trained in the European tradition by starting work at age fifteen in his father's Seattle furniture shop. Through this training, he learned cabinetmaking techniques, a respect for traditional furniture, and shop management skills. After high school, Sodergren took evening classes in production illustration and perspective drawing. In 1947, when his father had returned to Sweden, he took over the shop and began a fifty-five-year career in furniture making.

Although his father had made furniture primarily in historical styles, Sodergren was influenced in his early career by the Scandinavian Modern designs of Hans Wegner, Bruno Mathsson, Finn Juhl, and George Nelson. By the early 1950s, his work was exhibited widely in the Northwest and throughout the United States. In 1951, he joined the faculty of the art department at the University of Washington, where he taught furniture design for more than twenty-five years. He continued showing work at Seattle's Northwest Gallery of Fine Woodworking through the 1980s.

From his independent shop, where he employed some 150 apprentices over the course of his career, Sodergren refined his designs for limited production, including his sculptured chairs, designed between 1951 and 1953 and built to order until about 1980. Other production designs included a laminated folding bench with leather seat and his series of *tansu* chests, which he began making about 1970 (see cat. no. 31). Sodergren had repaired antique *tansu* chests before he began making his own, and throughout the 1970s and 1980s he produced several hundred chests in a variety of sizes and configurations. The chests offered nearly unlimited possibilities for showcasing exotic woods and elaborate metal hardware, which Sodergren made himself.

He enjoyed combining materials; his furniture has incorporated not only wood but also brass, bronze, aluminum, ceramics, and leather. According to Sodergren, finding the right mix of materials was an organic part of the design process. He wrote in 1976, "Bringing the actual materials together is the only way to tell if they will 'like each other.' Each material suggests a way to assist the other in providing an integration of design detail as a construction method or decoration that adds strength and durability."

SELECT REFERENCES

Portland Art Museum, *Works in Wood by Northwest Artists*, exh. cat. (Portland, Ore.: Portland Art Museum, 1976).

Scott Landis, "Design in Context: Woodworkers of the Northwest," in *Fine Woodworking Design Book Five* (Newtown, Conn.: Taunton Press, 1990), 146–83.

Margaret Minnick, E-mail communication to Edward S. Cooke, Jr., September 26, 2002.

ROSANNE SOMERSON

Born 1954, Philadelphia, Pennsylvania

Somerson has combined making and teaching throughout her career, seeking personal expression in her own work and encouraging students to formulate their own ideas. As an undergraduate at the Rhode Island School of Design (RISD), she intended to major in photography but felt limited by two-dimensional work. After taking a woodworking class, Somerson decided she wanted to make furniture, although the school did not offer an undergraduate major in furniture design. She majored first in sculpture and later in industrial design, trying to fit in as many woodworking courses as possible.

Frustrated with RISD's programs, Somerson took a semester off to study furniture full-time at the Peters Valley Craftsmen workshops.

After graduation, she was an assistant editor at *Fine Woodworking* magazine and later worked on Tage Frid's book series. She taught woodworking to elementary school students and also to adults (through Harvard University's continuing education program and at the Boston Architectural Center). After subletting shop space at the Emily Street cooperative in Cambridge, she and her husband, Alphonse Mattia, set up shop in their own house in Roslindale, Massachusetts, in 1979. With her own studio, Somerson was able to pursue furniture making as a full-time career.

Her early works, large and technically complex, displayed the technical skills she had learned from Tage Frid at RISD. She gained important exposure from showing her work in a number of venues: in 1979, at Richard Kagan Gallery in Philadelphia and the Danforth Museum in Framingham, Massachusetts; in the 1981 "Woodforms" show at the Brockton Art Museum; and, in 1982, at Workbench Gallery. Her designs were inspired by eclectic influences including Egyptian artifacts, African baskets, Japanese architecture, and Art Deco graphics.

In the mid-1980s, Somerson began to explore smaller forms that evoke an intimate response from the viewer. Valuing function and longevity as well as emotional content, she used surface decorations carefully, according to the intended use of the object. When she and Mattia moved their home and studio to rural Westport, Massachusetts, in 1986, and Somerson gave birth to their daughter, her work evolved to draw on natural surroundings and themes of memory and emotion. She returned to larger forms such as benches and daybeds but used layers of detail to encourage viewers to interact closely with each piece. Somerson has headed RISD's graduate program in furniture since 1985. At the same time, she has continued to make furniture with the help of part-time assistants, producing a mix of commissions and exhibition work.

EDUCATION
Rhode Island School of Design, Providence, BFA (industrial design) 1976.

TEACHING
Harvard University, Center for Continuing Education, teaching fellow, 1977–78.

Boston Architectural Center, woodworking instructor, 1981.

Rhode Island School of Design, Providence, graduate furniture design program, 1985–present; department head, furniture design department, 1995–present.

SELECT REFERENCES
Brockton Art Museum/Fuller Memorial, *Woodforms: Contemporary Hand-Crafted Furniture of Original Design*, exh. cat. (Brockton, Mass.: Brockton Art Museum/Fuller Memorial, 1981), 21.

Joy Cattanach Smith, "Furniture: A Sculptural Medium," *Art New England* 7 (December/January 1986): 4–5.

Rosanne Somerson, "Rosanne Somerson: Furniture Maker," *Women Artists News* 12 (fall–winter 1987): 16–18.

Cooke 1989, 116–19.

Peter Joseph Gallery, *Rosanne Somerson: Earthly Delights*, exh. cat. (New York: Peter Joseph Gallery, 1993).

Mary Frakes, "Alphonse Mattia, Rosanne Somerson," *American Craft* 53, no. 6 (December 1993–January 1994): 38–43, 64–65.

WILLIAM WALKER

Born 1957, Norwalk, Connecticut

William Walker developed an interest in building things as a child, in part due to the influence of his grandfather, an amateur boatbuilder. Exposure to the work of a guitar maker in Beaufort, North Carolina, in 1978 inspired Walker to "get some tools, books, and wood" and to try his hand at fine woodworking. After a few years, he chose to study at the College of the Redwoods, where he found James Krenov to be an invaluable mentor. From Krenov, Walker gained technical skills (particularly in the use of hand tools), an ability to translate ideas into objects with confidence, and a sense of responsibility for continuing his education in furniture making.

After his studies with Krenov, he evolved his own style and work process that became increasingly direct and simple. In his earlier work, he tended to rely on dramatic materials or displays of elaborate technique, but the work of mid-twentieth-century Danish designer Hans Wegner influenced him to seek more streamlined methods and to be "more aware of what work shouldn't happen." Wharton Esherick and Hank Gilpin, Finnish architect Alvar Aalto, and the work of contemporary studio makers shown at the Pritam and Eames Gallery have also been key influences.

Walker began his career in a collective shop in downtown Seattle but now maintains a studio near his home on Bainbridge

Island, outside the city. Although he occasionally serves as a guest lecturer for furniture design at the University of Washington and has taught workshops at the College of the Redwoods, his studio work is his primary focus. Working with one full-time employee and one apprentice, Walker produces speculative work for gallery shows about every four years but relies largely on commissions. He still works "maniacally and singularly on a project from time to time" and hopes that he "will always connect to the same joy of creating that launched this career twenty years ago."

EDUCATION
Duke University, Durham, N.C., BA 1978.

College of the Redwoods, Fort Bragg, Calif., 1982–84.

SELECT REFERENCES
William Walker, biographical questionnaire, October 7, 2002, Department of Art of the Americas files, MFA.

WALKER T. WEED

Born 1918, Glen Ridge, New Jersey

Self-taught in furniture making, Weed credits his Yankee grandmother for getting him started: "She communicated to me her enthusiasm for her collection of good antique furniture and her knowledge about its construction. She was also very handy with tools." At the age of twelve, he had his own woodshop and was producing a line of coffee tables priced at five dollars. His formal training in cabinetmaking ended with six- and seventh-grade shop classes in Montclair, New Jersey.

After high school, Weed attended Dartmouth, majoring in modern English literature. World War II intervened, but Weed chose to pursue cabinetmaking after service in the army. He opened the Gilford Workshop in New Hampshire in 1948, working with Gary Allen and Gus Pitout until 1951, making primarily reproductions of Early American pine furniture.

He maintained his own shop from 1951 through 1965, with the collaboration of his wife Hazel and the assistance of their two children. An extended trip to Norway, Denmark, and Sweden during 1960 and 1961 (and a later visit in 1973) allowed Weed the opportunity to study Scandinavian work firsthand. In 1962, he

■ Fig. 44. Walker T. Weed.
■ Fig. 45. Stephen Whittlesey.
■ Fig. 46. Edward Zucca.

EDUCATION

Dartmouth College, Hanover, N.H., BA 1940.

TEACHING

Hopkins Center, Dartmouth College, Hanover, N.H., 1962–81.

SELECT REFERENCES

C. B., "Walker Weed, Yankee Cabinetmaker," *Craft Horizons* 17, no. 1 (February 1957): 37–39.

Walker Weed: A Retrospective Exhibition, 1950–1981, exh. cat. (Hanover, N.H.: Hopkins Center, Dartmouth College Museum and Galleries, 1981).

Richard Starr, "Portfolio: Walker Weed, a Retrospective of Quiet Woodworking," *Fine Woodworking*, no. 38 (January–February 1983): 66–69.

"Honoring Excellence: The American Craft Council Awards: Walker Weed," *American Craft* 52, no. 4 (August–September 1992): 14.

started teaching at Dartmouth in New Hampshire and, in 1964, he became the director of the crafts program at Hopkins Center there, a position he held until his retirement in 1981.

Weed's work was exhibited in 1955 at the Worcester Art Museum and again in 1957 in the "Furniture by Craftsmen" exhibition at the Museum of Contemporary Crafts in New York. These and many subsequent exhibitions established his reputation as a solid woodworker in the best New England tradition. In addition to the influence of Scandinavian work and Shaker furniture, the work of George Nakashima in the early 1950s exerted its impact on Weed's deceptively simple, elegant objects. In 1983, he expressed the sentiments of many of his generation of woodworkers: "We are overwhelmed these days by people trying to do something different just to make a splash. I have always objected to the emphasis on doing a striking or new design instead of concentrating on good established things. It would be better to teach a student to make a good wheelbarrow than a very fancy highboy." He used conventional joinery techniques, relied "on machines when they can do the job better or more quickly," and favored native woods.

Weed's quiet, unassuming, modest nature is reflected in his work. As Richard Starr has noted, "Walker Weed's furniture would be better known if fame depended on quality rather than on showmanship."

STEPHEN WHITTLESEY

Born 1938, Norwood, Massachusetts

Stephen Whittlesey's fascination with recycling wooden objects in his sculptural furniture derives from his rural Massachusetts childhood. He recalls that on the local farms where he worked in his youth, "things were fixed, not thrown away, and frequently they were fixed by using stuff that was lying behind some shed. My creations out of salvaged wood have grown out of that making-do-with-what-you-have kind of thinking."

His furniture incorporates remnants of such disparate objects as old staircases, industrial conveyor belts, floor-

boards, abandoned boat hulls, and decaying porches with peeling paint. Whittlesey gathers his raw materials from the New England countryside. In his Cape Cod studio, he identifies how the objects trigger particular emotions and develops ways of using the objects in new forms to convey those emotions or ideas.

Whittlesey, who trained in sculpture and painting at Columbia University in the 1960s, approaches his work with a conceptual bent, explaining that "when I begin a piece, I don't think about whether it can hold a TV set or seat six people, but what it can say about us and the way we live." Since the 1970s, he has created semifunctional furniture that reveals the history of the found objects he incorporates and that also expresses his own life experiences. For example, the fluid lines of a canoe he paddled as a child inspired the form of several objects assembled from old wood. Like other studio furniture makers of the second generation, he is concerned with themes of memory and narrative, often with a sense of whimsy. His work is not, however, simply a tribute to old-fashioned rural life. As Whittlesey explains, "This isn't nostalgia. It is carrying a story forward in a different fashion, re-telling the stories and myths of old familiar forms."

EDUCATION

Columbia University, BA (creative writing and English literature, minor in studio art) 1962.

Columbia University, MFA (painting and sculpture) 1965.

TEACHING

University of Massachusetts, Dartmouth, Program in Artisanry, 1992–present.

SELECT REFERENCES

Lisa Hammel, "Angels, Steeples, and Other Presences," *American Craft* 41, no. 6 (December 1986–January 1987): 30–37.

Mark Swan, "From Salvage to Sculpture: Stephen Whittlesey Makes Art from Debris," *Woodwork*, no. 9 (spring 1991): 32–36.

Michael Rush, "Stephen Whittlesey," *American Craft* 58, no. 3 (June–July 1998): 47–49.

EDWARD ZUCCA

Born 1946, Philadelphia, Pennsylvania

Edward Zucca's humorous and satirical furniture has been inspired by eclectic sources ranging from childhood space guns, windup toys, and Erector Sets to pre-Columbian architecture. As a child, he was fascinated by building and design and enjoyed assembling model kits, but he did not encounter woodworking until he enrolled at the Philadelphia College of Art (PCA) in the 1960s. While the PCA program provided a foundation in all media, Zucca concluded that the "slow, step-by-step process" of woodworking was most appealing. Under the guidance of instructors Daniel Jackson and Robert Worth, he mastered traditional furniture making techniques and also learned to use subtractive shaping to create contemporary forms.

After graduating from PCA, Zucca held a variety of short-term teaching and woodworking jobs, including a year spent as artist-in-residence at Penland School of Crafts in North Carolina. Beginning in 1974, he operated his own shop, where he designed and built furniture primarily for commissions, and continued to teach short courses and workshops. His work was included in numerous exhibitions, including landmark shows such as "New Handmade Furniture" (1979) and "Material Evidence" (1984).

Zucca's style matured in the years after college. The PCA program did not teach historical furniture, and his early work was largely influenced by "the pseudo–Art Nouveau Psychedelic mélange of the '60s." In the 1970s, he began to explore a wider range of design sources. After a trip to Mexico in 1971, Zucca became intrigued by pre-Columbian architecture, and he chose to incorporate crisp geometric shapes and the stepped forms of Mayan temples in his work. During the 1970s and 1980s, he borrowed from other historical influences, including Egyptian artifacts and Shaker furniture, as well as twentieth-century appliances and automobiles, and Art Deco design.

Zucca exhibited his work at several important galleries—including the Elements, Workbench, Snyderman, Pritam and Eames, and Peter Joseph—in the 1980s and 1990s. Although he has continued to rely on traditional woodworking skills, he has experimented with a wide variety of surface finishes, including painting wood to simulate metal or stone. He has also incorporated other objects in his work, including dollar bills, postage stamps, and electronic instruments that lend a decorative effect as well as a humorous storytelling aspect.

EDUCATION
Philadelphia College of Art, Philadelphia, Pa., BFA 1968.

TEACHING
Philadelphia College of Art, summer 1968.

Rhode Island School of Design, Providence, 1971–72.

Massachusetts College of Art, Boston, furniture design and woodworking, 1975.

Boston University, Program in Artisanry, 1979.

SELECT REFERENCES
Brockton Art Museum/Fuller Memorial, *Woodforms: Contemporary Hand-Crafted Furniture of Original Design*, exh. cat. (Brockton, Mass.: Brockton Art Museum/Fuller Memorial, 1981), 29.

Michael Stone, "Skill at Play: Edward Zucca," *American Craft* 41, no. 3 (June–July 1981): 2–5.

M. S., "In Putnam, Conn....," *Fine Woodworking*, no. 30 (September–October 1981): 93–97.

Cooke 1989, 128–31.

Peter Joseph Gallery, *Edward Zucca*, exh. cat. (New York: Peter Joseph Gallery, 1991).

Select Schools and Programs in Furniture Making and Woodworking

Note to the Reader

Although a number of studio furniture makers were self-taught or had training in other art media, many studied furniture making in academic programs. This list, arranged alphabetically, is limited to schools and educational centers that offered strong programs in woodworking and/or furniture making prior to 1990. Both degree-granting institutions and workshop centers are included.

In addition to the select references given below (which are cited chronologically), other sources consulted include advertisements in the magazines *Craft Horizons* (later titled *American Craft*) and *Fine Woodworking* between the years 1940 and 1990, as well as brochures, press releases, course catalogues, and other materials in the research files of the Art of the Americas Department, Museum of Fine Arts, Boston (MFA files). Notes from telephone interviews can also be found in these files. Further information was found on the Web sites of many schools and programs.

Anderson Ranch Arts Center

Founded 1966, Snowmass Village, Colorado

Located ten miles west of Aspen on the site of a former cattle and sheep ranch, Anderson Ranch Arts Center was founded in 1966 by Paul Soldner as a summer ceramics workshop. After a group of artists converted the historic barns into studios and gallery space, the ranch added numerous workshops and incorporated as a nonprofit visual arts community in 1973. By the late 1970s, a number of leading furniture makers taught at the ranch. Beginning in 1975, Sam Maloof gave a series of popular annual workshops and developed a strong relationship with the ranch. He was honored in 1986 with the opening of the Sam Maloof Woodbarn facility, and in 1987 he and his wife established the Sam and Alfreda Maloof Scholarship Fund to support students at the ranch. By the late 1980s, Anderson Ranch began to operate year-round; today it offers intensive workshops in a wide range of media, including a strong program in furniture and woodworking.

Select References

"Woodworking and Furniture Making Craft Schools," *Country Journal* (January–February 1991): 46–47.

Elizabeth Heilman Brooke, "A Ranch in the Rockies for Famed Artists and Novices," *New York Times*, August 1, 2000, MFA files.

Jeremy Adamson, *The Furniture of Sam Maloof,* exh. cat. (Washington, D.C.: Smithsonian American Art Museum, 2001), 148, 179, 209.

Appalachian Center for Crafts

Founded 1979, Smithville, Tennessee

Founded in 1979 by the Tennessee Arts Commission with a federal grant, the Appalachian Center for Crafts became a division of Tennessee Technological University in 1985. From the beginning, the center offered a BFA in crafts with a choice of concentrations, including wood, glass, metal, fiber, and clay. Under the guidance of faculty including Thomas Hucker, Wendy Maruyama, Trent Whittington, and Graham Campbell, the wood curriculum has emphasized contemporary studio furniture, including design and construction, sculpture, and hand-tool woodworking. A strong summer workshop series has offered instruction in traditional crafts as well as programs in contemporary woodworking; an ongoing artist-in-residence program has brought emerging artists to the campus to work and teach.

Select References

"Appalachian Dedication," *Craft Horizons* 39, no. 2 (April 1979): 45.

"Thirteen States," *Fine Woodworking,* no. 21 (March–April 1980): 84.

"Woodworking and Furniture Making Craft Schools," *Country Journal* (January–February 1991): 46–47.

"Appalachian Center for Crafts: History and Mission," http://craftcenter.tntech.edu/history.html, accessed December 16, 2001.

Wendy Maruyama, E-mail communication, August 6, 2002.

Graham Campbell, telephone interview, August 8, 2002.

Brookfield Craft Center

Founded 1954, Brookfield, Connecticut

The Brookfield Craft Center was founded in the post–World War II period by Nancy DuBois Hagmayer as a school and gallery intended primarily for New England craftspeople. Located in a converted eighteenth-century gristmill, the center has, since its founding, offered short-duration workshops in a variety of craft media, including woodworking. The center has defined woodworking in the broadest possible terms; guest faculty have provided instruction in diverse subjects such as rustic furniture, contemporary design, Windsor chairs, Japanese hand tools, furniture repair and restoration, wood sculpture, turning, and wood-boat building. Temporary exhibitions have been used to complement the center's programs and highlight the work of guest faculty.

Select References

"Brookfield's Silver Anniversary," *American Craft* 39, no 5 (October–November 1979): 80.

Kenneth A. Simon, *The New England Handcraft Catalog* (Chester, Conn.: Globe Pequot Press, 1983), 277.

"Woodworking and Furniture Making Craft Schools," *Country Journal* (January–February 1991): 46–47.

http://www.brookfieldcraftcenter.org, accessed March 19, 2002.

Jack Russell, telephone interview, August 14, 2002.

BUCKS COUNTY COMMUNITY COLLEGE

BCCC founded 1964, Newtown, Pennsylvania; Fine Woodworking Program founded 1978

The woodworking program at BCCC is a product of the strong tradition of craft and furniture making in the Bucks County region; the studios of Wharton Esherick, George Nakashima, and Robert Whitley are nearby, as are a number of commercial furniture manufacturers. Since 1982, the BCCC program has offered a two-year associate's degree intended to prepare students for a variety of careers in woodworking. As part of a community college, the program has welcomed students of all ages, a large number of women and international students, as well as many hobbyists and students seeking a career change. Under Mark Sfirri, who has headed the program since 1982, the curriculum balances studio work, art history, design, and technical skills involving both hand and machine tools.

SELECT REFERENCES
Knock on Wood, student publication of the BCCC Woodshop, no. 10 (October 1998).
Michael Rush, "Philadelphia Wood," *American Craft* 59, no. 1 (February–March 1999): 80–83, 94.
http://www.bucks.edu, accessed August 12, 2002.
Mark Sfirri, telephone interview with the author, August 21, 2002.

CALIFORNIA COLLEGE OF ARTS AND CRAFTS

CCAC founded 1907, Oakland, California; woodworking program founded 1977

The CCAC woodworking program began when Skip Benson, a graduate of the School for American Craftsmen at the Rochester Institute of Technology, took over the shop, which had previously been used for vocational and architectural work. He instituted a new major in woodworking in 1977, with a curriculum based on that at RIT and focusing on technical skills. In the 1980s, faculty members Gail

Fredell, Wendy Maruyama, and Tom Loeser emphasized a more conceptual approach to furniture making. In the early 1990s, the program saw a number of faculty changes, with various instructors emphasizing theory or technique to differing degrees. In the mid-1990s, CCAC began to add design programs in other areas, such as architecture and graphic design. Since program head Donald Fortescue was hired in 1997, the woodworking program has spanned both industrial design and studio/fine arts approaches.

SELECT REFERENCES
Glenn Adamson, "California Dreaming," in *Furniture Studio: The Heart of the Functional Arts,* ed. John Kelsey and Rick Mastelli (Free Union, Va.: Furniture Society, 1999), 32–42.
Donald Fortescue, telephone interview, September 16, 2002.

CALIFORNIA STATE UNIVERSITY, LONG BEACH

Campus founded 1949; woodworking taught since 1969

During the 1960s and 1970s, the large art department at Cal State Long Beach offered instruction in a variety of media, including ceramics, painting, graphic design, metals, and fiber. Woodwork was added to the general craft curriculum in 1969, when John Snidecor joined the faculty. In the 1970s, the art department earned accreditation from the National Association of Schools of Art and Design, and in 1974 began to offer BFA and MFA degrees. Woodwork became a separate degree discipline in the mid-1980s. Furniture makers, woodworkers, and wood turners including John Cederquist, Frank Cummings, and Bob Trout are among the notable graduates from the program.

SELECT REFERENCES
http://www.art.csulb.edu, accessed December 31, 2001.
John Cederquist, telephone interview, August 21, 2002.
John Snidecor, telephone interview, August 28, 2002.

CALIFORNIA STATE UNIVERSITY, NORTHRIDGE

Campus founded 1958; Design in Wood Program founded 1958

The wood program at Cal State Northridge was founded within the department of art by Tom Trammel, who had previously taught woodworking at Cal State Los Angeles. In the late 1960s, Ralph Evans and Bob Smith joined the woodworking faculty, and the program grew to involve about 250 students in six or seven classes. California furniture makers and artists including Sam Maloof, Michael Jean Cooper, Gerry Glaser, and Jan DeSwart presented advanced workshops, and the program offered field trips to the studios of other California woodworkers. It also involved training in the fundamentals of woodworking and emphasized making one-off objects, while students exchanged ideas and studied art history along with students in other art disciplines.

SELECT REFERENCES
Merryll Saylan, "A Slightly Different History," unpublished manuscript, September 2002.
Pamela Weir Quiton, telephone interview, October 8, 2002.
Robert Smith, telephone interview, October 22, 2002.

WENDELL CASTLE SCHOOL OF WOODWORKING

Founded 1980, Scottsville, New York; closed 1988

Promising "more than an apprenticeship…more than a fine arts program," Wendell Castle opened a two-year residential school of fine woodworking at his studio near Rochester, New York, in 1980. Attempting to balance technical and creative elements, Castle's program was geared toward "artist-craftsmen" whose goal was to earn a living by making furniture. The curriculum covered woodworking techniques, creative design, drawing, and art history, as well as practical advice on setting up a shop and selling work in the marketplace. Castle and his associate faculty offered an intensive two-year course of study; in 1983 the school was accredited to award an associate's degree in occupational studies. The program also featured summer workshops by visiting faculty and sponsored exhibitions of student and faculty objects at area galleries.

SELECT REFERENCES

John Kelsey, "Editor's Notebook," *Fine Woodworking*, no. 22 (May–June 1980): 80–81.
Paul Bertorelli, "Two Schools: Castle and Krenov—Different Ideas about How to Teach," *Fine Woodworking*, no. 39 (March–April 1983): 103–4.
Wendell Castle, untitled essay, *Workshop* (summer 1983): 15.
A. U. Chastain-Chapman, "Fine Furniture Making," *American Craft* 44, no. 6 (December 1984–January 1985): 14–15.
Davira S. Taragin, Edward S. Cooke, Jr., and Joseph Giovannini, *Furniture by Wendell Castle*, exh. cat. (New York: Hudson Hills Press in association with the Founders Society, Detroit Institute of Arts, 1989).

COLLEGE OF THE REDWOODS

College founded 1964, Fort Bragg, California; Fine Furniture Program founded 1981

The Fine Furniture Program at the College of the Redwoods grew out of a series of summer workshops given by James Krenov in the summers from 1978 to 1980 for the Mendocino Woodworkers Association. A student, Michael Burns, recruited Krenov to head a new program in 1981 and remained to assist with teaching. Affiliated with the College of the Redwoods, a community college, the program has admitted about twenty students each year for a one-year nondegree course. In the 1980s, summer workshops and a few second-year positions were added for advanced students. Students have usually come to the school familiar with Krenov's writings and his approach to woodworking, which emphasizes the sensitive use of hand tools, refined traditional joinery, and understanding of wood as a medium for self-expression.

SELECT REFERENCES

Paul Bertorelli, "Two Schools: Castle and Krenov—Different Ideas about How to Teach," *Fine Woodworking*, no. 39 (March–April 1983): 103–4.
Michael Stone, "The Quiet Object in Unquiet Times," *American Craft* 44, no. 1 (February–March 1984): 39–43.
Michael A. Stone, *Contemporary American Woodworkers* (Salt Lake City, Utah: Gibbs M. Smith, 1986), 100–113.
Ross Day, "A Krenov Student's Notebook," *Fine Woodworking*, no. 146 (winter 2000–2001): 98–103.
James Krenov, *With Wakened Hands: Furniture by James Krenov and Students* (Fresno, Calif.: Cambium Press, 2000).

HAYSTACK MOUNTAIN SCHOOL OF CRAFTS

Founded 1950

Mary Beason Bishop founded Haystack as a research and studio program to nurture fine contemporary craftsmanship. In 1961, the school moved to a new campus designed by architect Edward Larrabee Barnes. Haystack has offered a variety of summer workshops taught by guest faculty in all craft media and in specialized subjects such as writing about crafts; there are also seminars covering the history of craft. Open to all levels of students, the workshops emphasize artistic growth and the development of new ideas. Workshops in wood have been offered consistently but were particularly prevalent in the 1950s under William J. Brown, and in the late 1970s and 1980s with guest faculty including Tage Frid, Jon Brooks, Donald McKinley, Bob Trotman, and Tom Hucker.

LOCATIONS

1950–61: Liberty, Me.
1961–present: Deer Isle, Me.

SELECT REFERENCES

"Haystack to Move," *Craft Horizons* 21, no. 1 (January–February 1961): 52.
"Travel and Study," *Craft Horizons* 25, no. 3 (May–June 1965): 27–28.
Kenneth A. Simon, *The New England Handcraft Catalog* (Chester, Conn.: Globe Pequot Press, 1983), 280.
Karen S. Chambers, "Haystack: That Certain Feeling," *Craft International* (October–November–December 1985): 28.
Stuart Kestenbaum, telephone interview, August 21 and 26, 2002.

HOOSUCK DESIGN AND WOODWORKING / KIRBY STUDIOS

Founded in 1976, North Adams, Massachusetts; closed 1987

Ian Kirby, a woodworker trained in England in several design and furniture programs, moved to the United States in 1973, where he taught, practiced, consulted, and wrote about woodworking. In 1976, he joined a craft enterprise in a converted mill in North Adams, Massachusetts, a depressed mill town where Mary Ann Beinecke had founded the Hoosuck Community Resources Corporation in an effort to revitalize the area through arts programs. Kirby ran Hoosuck Design and Woodworking in North Adams until 1978, at which time he moved the program to Bennington, Vermont, and renamed it Kirby Studios. The new independent program emphasized a straightforward approach to design and technique that would prepare students for a career in furniture making. While both Hoosuck Design and Kirby Studios (which later moved to Atlanta, Georgia) offered full-time courses of study, Kirby has been well known for his intensive workshops.

LOCATIONS

1976–78: Hoosuck Design and Woodworking, North Adams, Mass.
1978–83: Kirby Studios, Bennington, Vt.
1983–87: Kirby Studios, Atlanta, Ga.

SELECT REFERENCES

Mary and Harvey Flad, "Hoosuck: A Community Story," *Craft Horizons* 37, no. 2 (April 1977): 20–21, 61.
Rosalind Freer and Ian Kirby, information packet for prospective students, 1985–86, Department of Art of the Americas files, MFA.
"Profile: Ian Kirby," *Woodworker West* (January–February 1994), accessed at http://www.wood-west.com/web/Kirby/html, on August 9, 2002.
Larry Grainger, "Ian Kirby Biography," E-mail communication, August 15, 2002.
Ian Kirby, telephone interview, August 15, 2002.

LEEDS DESIGN WORKSHOPS

Founded 1977, Easthampton, Massachusetts; closed 1989

David Powell, founder of Leeds Design Workshops, was born in England, trained in furniture making under Edward Barnsley, and also studied at the Royal College of Art in London. After running his own shop in London for fifteen years, Powell moved to Putney, Vermont, and to Northampton, Massachusetts, in 1969. He and John Tierney, formerly an administrator at Boston University's Program in Artisanry, established Leeds Design Workshops as a furniture making program that accommodated both interns and resident professionals. Up to twenty-one interns were accommodated in a full-time, two-year course of study that emphasized traditional cabinetmaking techniques. Resident designer-makers could operate their own businesses from private studios at the workshops while teaching interns and sharing machine-shop equipment.

SELECT REFERENCES
Brockton Art Museum/Fuller Memorial, *Woodforms: Contemporary Hand-Crafted Furniture of Original Design,* exh. cat. (Brockton, Mass.: Brockton Art Museum/Fuller Memorial, 1981), 18.
Kristina Madsen, telephone interview, September 23, 2002.

MURRAY STATE UNIVERSITY

University founded 1922, Murray, Kentucky; Functional Design/Wood Program founded 1982

A Canadian-born woodworker and sculptor, Paul Sasso began teaching at Murray State in 1981 and soon converted a course in materials and design to an undergraduate program in furniture design and construction. From the beginning, the Functional Design/Wood Program has emphasized contemporary decorative arts and trained students in studio furniture making. The wood program has grown over the years and, in 1993, gained larger studio space in the former industrial education shop. The flexible curriculum requires only one basic design course, after which students can pursue their interests in a series of advanced courses.

The program is part of the department of art, which offers bachelor's degrees in art education and studio art.

SELECT REFERENCES
http://www.mursuky.edu, accessed December 13, 2001.
Paul Sasso, "Functional Design/Wood, Department of Art, Murray State University, Murray, Kentucky," fax transmission, August 23, 2002.

NORTH BENNET STREET SCHOOL

Founded 1885, Boston, Massachusetts; cabinetmaking program founded 1951

Incorporated in 1885, the North Bennet Street Industrial School originally offered social services and vocational training to the immigrant community of Boston's North End. After World War II, the school introduced trade classes for veterans on the GI Bill, including a course in fine traditional woodworking that was established in 1951 by George Fullerton, a master craftsman who had worked at several custom furniture shops. He focused on teaching students hand skills rather than design. In 1985, the same year in which the school gave up its social service functions to focus on professional craft training, dropping the word "Industrial" from its name, Fullerton retired. His former student, Lance Patterson, continues to head the two-year woodworking program. Accredited as a trade school since 1982, North Bennett continues to offer one of the most comprehensive courses of study in traditional cabinetry in the country.

SELECT REFERENCES
John Kelsey, "Woodworking Education," *Fine Woodworking,* no. 26 (January–February 1981): 88–89.
John Lively, "North Bennet Street Industrial School: Learning Cabinetry the Traditional Way," *Fine Woodworking,* no. 28 (May–June 1981): 66–67.
A. U. Chastain-Chapman, "Period Pieces," *American Craft* 45, no. 4 (August–September 1985): 32–39.
Sarah Henry and Mary A. Williams, with Laura Stanton, ed., *North Bennet Street School: A Short History 1885–1985* (Boston, Mass.: Chadis Printing, 1985).
Lance Patterson, telephone interview, August 23, 2002.

PENLAND SCHOOL OF CRAFTS

Founded 1929, Penland, North Carolina

With a residential campus of about four hundred acres in the mountains of western North Carolina, Penland is the oldest and one of the largest craft education centers in the nation. Teacher Lucy Morgan founded Penland Weavers in 1923 and expanded the instruction to include other crafts, creating Penland School in 1929. Since that time, the school has offered dozens of workshops each year in craft and fine arts media, including woodworking. Courses at Penland can be used to earn graduate and undergraduate academic credit through East Tennessee State University. Under the directorship of Bill Brown, Penland's programs grew to attract students from sixty foreign countries as well as leading instructors. Sam Maloof, Wendy Maruyama, John McNaughton, Seth Stem, Dan Rodriquez, and others offered furniture making and woodworking programs in the 1970s and 1980s.

SELECTED REFERENCES
"Travel and Study," *Craft Horizons* 25, no. 3 (May–June 1965): 28, 37.
"Penland School of Crafts," *Craft Horizons* 26, no. 3 (June 1966): 57–58.
"Penland Celebrates Its 50th," *American Craft* 39, no. 5 (October–November 1979): 80.
Linda Darty, "The Dream of Miss Lucy Morgan," *American Craft* 41, no. 5 (October–November 1981): 2–3.
"Woodworking and Furniture Making Craft Schools," *Country Journal* (January–February 1991): 46–47.

PETERS VALLEY CRAFT EDUCATION CENTER

Founded 1970, Layton, New Jersey

Peters Valley Craft Education Center began as a cooperative venture of the National Park Service and a local group of craftspeople and educators called the Peters Valley Craftsmen. The Park Service acquired a collection of historic buildings and converted them to studios, demonstration and retail spaces, as well as dormitories for instructors and students. Resident craftsmen live in the village year-round, producing work, training interns, and teaching summer workshops. In addition to the classes taught by residents, Peters Valley attracts visiting artists to give seminars in a variety of craft media. Woodworking has been offered since the school's first year; residents and instructors have included Bob March, Wayne Raab, Karl Seemuller, Alphonse Mattia, and Howard Werner.

SELECT REFERENCES

Maribelle Rhodes, "A Community of Crafts: Peters Valley," *Craft Horizons* 31, no. 2 (April 1971): 38, 62.

Joanna Shaw-Eagle, "Peters Valley Celebrates Artistic/$$$ Success," *Craft Horizons* 38, no. 8 (December 1978): 43.

Bob March, telephone interview, August 26, 2002.

PHILADELPHIA COLLEGE OF ART (PCA)

See "University of the Arts."

PROGRAM IN ARTISANRY

Founded 1975, Boston, Massachusetts

While at Boston University, the Program in Artisanry (PIA) was a dynamic center of the studio furniture movement. Students were admitted on the basis of their portfolios and prior experience. The program offered them access to the academic resources of the university, but it was primarily studio-based. PIA was unique among craft programs in that it offered academic degrees (AFA, BFA, and, after 1983, MFA), and a flexible, graduate-level certificate of mastery to accommodate students who did not fit traditional academic classification. Jere Osgood and Alphonse Mattia, the longest-serving faculty at PIA, demanded high standards of technique and aesthetics and encouraged students to take a personal approach to making objects. Student work was frequently exhibited at major East Coast galleries. After Boston University closed the program in 1985, it moved to two other Massachusetts schools. Many graduates have settled in the Boston area and continue to make studio furniture.

LOCATIONS

1975–85: Boston University, Boston, Mass.
1985–88: Swain School of Design, New Bedford, Mass.
1988–present: Southeastern Massachusetts University, Dartmouth, Mass. / University of Massachusetts, Dartmouth, Mass.

SELECT REFERENCES

Jane Steinberg, "Comprehensive Craft Program Begins at Boston University," *Craft Horizons* 35, no. 2 (April 1975): 6.

Leon Nigrosh and Dick Sauer, "Massachusetts," *Craft Horizons* 37, no. 2 (April 1977): 54.

Dick Sauer, "Boston," *Craft Horizons* 39, no. 2 (April 1979): 64.

Review of PIA exhibition, *Fine Woodworking*, no. 28 (May–June 1981): 90–91.

David Sanders, "Portrait of a Program: Woodworking and Furniture Design at Boston University's Program in Artisanry," *The Workshop* (fall 1983).

Kenneth A. Simon, *The New England Handcraft Catalog* (Chester, Conn.: Globe Pequot Press, 1983), 281–82.

Roger Holmes, "BU to Close Artisanry Program," *Fine Woodworking*, no. 52 (May–June 1985): 102–4.

Alphonse Mattia, interview, August 7, 2002.

RHODE ISLAND SCHOOL OF DESIGN (RISD)

School of Design founded 1877, Providence, Rhode Island; furniture program founded 1962

RISD's historic mission as a school of design included a commitment to applying art to industry, and from 1962 to 1996 its furniture program was housed in the industrial design department. In 1962, the Danish-born instructor Tage Frid was recruited from the School for American Craftsmen in Rochester to teach at RISD, where he trained students in woodworking techniques and a Scandinavian Modern approach to design. At his retirement in 1985, his former student, Rosanne Somerson, became the program head. In 1996, a separate furniture design department was created, offering both a BFA and an MFA. The program continues Frid's legacy of hands-on technical training but also encourages interdisciplinary work and a multimedia approach to design.

SELECT REFERENCES

Tage Frid, "Woodworking Thoughts: Musings of a Designer-Craftsman-Teacher," *Fine Woodworking* 1, no. 1 (winter 1975): 31–32.

Kenneth A. Simon, *The New England Handcraft Catalog* (Chester, Conn.: Globe Pequot Press, 1985), 286–87.

"Rhode Island's Embarrassment of Riches," *Fine Woodworking*, no. 95 (August 1992): 100.

"Furniture, Focus of a New Major," *RISD Views* (fall 1995): 18–19.

"Rhode Island School of Design Announces the Creation of the Department of Furniture Design," brochure, 1996.

"The Master Class," *Metropolis* (May 1997): 82–83, 123–26.

Hank Gilpin, "Professor Frid," *Fine Woodworking*, no. 146 (winter 2000–2001): 80–85.

ROCHESTER INSTITUTE OF TECHNOLOGY (RIT)

See "School for American Crafts."

SAN DIEGO STATE UNIVERSITY

University founded 1897, San Diego, California; furniture design program founded 1967

Jack Rogers Hopkins taught the first woodworking classes at San Diego State in 1967; he was succeeded by Larry Hunter, who incorporated woodworking into the crafts department. Under Hunter's direction, the program flourished in the "anything goes" style of California woodworking that emerged in the 1970s. In 1989, Wendy Maruyama took over, becoming one of the first women to head a college-level furniture program. Although it has been viewed as more experimental than its East Coast counterparts, the curriculum gives equal weight to creativity and technical skills. Undergraduate art majors may concentrate in furniture through the applied design program, while graduate students in furniture design earn an MFA in an intensive three-year program.

SELECT REFERENCES

http://art.sdsu.edu/art/emphasis/furniture/geninfo.html, accessed December 13, 2001.

Wendy Maruyama, E-mail transmission, August 6, 2002.

School for American Crafts (SAC)

Founded 1943, Hanover, New Hampshire

In 1943, Aileen Osborn Webb, a lifelong patron of American crafts, led the American Craftsmen's Educational Council to establish the SAC at Dartmouth College. Initially, the program was intended to train craftsmen to earn a living in ceramics, woodworking, metalworking, or weaving through a "modernized revival of the apprentice system." Beginning in 1948, SAC offered the first four-year college degree (BS) in crafts. It remained the only degree-granting program in furniture until 1962, when it was joined by the Rhode Island School of Design. SAC eventually made its permanent home at the Rochester Institute of Technology in New York, with Tage Frid as the head of the wood program until 1962. Frid's successors, Bill Keyser and Wendell Castle, continued to emphasize woodworking technique through the 1970s and 1980s. In recent years, under Rich Tannen and Andy Buck, the program has maintained its commitment to technical expertise while placing even greater attention on experimentation and content.

LOCATIONS

1943–46: Dartmouth College, Hanover, N.H.
1946–50: Alfred University, Alfred, N.Y.
1950–present: College of Fine and Applied Arts, Rochester Institute of Technology, Rochester, N.Y.

SELECT REFERENCES

"The School for American Craftsmen, New England Division, Hanover, N.H.," *Craft Horizons* 4, no. 10 (August 1945): 4–9, 35.
"Alfred University," *Craft Horizons* 5, no. 13 (May 1946): 37.
"The School for American Craftsmen," *Craft Horizons* 6, no. 14 (August 1946): 35.
Elizabeth Geen, "An Educator's Analysis," *Craft Horizons* 8, no. 21 (May 1948): 14–15.
"Important Announcements," *Craft Horizons* 9, no. 3 (autumn 1949): 30.
"Furniture from the School for American Craftsmen," *Craft Horizons* 12, no. 1 (January 1952): 40–41.
Harold Brennan, "The School for American Craftsmen," *Craft Horizons* 20, no. 3 (May–June 1960): 21–24.
"Travel and Study," *Craft Horizons* 25, no. 3 (May–June 1965): 27–28, 37–41.
Aileen O. Webb, "School for American Craftsmen 25th Anniversary," *Craft Horizons* 36, no. 1 (February 1976): 40–43, 71–72.
Rich Tannen, telephone interview, August 23, 2002.

Sheridan College, School of Crafts and Design

Founded 1967, Mississauga, Ontario

Located near Toronto, Sheridan College hosts a woodworking program that has been the largest and most successful effort of its kind in Canada since it was established in September 1967 with impetus from the Ontario Craft Foundation. The School of Crafts and Design (SOCAD) has included furniture making from the beginning, as one of its core offerings along with ceramics, textiles, and jewelry. Donald Lloyd McKinley was the first director and the furniture studio master for thirty years, until his retirement in 1995. Later members of the faculty have included Stephen Hogbin, Stephen Harris, Chris Sorenson, and Michael Fortune. The three-year program of study currently has seven faculty members.

SELECT REFERENCES

Tom Hurley, "Furniture-Making in Toronto," *Fine Woodworking*, no. 73 (November–December 1988): 42–47.
James Strecker, ed., *Sheridan: The Cutting Edge in Crafts* (Erin, Ontario, Canada: Boston Mills Press, 1999).
Karen R. White, *Donald Lloyd McKinley: A Studio Practice in Furniture* (Oakville, Ontario, Canada: Oakville Galleries, 2000).

University of the Arts (formerly Philadelphia College of Art)

Philadelphia College of Art founded 1876, Philadelphia, Pennsylvania; merged with Philadelphia College of Performing Arts to become the University of the Arts, 1987

Originally affiliated with the Philadelphia Museum of Art, the Philadelphia College of Art (PCA) became independent in 1964. In that year, Daniel Jackson was hired to teach dimensional design and started the furniture making program. Jackson's teaching incorporated his technical training under Tage Frid at the Rochester Institute of Technology, as well as his own interests in sculpture and conceptual design. After Jackson left PCA in 1976, the program was led by Bob DeFuccio in the late 1970s, and by Michael Hurwitz, Richard Kagan, and Peter Pierobon in the 1980s; these instructors continued to emphasize technique and design in furniture making. In the 1990s, Jack Larimore and Roy Superior, both self-taught in woodworking, emphasized imaginative, multidisciplinary work rather than the more technical aspects of furniture making. The program became a "wood" program in the crafts department of the College of Art and the design department at the University of the Arts.

SELECT REFERENCES

Edward S. Cooke, Jr., *New American Furniture: The Second Generation of Studio Furnituremakers*, exh. cat. (Boston, Mass.: Museum of Fine Arts, 1989), 17–18.
Michael Rush, "Philadelphia Wood," *American Craft* 59, no. 1 (February–March 1999): 80–83, 94.
http://www.uarts.edu/home/hist.html, accessed December 13, 2001.
Jack Larimore, telephone interview, August 27, 2002.
Richard Kagan, telephone interview, August 28, 2002.
Roy Superior, telephone interview, August 28, 2002.

University of Wisconsin

University founded 1848, Madison, Wisconsin; woodworking program founded 1965

The University of Wisconsin department of fine arts, part of the School of Education, grew after World War II to serve veterans taking advantage of the GI Bill. When C. R. "Skip" Johnson was hired to start a woodshop in 1965, he tried to give students a basic understanding of woodworking in a fine arts context through creative, problem solving assignments. In the late 1960s, the school began to offer an MFA in addition to the BFA. After Johnson's retirement in 1991, Tom Loeser took over the furniture making program. Because woodworking there has always been part of a multidisciplinary department in a large research university, individuals studying furniture learn to define and defend their original work through critiques from students involved in other art disciplines.

SELECT REFERENCES

Tom Loeser, "Finding Your Own Direction: Five Stories of Life after Graduation," *Woodwork*, no. 72 (December 2001): 35–40.
C. R. "Skip" Johnson, telephone interview, August 26, 2002.
Tom Loeser, telephone interview, August 26, 2002.

Virginia Commonwealth University

University incorporated 1968, Richmond, Virginia; craft program founded 1968

The wood program at VCU was founded by Alan Lazarus soon after the university was incorporated in 1968. Wood was one of several media represented in the craft department in the School of the Arts, which offered both BFA and MFA degrees. Lazarus was succeeded by Joe DiStefano, Alphonse Mattia, and finally Bill Hammersley, who continues to head the program. Over the years, the curriculum has shifted from an emphasis on cabinet-making techniques to a stronger focus on form and individual expression in the process. The program thus has allowed students to pursue interests ranging from sculpture to commercial design, and all students are encouraged to work in a wide range of media.

SELECT REFERENCES

Carol Sesnowitz, "VCU History," E-mail communication, September 3, 2002.

Bill Hammersley, telephone interview, September 30, 2002.

Worcester Center for Crafts

Worcester Employment Society founded 1874, Worcester, Massachusetts; School for Professional Crafts founded 1977

The WCC evolved from a late-nineteenth-century charitable organization intended to promote welfare through work; by 1949 the institution redirected its mission to the field of craft training, including woodworking. After moving to a new building in 1960, the craft studios and programs expanded. Since the 1960s, the WCC has offered a wide array of summer and weekend workshops taught by leading craftspeople and has organized many important exhibitions. In 1977, the center opened its School for Professional Crafts, which offers a two-year associate's degree through an affiliation with Becker College, as well as a nondegree track. The woodworking curriculum includes traditional techniques, hand tools and machinery, a strong design component, and business and marketing classes to prepare students to become professional furniture makers.

SELECT REFERENCES

Kenneth A. Simon, *The New England Handcraft Catalog* (Chester, Conn.: Globe Pequot Press, 1983), 283.

Charles L. Taggart to Jonathan L. Fairbanks, correspondence and brief history of school, September 6, 1996, Department of Art of the Americas files, MFA.

Robert March, telephone interview, August 26, 2002.

http://www.craftcenter.worcester.org, accessed August 29, 2002.

Worcester Center for Crafts, *The Chair,* exh. cat. (Worcester, Mass.: Worcester Center for Crafts, 2002).

AMERICA HOUSE

Founded 1940, New York, New York; closed 1971

America House, run by the American Craftsmen's Council, was the earliest major retail outlet for American crafts, including furniture. Founded by Aileen O. Webb, with architect David Campbell and pewter craftsman Lawrence Eichner, America House was originally a cooperative but soon became a private corporation. The shop sold one-of-a-kind pieces as well as those created in limited and quantity production. Works were sometimes purchased outright by the shop but more often sold on consignment. During the 1960s, America House opened five branches and expanded its services to include a mail-order catalogue, a retail gift shop at the Museum of Contemporary Crafts, and an architectural interior design service. Due to mounting expenses, America House closed in 1971.

LOCATIONS

1940–43: East 54th Street, New York, N.Y.
1943–60: 485 Madison Avenue at 52nd Street, New York, N.Y.
1960–71: 44 West 53rd Street, New York, N.Y.

SELECT REFERENCES

"America House Moves," *Craft Horizons* 2, no. 3 (November 1943): 1.
Charles Burwell, "The New America House and Its Policies," parts 1 and 2, *Craft Horizons* 20, no. 5 (September–October 1960): 50–51, and *Craft Horizons* 20, no. 6 (November–December 1960): 56–57.
La Mar Harrington, "New America House," *Craft Horizons* 24, no. 5 (September–October 1964): 62.

Harriet Cohen, "America House: An Appreciation," *Craft Horizons* 31, no. 2 (April 1971): 11, 57.
Aileen O. Webb, "America House 1940–1971," *Craft Horizons* 31, no. 2 (April 1971): 11.

CLARK GALLERY

Founded 1976, Lincoln, Massachusetts

Meredyth Hyatt Moses founded Clark Gallery in an affluent suburb of Boston. As she and codirector Pamela Clark Cochrane began to concentrate on New England artists, Moses became particularly interested in studio furniture in the early 1980s. In the mid-1980s, Clark Gallery began to collaborate with Gallery NAGA in Boston on furniture shows; Moses and NAGA director Arthur Dion have actively sought out new talent among the city's younger generation of furniture makers, shown nationally prominent furniture makers, and worked to develop new collectors of studio furniture.

SELECT REFERENCES

"Yankee Unique: Local Artisans Create a New England Tradition," *Boston Globe*, January 10, 1986.
Christine Temin, "Opulence Rules at Furniture Show," *Boston Globe*, January 5, 1989.
Meredyth Hyatt Moses, telephone interview, August 28, 2002.

THE EGG AND THE EYE

Founded 1965, Los Angeles, California; reorganized 1974

This gallery's unusual name refers to its origins as a restaurant known for its omelets and its changing art exhibitions. Founders Edith Wyle and Bette Chase showed international folk art as well as the work of leading American crafts-people, including California woodworkers Sam Maloof, John Cederquist, and Jack Rogers Hopkins. By 1974, The Egg and the Eye had become an educational association for the promotion of contemporary crafts and folk art. It reorganized as the Los Angeles Craft and Folk Art Museum and is now owned by the city.

SELECT REFERENCES

Bernard Kester, "Los Angeles," *Craft Horizons* 34, no. 4 (August 1974): 32.
"The Egg and the Eye Eyes Its Aims and Fame," *Craft Horizons* 34, no. 6 (December 1974): 9.

ELEMENTS GALLERY

Founded 1973, Greenwich, Connecticut; closed 1993

The Elements Gallery was a pacesetting crafts gallery when there were few others in the New York area. Founders Kay Eddy, Betsy Beasley, and Emily Toohey opened the first Elements Gallery in a converted stable in Greenwich, Connecticut, in 1973, then opened another branch in 1977 in New York, where they could present more adventurous work. Three years after moving to Tribeca, an emerging arts neighborhood, the New York Elements Gallery closed. The Greenwich gallery continued to show functional crafts until 1993.

LOCATIONS

1973–93: Greenwich, Conn.
1977–82: 766 Madison Ave., New York, N.Y.
1982–85: 90 Hudson St., New York, N.Y.

SELECT REFERENCES

"Showcase for Crafts Ends New York Run," *American Craft* 45, no. 4 (August–September 1985): 93.
Tommy Simpson, telephone interview, August 20, 2002.

NOTE TO THE READER

Although many studio furniture makers have sold their work directly to customers through commissions, private sales at their own shops or showrooms, or craft and furniture shows, art galleries have played an important role in promoting studio furniture to a wider audience. Galleries included in this list, arranged alphabetically, were prominent in the field of studio furniture prior to 1990. The success and growth of the field during the 1980s broadened the market of collectors and led to the opening of many new galleries (not included here) after 1990.

Select references for each entry are listed in chronological order. In addition to the references given below, other sources consulted include advertisements in *Craft Horizons* (later *American Craft*) and *Fine Woodworking* magazines in the years from 1940 to 1990, as well as press releases and exhibition announcements in the research files of the Art of the Americas Department, Museum of Fine Arts, Boston (MFA files). Notes from telephone interviews can also be found in these files.

Fairtree Gallery

Founded 1971, New York, New York; closed 1976

Fairtree Gallery, the sister gallery of Galeria del Sol in Santa Barbara, California, was operated by the Fairtree Fine Crafts Institute, a nonprofit organization created and funded by Betty and Stanley Sheinbaum in 1971. Under the direction of furniture maker and gallery designer Stan Reifel, the Fairtree Gallery exhibited the work of hundreds of craftspeople and presented workshops and craft demonstrations. Educational director Jackie Springwater gave slide presentations in area schools and colleges in an effort to educate New Yorkers about handmade functional objects. After operating at a loss, supported by the Sheinbaums, the gallery closed in 1976.

SELECT REFERENCES
"Craftsmen of New York, Fairtree Gallery," *Craft Horizons* 33, no. 6 (December 1973): 53–54.
Larry Grobel, "Profile: Fairtree's Stan Reifel," *Craft Horizons* 35, no. 3 (June 1975): 10.
"Sheinbaum Tells Why Fairtree Gallery Closes in New York," *Craft Horizons* 36, no. 1 (February 1976): 66–67.
Tommy Simpson, telephone interview, August 20, 2002.

Galeria del Sol

Founded 1967, Santa Barbara, California; closed 1976

Galeria del Sol was the first of a pair of craft galleries owned by Betty and Stanley Sheinbaum; Fairtree Gallery, founded in New York in 1971 was its East Coast counterpart. Betty Sheinbaum, inspired by the craft movement in California in the 1960s, opened Galeria del Sol as a showcase for arts in "other media" that "didn't fit into the conventions of easel painting or sculpture." Exhibitions included furniture by Arthur Espenet Carpenter. The gallery was a nonprofit venture intended to educate the public about studio crafts; in 1971 it became part of the Sheinbaum's Fairtree Fine Crafts Institute. After operating at a loss for several years, the gallery closed in 1976.

SELECT REFERENCES
Bernard Kester, "Los Angeles," *Craft Horizons* 33, no. 6 (December 1973): 45.
Larry Grobel, "Profile: Fairtree's Stan Reifel," *Craft Horizons* 35, no. 3 (June 1975): 10.
"Sheinbaum Tells Why Fairtree Gallery Closes in New York," *Craft Horizons* 36, no. 1 (February 1976): 66–67.
"New Era Begins as Galeria del Sol Ends," *Craft Horizons* 36, no. 6 (December 1976): 6.

Gallery Fair

Founded 1977, Mendocino, California

Gallery Fair was founded by Bill and Lynette Zimmer in Mendocino, California, where a strong woodworking community developed in the 1970s. The gallery has shown studio furniture as well as other crafts and art media by many prominent makers. Still in its original location, the gallery has changed its name to the William Zimmer Gallery.

SELECT REFERENCES
http://www.williamzimmergallery.com, accessed September 23, 2002.

Gallery Henoch

Founded 1982, New York, New York

George Henoch Schechtman opened the Christopher Street Gallery in Greenwich Village in 1966 but moved the gallery to Madison Avenue in the 1970s, renaming it the Christopher Gallery. In 1982, Shechtman opened Gallery Henoch in the emerging Soho art scene. From its Wooster Street location, Gallery Henoch presented the work of studio furniture makers including Richard Scott Newman, Kristina Madsen, Thomas Hucker, Silas Kopf, and John Dunnigan, in shows such as "Master Furniture Makers of the Eighties." The gallery, located in Chelsea since the fall of 2000, continues to show studio furniture along with other contemporary art.

SELECT REFERENCES
"Trio in Soho," *Fine Woodworking*, no. 48 (September–October 1984): 116.
http://www.galleryhenoch.com/about.html, accessed August 8, 2002.

Gallery NAGA

Founded 1977, Boston, Massachusetts

Gallery NAGA was founded in 1977 on Boston's Newbury Street as the cooperative gallery of the Newbury Associated Guild of Artists (NAGA). In 1982, it became a private gallery, with Arthur Dion as director. The gallery grew during the period when graduates of Boston University's Program in Artisanry made the city a flourishing center of the studio furniture movement. In 1985, Deborah Daw helped Dion organize the gallery's first exhibition of studio furniture, "Elegant Wit: Contemporary New England Furniture," which showed the work of seven leading regional furniture makers. Since 1989, Gallery NAGA has collaborated with Clark Gallery in Lincoln, Massachusetts, for all of its studio furniture shows.

SELECT REFERENCES
Christine Temin, "An Exhibit with Wit and Whimsy," *Boston Globe*, September 13, 1985.
Arthur Dion and Meredyth Hyatt Moses, "Contemporary Furniture: Thirteen Major Figures," in *Visual, Tactile, and Functional: Contemporary Furniture in Boston Galleries, 1989–1990*, exh. cat. ([Boston, Mass.]: Meridien Printing, [1990]).
Arthur Dion, "Something Living That Has Paused," in *Judy Kensley McKie: New Furniture*, exh. cat. (Boston, Mass.: Gallery NAGA and Clark Gallery, 1995).
Arthur Dion, telephone interview, September 3, 2002.

The Hand and the Spirit Crafts Gallery

Founded 1972, Scottsdale, Arizona; sold 1998 and renamed Gallery Materia

Joanne Rapp and her partner Star Sacks opened The Hand and the Spirit Crafts Gallery on Bishop's Lane in Scottsdale, after spending more than a year researching contemporary craft artists and their work. Rapp wished to create a gallery that showed "respect for the object" and focused on wood, textiles, and clay. In the 1970s, when few galleries were showing furniture, The Hand and the Spirit showed the work of George Nakashima, Wendell Castle, Sam Maloof, and Garry Knox Bennett. In the 1980s, the gallery showed more experimental pieces as well as more work by California artists like Wendy Maruyama. In the 1990s, the gallery began to increase its number of group shows.

SELECT REFERENCES

Joanne Rapp, telephone interview, September 24, 2002.

HOKIN KAUFMAN GALLERY

Founded 1982, Chicago, Illinois; closed 1994

Lori Kaufman inaugurated her gallery in 1982 with a show of artist-designed furniture entitled "Made in Chicago." The gallery was founded in the River North area of Chicago, then a developing art scene, and was the first in the city to show studio furniture. Through her annual furniture shows, "Furniture of the Eighties," Kaufman worked to develop awareness of functional art in the conservative Chicago market. These exhibitions displayed innovative work by furniture makers from Chicago and across the nation, including Tom Tedrowe, Wendell Castle, David Ebner, John McNaughton, and Bob Trotman.

SELECT REFERENCES

"Events," *Chicago Tribune,* January 22, 1989.
Chris Vartanian, "Furniture of the Eighties Means Functional Sculpture," *Chicago Sun-Times,* January 22, 1989.
Stephen Luecking, "Furniture of the Eighties," *New Art Examiner* 16 (April 1989): 47–48.
Lori Kaufman, telephone interview, August 23, 2002.

RICHARD KAGAN GALLERY

Founded 1973, Philadelphia, Pennsylvania; closed 1983

Although Richard Kagan considered himself a furniture maker first and a gallery owner second, his gallery created an important forum for the studio furniture movement because it was the first gallery in the United States dedicated exclusively to fine woodworking. Kagan opened the gallery in 1973, subsidizing it with his workshop profits. Kagan showed his own work and pieces by leading furniture makers Wendell Castle, Daniel Jackson, Jere Osgood, Tom Hucker, Judy McKie, and others. He offered about three exhibitions each year at his South Street location, focusing on educating the public about furniture making.

SELECT REFERENCES

John Kelsey, "Craftsman's Gallery: Shop/Gallery Combination Works," *Fine Woodworking* 1, no. 3 (summer 1976): 10.
Carol Shutt, "Hardwood Furniture and Objects," *Craft Horizons* 36, no. 4 (August 1976): 61.
Robert DeFuccio, "Five Chairs: One View," *Fine Woodworking,* no. 14 (January–February 1979): 58–60.
Michael Rush, "Philadelphia Wood," *American Craft* 59, no. 1 (February–March 1999): 80–83.
Richard Kagan, telephone interview, August 28, 2002.

MEREDITH GALLERY

Founded 1977, Baltimore, Maryland

Meredith Gallery continues to occupy the historic Baltimore town house in which it opened in 1977. When Judith Lippman founded the gallery, she showed many different media, including painting, sculpture, and ceramics. In the early to mid-1980s, her daughter Mandy introduced her to the field of studio furniture. Soon, the gallery mounted several shows featuring the work of Judy Kensley McKie, Michael Hurwitz, Rosanne Somerson, Alphonse Mattia, Ronald Puckett, and other second-generation East Coast studio furniture makers. Since the 1980s, the gallery has continued to focus on showing contemporary furniture in "room settings" in its town house.

SELECT REFERENCES

http://www.meredithgallery.com, accessed August 8, 2002.
Judith Lippman, telephone interview, October 1, 2002.

ALEXANDER F. MILLIKEN GALLERY

Founded 1977, New York, New York; closed 1990

Alexander Milliken, a prominent dealer of fine arts, initially featured sculpture and paintings in his Soho gallery but soon began to focus on selling "masterpieces" by contemporary artists. Milliken sought out artists who were the best in the world, regardless of nationality or media. In 1980, he began to represent Wendell Castle, who was then beginning to focus on historically based fine furniture.

Milliken successfully promoted Castle's work over the next ten years, garnering public interest with shows of pieces such as his tall clock series; the gallery also exhibited the work of Castle's students. By generating excitement (and high prices) for Castle's work, Milliken contributed to the rapid growth of the studio furniture market in the 1980s.

SELECT REFERENCES

Davira S. Taragin, Edward S. Cooke, Jr., and Joseph Giovannini, *Furniture by Wendell Castle,* exh. cat. (New York: Hudson Hills Press in association with the Founders Society, Detroit Institute of Arts, 1989), 58–59 and passim.
Alexander Milliken, telephone interview, September 9, 2002.

MOGUL GALLERY

See "Franklin Parrasch Gallery."

NORTHWEST GALLERY OF FINE WOODWORKING

Founded 1980, Seattle, Washington

The Northwest Gallery of Fine Woodworking was founded by David Gray and a group of about twenty-five woodworkers who were frustrated with the difficulty of placing their work in local art galleries. Since its beginning, the gallery, originally staffed by the woodworkers themselves, has sold furniture and wood sculpture made by the cooperative's members. The initial location was Seattle's Pioneer Square, at the time a redeveloping inner-city area. Following the success of the first store, the group opened a second space in 1989 on the east side of Seattle; after two relocations, it continues in Bellevue.

LOCATIONS

1980–present: Pioneer Square, Seattle, Wash.
1989–93: Gillman Village, Issaquah, Wash.
1993–96/97: Kirkland, Wash.
1996/97–present: Bellevue, Wash.

SELECT REFERENCES

"Connections," *Fine Woodworking,* no. 26 (January–February 1981): 47.
A. U. Chastain-Chapman, "Fine Furnituremaking," *American Craft* 44, no. 6, (December 1984–January 1985): 12.
http://www.nwfinewoodworking.com, accessed August 8, 2002.
Christopher Brooks, telephone interview, August 26, 2002.

FRANKLIN PARRASCH GALLERY (formerly Mogul Gallery)

Founded 1986, Washington, D.C.

When Franklin Parrasch first encountered studio furniture, he was fascinated by its relationship to contemporary installation art. After finishing graduate school, he opened Mogul Gallery to exhibit studio furniture in a fine arts context; in 1988, it was renamed Franklin Parrasch Gallery. In the fall of 1989, he moved the gallery to New York in order to gain greater recognition for furniture makers in the art world. Parrasch has often presented "challenges" or "disciplines" to the artists he represents, asking them to create new work based around particular themes.

LOCATIONS
1986–1989: Washington, D.C.
1989–present: New York, N.Y.

SELECT REFERENCES
Mogul Gallery, *A Traditional Move*, exh. cat. (Washington, D.C.: Mogul Gallery, 1987).
"Shops and Galleries," *American Craft* 50, no. 1 (February–March 1990): 24.
Franklin Parrasch, telephone interview, August 14, 2002.

ELAINE POTTER GALLERY

Founded 1978, San Francisco, California; closed 1989

Elaine Potter, a passionate advocate for contemporary crafts, opened the Contemporary Artisans Gallery on Bush Street in San Francisco in 1978. In 1979, she mounted her first furniture show, featuring Garry Knox Bennett's controversial *Nail Cabinet*. In 1984, the gallery was renamed the Elaine Potter Gallery and moved to Hayes Street, where it remained until she sold it in 1989. The gallery exhibited ceramics, glass, fiber, and metal as well as studio furniture. Potter has been described by colleagues as a "driving force" in the craft field, with a strong commitment to supporting emerging artists.

LOCATIONS
1978–84: Bush Street, San Francisco, Calif.
1984–89: Hayes Street, San Francisco, Calif.

SELECT REFERENCES
"Elaine Potter, 55, Craft Retailer and Advocate," obituary, *American Craft* 51, no. 6 (December 1991–January 1992): 62–63.
Sylvia Bennett, telephone interview, August 27, 2002.

PRITAM AND EAMES GALLERY

Founded 1981, East Hampton, New York

In 1979, Bebe Pritam Johnson and her husband, Warren Eames Johnson, spent a year meeting with craftspeople and researching ideas for a gallery specializing in handmade furniture. Their inaugural show in 1981 featured the work of thirty established furniture makers, many from the Northeast. The gallery has catered to the affluent and culturally oriented clientele of the Hamptons and promoted its stable of artists through thematic shows. Pritam and Eames has been among the most successful galleries devoted exclusively to furniture; it celebrated its twentieth anniversary in 2001.

SELECT REFERENCES
"Connections," *Fine Woodworking*, no. 28 (May–June 1981): 40.
Rick Mastelli, "New Furniture: A Gallery Opens on Long Island," *Fine Woodworking*, no. 31 (November–December 1981): 95.
Sarah Bodine, "Beyond the Final Polish: The Marketing of Handmade Furniture," *The Workshop* (fall 1983).
Helen A. Harrison, "The Desk at Pritam and Eames," *The Workshop* (fall 1983).
Jonathan Binzen, "Pritam and Eames," *American Craft* 61, no. 5 (October–November 2001): 96–98.

BERTHA SCHAEFER GALLERY

Founded 1944, New York, New York; closed 1971

Bertha Schaefer's gallery was one of the earliest art galleries to explore the link between studio furniture and the fine arts. She founded the gallery in 1944 to show contemporary American art but later expanded her vision to show contemporary paintings and sculpture from around the world. Schaefer, who designed modern interiors and furniture, believed that interior design should be more closely linked to the fine arts through a careful study of design elements in painting and sculpture. To this end, she organized a series of exhibits called "The Modern Home Comes Alive" and showed hand-sculptured furniture by Wharton Esherick in the early 1950s.

SELECT REFERENCES
Bertha Schaefer, "The Modern House Comes Alive," *Craft Horizons* 13, no. 5 (September–October 1953): 30–33.
"Bertha Schaefer," *Arts Magazine* 45 (April 1971): 53.
"Bertha Schaefer, 1895–1971," obituary, *Craft Horizons* 31, no. 4 (August 1971): 4.
Edward S. Cooke, Jr., "Women Furniture Makers: From Decorative Designers to Studio Makers," in Pat Kirkham, ed., *Women Designers in the USA, 1900–2000*, exh. cat. (New Haven and London: Yale University Press, for the Bard Graduate Center for Studies in the Decorative Arts, New York, 2000), 295–96.

SHOP ONE

Founded 1953, Rochester, New York; closed 1976

Shop One was founded by a group of four designer-craftsmen—metalsmith Jack Prip, furniture maker Tage Frid, potter Frans Wildenhain, and jeweler Ronald Pearson—all faculty or graduates of the School for American Craftsmen at Rochester Institute of Technology. Over the years, local craftspeople were added as associate members; in 1972, metalworker Tom Markusen and furniture maker Wendell Castle became part-owners. The gallery was one of the earliest and longest-running retail outlets for American crafts. Owned by craftspeople and staffed by their spouses, the gallery allowed customers to deal directly with the makers of the objects on view and helped educate the public about the emerging studio craft movement.

SELECT REFERENCES
C. B., "Shop One," *Craft Horizons* 16, no. 2 (March–April 1956): 19–23.
"Shop One," *Craft Horizons* 31, no. 6 (December 1971): 6.
Allan Peterson, "Five Owners," *Craft Horizons* 32, no. 3 (June 1972): 57.
"The Decade: Change and Continuity," *Craft Horizons* 36, no. 3 (June 1976): 52.
http://www.youllputyoureyeout.com/shopone-heirlooms.html, accessed September 4, 2002.

SNYDERMAN GALLERY/THE WORKS

The Works Gallery founded 1965, Philadelphia, Pennsylvania

Snyderman Gallery founded 1983, Philadelphia, Pennsylvania

The galleries founded by Rick and Ruth Snyderman have been a vital part of the Philadelphia craft scene since the 1960s. The Works Gallery, founded in 1965 by Ruth and a partner, Rosemarie Philips (who left in 1966), was among the earliest galleries dedicated to crafts. In its first decade, it showed international crafts along with contemporary American objects. After Rick joined his wife's venture, the couple moved the Works to the thriving artists' community on South Street in 1972. By the late 1970s, the Snydermans began to focus exclusively on American studio crafts, including furniture.

In 1983, they opened the Snyderman Gallery next door to the Works. Under Rick's management, Snyderman Gallery has concentrated on furniture and glass, while the Works, directed by Ruth, has focused on ceramics, jewelry, and fiber. In 1992, the expanding Snyderman Gallery moved to a larger space in the Old City section of Philadelphia; in 1996 the Works moved to the same location. While the galleries are operated independently, they collaborate on special projects and off-site exhibitions.

LOCATIONS (THE WORKS GALLERY)
1965–72: Locust Street, Philadelphia, Pa.
1972–96: South Street, Philadelphia, Pa.
1996–present: Cherry Street, Philadelphia, Pa.

LOCATIONS (SNYDERMAN GALLERY)
1983–92: South Street, Philadelphia, Pa.
1992–present: Cherry Street, Philadelphia, Pa.

SELECT REFERENCES
Victoria Donohue, "New South Street Crafts Gallery to Feature Large Works of Art," *Philadelphia Inquirer*, October 23, 1983.
Victoria Donohue, "Craft Gallery's Exhibit Features Varied Works in Wood and Glass," *Philadelphia Inquirer*, February 3, 1984.
"Shops and Galleries," *American Craft* 50, no. 5 (October–November 1990): 26.
Michael Rush, "Philadelphia Wood," *American Craft* 59, no. 1 (February–March 1999): 80–83.
http://www.snyderman-works.com/snyderman/about/history/snyderman.html, accessed August 8, 2002.

SOCIETY OF ARTS AND CRAFTS, BOSTON

Founded 1897, Boston, Massachusetts

The Society of Arts and Crafts (SAC) is the oldest nonprofit craft organization in America, dedicated since its founding to promoting fine contemporary craftsmanship. It began with the first craft exhibition in the country in 1897 and has continued to offer educational exhibitions and retail gallery space for craft artists. In the 1970s and 1980s, the society organized several important exhibitions of contemporary woodwork and furniture, including work by students and faculty at Boston University's Program in Artisanry. It continues to maintain a gallery on Newbury Street in the city.

SELECT REFERENCES
Jere Osgood, "Yankee Diversity," *Fine Woodworking* 1, no. 3 (summer 1976): 26–27.
Wendy Kaplan, ed., *"The Art That Is Life": The Arts and Crafts Movement in America, 1875–1920*, exh. cat. (Boston: Museum of Fine Arts, 1987).
Marilee Boyd Meyer et al., *Inspiring Reform: Boston's Arts and Crafts Movement*, exh. cat. (Wellesley, Mass.: Davis Museum and Cultural Center, Wellesley College, 1997).
http://www.societyofcrafts.org, accessed August 8, 2002.

SWAN GALLERIES

Founded mid-1980s, Philadelphia, Pennsylvania; closed

This Philadelphia gallery advertised studio furniture shows in the mid-1980s, including an invitational exhibition "Chairs," featuring the work of makers including John Dunnigan, Lee Weitzman, and David Ebner.

TEN ARROW

Founded 1972, Cambridge, Massachusetts; closed 1993

Betty Tinlot founded her gallery Ten Arrow at 10 Arrow Street in Cambridge, Massachusetts, after working as the manager for Shop One in Rochester, New York, from 1960 to 1969. Her time at Shop One enabled Tinlot to develop a collector's eye and a sense of the craft marketplace, which helped in maintaining her gallery successfully for over twenty years.

At Ten Arrow, beginning in the early 1980s, Tinlot held several shows of studio furniture, including work by such established makers as Wendell Castle and Jon Brooks, in addition to new artists such as Kristina Madsen and Wendy Stayman.

SELECT REFERENCES
Deborah Daw, "Criteria for Collecting Crafts," *Art New England* (1981).
Ruth Walkey, telephone interview, September 3, 2002.
http://www.youllputyoureyeout.com/bettytinlot.html, accessed September 4, 2002.

WORKBENCH GALLERY

Founded 1980, New York, New York; closed 1988

The Gallery at Workbench began in 1980 when Warren Rubin, chairman of the Workbench chain of retail furniture stores, organized a one-man show of work by Garry Knox Bennett in conjunction with Workbench's twenty-fifth anniversary. In 1981, Workbench opened a nonprofit gallery to show the work of contemporary craftsmen and create a new market for studio furniture. Under the direction of Bernice Wollman, with codirectors Judy Coady and Patricia Pullman, the gallery offered several important exhibitions, including "Women Are Woodworking" (1983) and "Material Evidence: New Color Techniques in Handmade Furniture" (1985). The gallery closed in 1989, when numerous retail outlets for studio crafts made it unnecessary to maintain a nonprofit gallery.

SELECT REFERENCES
"New Showpieces and New Cracks in the Marketing Barriers," *Fine Woodworking*, no. 28 (May–June 1981): 88–91.
Sarah Bodine, "Beyond the Final Polish: The Marketing of Handmade Furniture," *The Workshop* (fall 1983).
Judy Coady, "One Gallery Tells What It Can Sell," *Fine Woodworking*, no. 43 (November–December 1983): 104–6.
"Shops and Galleries," *American Craft* 48, no. 2 (April–May 1988): 13.
"Shops and Galleries," *American Craft* 48, no. 6 (December 1988–January 1989): 64–65.

CHRONOLOGY OF SELECT EXHIBITIONS

Between 1940 and 1990, an increasing number of studio furniture exhibitions held at museums (and a few other nonprofit institutions) contributed to the development of the field. Although some exhibitions traveled to more than one venue, usually only the original venue is listed here. The numerous exhibitions sponsored by commercial galleries during this same period are not included in this list.

1940

"America at Home." World's Fair, New York, N.Y.

1943

"An Exhibition of Contemporary New England Handicrafts." Worcester Art Museum, Worcester, Mass.

1944

"An Exhibition of Contemporary American Crafts." Baltimore Museum of Art, Baltimore, Md.

1946

"The Master Craftsmen of Tomorrow." America House Gallery, New York, N.Y.

1948

"Furniture of Today." Rhode Island School of Design, Providence.

1950 and later

"Young Americans." American Craftsmen's Educational Council, held at various locations.

1950–54

"Good Design." Museum of Modern Art, New York, N.Y.

1951

"Contemporary Furniture—The School for American Craftsmen, Rochester, New York." America House Gallery, New York, N.Y.

1953

"Designer-Craftsmen U.S.A. 1953" American Craftsmen's Educational Council and the Brooklyn Museum, Brooklyn, N.Y.

1954

"The Arts of Daily Living." Los Angeles County Fair, Los Angeles, Calif.

1955

"California Design," first in a series of eleven exhibitions at the Pasadena Art Museum, Pasadena, Calif.

"New England Craft Exhibition—1955." Worcester Art Museum, Worcester, Mass.

1956

"California Design Two." Pasadena Art Museum, Pasadena, Calif.

"Craftsmanship in a Changing World." Museum of Contemporary Crafts, New York, N.Y.

1957

"California Design Three." Pasadena Art Museum, Pasadena, Calif.

"Designer-Craftsmen of Western New York." Buffalo Fine Arts Academy, Buffalo, N.Y.

"Furniture by Craftsmen." Museum of Contemporary Crafts, New York, N.Y.

1958

"American Artists and Craftsmen." American Pavilion, Brussels World's Fair, Brussels, Belgium.

"California Design Four." Pasadena Art Museum, Pasadena, Calif.

1959

"California Design Five." Pasadena Art Museum, Pasadena, Calif.

"The Furniture and Sculpture of Wharton Esherick." Museum of Contemporary Crafts, New York, N.Y.

"Sixth Annual Kansas Designer-Craftsman Exhibition." University of Kansas, Lawrence.

1960

"California Design Six." Pasadena Art Museum, Pasadena, Calif.

"Designer-Craftsmen U.S.A. 1960." American Craftsmen's Council, at the Museum of Contemporary Crafts, New York, N.Y.

"Rochester–Finger Lakes Exhibition." Memorial Art Gallery, University of Rochester, Rochester, N.Y.

1961

"American Crafts—New Talent." University of Illinois, Urbana.

"California Design Seven." Pasadena Art Museum, Pasadena, Calif.

"Contemporary Craftsmen of the Far West." Museum of Contemporary Crafts, New York, N.Y.

1962

"California Design Eight." Pasadena Art Museum, Pasadena, Calif.

"Craftsmen of the Central States." Fort Worth Art Center, Fort Worth, Tex.

"Young Americans 1962." Museum of Contemporary Crafts, New York, N.Y.

1963

"Craftsmen of the Eastern States." Museum of Contemporary Crafts, New York, N.Y. Combined two regional exhibitions: "Craftsmen of the Northeastern States," Worcester Art Museum, Worcester, Mass.; "Craftsmen of the Southeastern States," Atlanta Art Association, Atlanta, Ga.

1964

"The American Craftsman." Museum of Contemporary Crafts, New York, N.Y.

"Amusements Is." Museum of Contemporary Crafts, New York, N.Y.

"Craftsmanship Defined." Philadelphia Museum College of Art, Philadelphia, Pa.

"Designed for Production: The Craftsman's Approach." Museum of Contemporary Crafts, New York, N.Y.

"First World Congress of Craftsmen." American Craftsmen's Council at Columbia University, New York, N.Y.

New York World's Fair, Flushing Meadows, Queens, N.Y.

"1964 Rochester–Finger Lakes Exhibition." Memorial Art Gallery of the University of Rochester, Rochester, N.Y.

1965

"American Craftsmen/1965: Festival of Contemporary Crafts." Krannert Art Museum, University of Illinois, Champaign.

"California Design Nine." Pasadena Art Museum, Pasadena, Calif.

"1965 Rochester–Finger Lakes Exhibition." Memorial Art Gallery of the University of Rochester, Rochester, N.Y.

1966

"The Bed." Museum of Contemporary Crafts, New York, N.Y.

"Craftsman-Designer-Artist." Upton Gallery, State University College, Buffalo, N.Y.

"Craftsmen U.S.A '66." Organized by the American Craftsmen's Council. Held at six regional centers: Delaware Art Center, Wilmington, Del.; North Carolina Museum of Art, Raleigh, N.C.; Dallas Museum of Fine Arts, Dallas, Tex.; Contemporary Crafts Association, Portland, Ore.; Los Angeles County Museum of Art, Los Angeles, Calif.; Milwaukee Art Center, Milwaukee, Wis. National exhibition at the Museum of Contemporary Crafts, New York, N.Y.

"Design: Wood." Museum West of the American Craftsmen's Council, San Francisco, Calif.

"Fantasy Furniture." Museum of Contemporary Crafts, New York, N.Y.

"1966 Rochester–Finger Lakes Exhibition." Memorial Art Gallery of the University of Rochester, Rochester, N.Y.

"Wendell Castle/Wharton Esherick/Sam Maloof/Marcelo Grassman." Renaissance Society, University of Chicago, Chicago, Ill.

1967

"Crafts 1967." Ball State University Art Gallery, Muncie, Ind.

"Craftsmen '67." Museum of the Philadelphia Civic Center, Philadelphia, Pa.

"Design and Aesthetics in Wood." Joe and Emily Lowe Art Gallery, Syracuse University, Syracuse, N.Y.

"Media Explored 1967: An Invitational Exhibition." Laguna Beach Art Association, Laguna Beach, Calif.

1968

"The American Craftsmen's Invitational Exhibition." Henry Art Gallery, University of Washington, Seattle.

"California Design Ten." Pasadena Art Museum, Pasadena, Calif.

"Objects Are...?" Museum of Contemporary Crafts, New York, N.Y.

"Second National Invitational Crafts Exhibition." Illinois State University, Normal.

1969

"Artist-Craftsmen of New York." First National Bank, New York, N.Y.

"Craft 1969." Memorial Art Gallery of the University of Rochester, Rochester, N.Y.

"Excellence of the Object." Honolulu Academy of Arts, Honolulu, Hawaii (cosponsored by the Museum of Contemporary Crafts, N.Y.).

"First Annual Craft Invitational Exhibit." University Center Gallery, Northern Illinois University, DeKalb.

"The Furniture of Wendell Castle." Wichita Art Museum, Wichita, Kans.

"Jonathan Brooks." Shop One, Rochester, N.Y.

"League of New Hampshire Craftsmen." Hargate Gallery, St. Paul's School, Concord, N.H.

"Objects: USA." National Collection of Fine Arts, Smithsonian Institution, Washington, D.C.

"Penland Resident Craftsmen." Penland School of Crafts, Penland, N.C.

"Rochester–Finger Lakes Exhibition." Memorial Art Gallery, University of Rochester, Rochester, N.Y.

"Young Americans." Museum of Contemporary Crafts, New York, N.Y.

1970

"Art in Other Media: Ceramic, Glass, Textile, Wood." Burpee Art Museum, Rockford, Ill.

"Artist-Craftsmen of New York." First National City Bank, New York, N.Y.

"Attitudes." Brooklyn Museum, Brooklyn, N.Y.

"Contemplation Environments." Museum of Contemporary Crafts, New York, N.Y.

"Contemporary Crafts." New Jersey State Museum, Trenton.

"Crafts 1970." Boston City Hall Galleries and Institute of Contemporary Art, Boston, Mass.

"Craftsmen '70." Museum of the Philadelphia Civic Center, Philadelphia, Pa.

"Daniel Jackson." Philadelphia Art Alliance, Philadelphia, Pa.

"Master Craftsmen: An Invitational Exhibition." State University of New York, Binghamton.

Philadelphia Council of Professional Craftsmen. Franklin Institute, Philadelphia, Pa.

"Sam Maloof." Long Beach Museum of Art, Long Beach, Calif.

"Virginia Craftsmen 1970." Virginia Museum of Fine Arts, Richmond.

1971

"California Design Eleven." Pasadena Art Museum, Pasadena, Calif.

1972

"New York State Craftsmen: 1972 Selection." Jointly sponsored by University Art Gallery, State University of New York, Albany, and the New York State Craftsmen.

"Woodenworks: Furniture Objects by Five Contemporary Craftsmen." Renwick Gallery, Smithsonian Institution, Washington, D.C.

1973

"A Comment on Contemporary Crafts." University of Wisconsin, Milwaukee.

"Craftsman Invitational 1973." Gallery of Contemporary Art, Winston-Salem, N.C.

"Craftsmen '73." Philadelphia Civic Center Museum, Philadelphia, Pa.

"Innovations: Contemporary Home Environments." La Jolla Museum of Contemporary Art, La Jolla, Calif.

"Old Orchard Midwest Craft Festival." Skokie, Ill.

"Paley/Castle." Fairtree Gallery of Contemporary Crafts, New York, N.Y.

1974

Contemporary woodworks show [no title given]. Craft Center, Worcester, Mass.

"Chairs in Motion." California State University Art Gallery, Fullerton.

"The Fine Art of Craftsmanship." Roberson Center for the Arts and Sciences, State University of New York, Binghamton.

"Fun and Fantasy '74." Xerox Square Exhibit Center, Rochester, N.Y.

"In Praise of Hands: Contemporary Crafts of the World," Ontario Science Center, Toronto, Canada.

"Nine Artisans." Bruce Gallery, Edinboro State College, Edinboro, Pa.

"Seven Contemporary Craftsmen." Friends of the Crafts, Seattle, Wash.

"Washington Designer-Craftsmen." Knoll International, Washington, D.C.

1975

"Arizona Crafts '75." Tucson Arts Center, Tucson, Ariz.

"Bed and Board: Contemporary Quilts and Woodwork." DeCordova and Dana Museum and Park, Lincoln, Mass.

"Change of Pace: Contemporary Furniture 1925–1975." Cincinnati Art Museum, Cincinnati, Ohio.

"Contemporary Crafts of the Americas." Colorado State University, Fort Collins.

"Craft Multiples." Renwick Gallery, Smithsonian Institution, Washington, D.C.

"Language of Wood." Buffalo Craftsmen and the Burchfield Center, State University of New York, Buffalo.

"SAC: Faculty and Alumni Exhibition." Bevier Gallery, Rochester Institute of Technology, Rochester, N.Y.

"Third Annual International Craft Show and Fair." New York Coliseum, New York, N.Y.

1976

"American Crafts '76: An Aesthetic View." Museum of Contemporary Art, Chicago, Ill.

"California Craftsmen '76." Monterey Peninsula Museum of Art, Monterey, Calif.

"California Design '76." Pacific Design Center, Los Angeles, Calif.

"Circa 1976: American Handcrafted Furnishings." Creative Arts Workshop, New Haven, Conn.

"Forty-first International Eucharistic Congress Exhibition of Liturgical Arts." Philadelphia Civic Center, Philadelphia, Pa.

"Of Growth and Form." Fort Wayne Public Library, Fort Wayne, Ind.

"Please Be Seated." Sam Maloof solo exhibition. Museum of Fine Arts, Boston, Mass.

"Virginia Craftsmen 1976." Virginia Museum of Fine Arts, Richmond.

"Works in Wood by Northwest Artists." Portland Art Museum, Portland, Ore.

1977

"American Crafts 1977." Philadelphia Museum of Art, Philadelphia, Pa.

Boston University's Program in Artisanry, works by faculty. Boston City Hall, Boston, Mass.

"Contemporary Works by Master Craftsmen." Museum of Fine Arts, Boston, Mass.

"Improbable Furniture." Institute of Contemporary Art, University of Pennsylvania, Philadelphia.

"L.A. Collects Folk Art." Craft and Folk Art Museum, Los Angeles, Calif.

"Paint on Wood: Decorated American Furniture since the Seventeenth Century." Renwick Gallery, Smithsonian Institution, Washington, D.C.

"Young Americans." Museum of Contemporary Crafts, New York, N.Y.

1978

"American Chairs: Form, Function, and Fantasy." John Michael Kohler Arts Center, Sheboygan, Wis.

"American Woodcarvers." Craft Center, Worcester, Mass.

"Board Feet." Lamont Gallery, Phillips Exeter Academy, Exeter, N.H.

"Contemporary Work by Master Craftsmen." Museum of Fine Arts, Boston, Mass.

"Sixteen American Woodcarvers." Worcester Craft Center, Worcester, Mass.

1979

"Art in Modern Handcrafts." Society for Art in Crafts, Verona, Pa.

Faculty Show. Worcester Craft Center, Worcester, Mass.

"New Handmade Furniture: American Furniture Makers Working in Hardwood." American Craft Museum, New York, N.Y.

"Paley/Castle/Wildenhain." Memorial Art Gallery, University of Rochester, Rochester, N.Y.

1980

"California Woodworking." Oakland Museum of Art Special Gallery, Oakland, Calif.

"It's About Time." Worcester Craft Center, Worcester, Mass.

"Sitting in Style: Wendell Castle, Tage Frid, Judy Kensley McKie, Contemporary Furniture in Cooperation with the Museum of Fine Arts." Society of Arts and Crafts, Boston, Mass.

"Woodworks I: New American Sculpture." Experiencenter, Dayton Art Institute, Dayton, Ohio.

1981

"Beyond Tradition: Twenty-fifth Anniversary Exhibition." American Craft Museum, New York, N.Y.

"The Fine Art of the Furniture Maker." Memorial Art Gallery, University of Rochester, Rochester, N.Y.

"For Love and Money: Dealers Choose." Pratt Manhattan Center Gallery, New York, N.Y.

"Furniture as Sculpture: Handcrafted Wood Furniture by Five Contemporary Artists." New Gallery of Contemporary Art, Cleveland, Ohio.

"Made in L.A." Craft and Folk Art Museum, Los Angeles, Calif.

"Recent Art Furniture." Buscaglia-Castellani Art Gallery, Niagara University, Niagara Falls, N.Y.

"Thirty Americans—An Invitational Exhibition: Clay, Fiber, Glass, Metal, Wood." Galveston Art Center, Galveston, Tex.

"Walker Weed: A Retrospective Exhibition 1950–1981." Dartmouth College Museum and Galleries, Hanover, N.H.

"Woodforms: Contemporary Hand-Crafted Furniture of Original Design." Brockton Art Museum/Fuller Memorial, Brockton, Mass.

1982

"Artists in Artisanry." Boston University, Boston, Mass.

"Chicago Furniture, 1982." Hyde Park Art Center, Chicago, Ill.

"New Views in Furniture: The Northeast." Worcester Craft Center, Worcester, Mass.

"Pattern: An Exhibition of the Decorated Surface." American Craft Museum II, New York, N.Y.

"Recent Art Furniture: Survey of Current Art Furniture in the Northeast." Buscaglia Castellani Art Gallery, Niagara University, Niagara Falls, N.Y.

"Woodworking in the Rockies." Colorado Springs Fine Arts Center, Colorado Springs.

1983

"Color/Wood." Brookfield Craft Center, Brookfield, Conn.

"Crafts: An Expanding Definition." J. M. Kohler Arts Center, Sheboygan, Wis.

"Furniture…by Philadelphia Woodworkers 1983." Society of Philadelphia Woodworkers and the Port of History Museum, Philadelphia, Pa.

"Material Allusion: Unlikely Material." Taft Museum, Cincinnati, Ohio.

"National Wood Invitational." Craft Alliance, St. Louis, Mo.

"Ornamentalism: The New Decorativeness in Architecture and Design." Hudson River Museum, Yonkers, N.Y.

1984

"American Contemporary Works in Wood '84." Dairy Barn Gallery, Southeastern Ohio Cultural Arts Center, Athens.

"Bentwood." Part I: "A History of Bentwood"; Part II: "Bentwood Today." Museum of Art, Rhode Island School of Design, Providence.

"Contemporary American Wood Sculpture." Crocker Art Museum, Sacramento, Calif.

"Contemporary Chairs." Boulder Center for the Visual Arts, Boulder, Colo.

"Furniture, Furnishings: Subject and Object." Museum of Art, Rhode Island School of Design, Providence.

"Living Treasures of California." Crocker Art Museum, Sacramento, Calif.

"New Works." Brockton Art Museum/Fuller Memorial, Brockton, Mass.

"Quiet Expressions in Wood. Furniture by the James Krenov Group." California Crafts Museum, San Francisco.

1985

"American Contemporary Works in Wood '85." Dairy Barn Gallery, Southeastern Ohio Cultural Arts Center, Athens.

"Contemporary American Wood Sculpture." Crocker Art Museum, Sacramento, Calif.

"Furniture, Furnishings: Subject and Object." Berkshire Museum, Pittsfield, Mass.

"Made in Syracuse Today: Contemporary Work in Wood." Everson Museum of Art, Syracuse, N.Y.

"Masterpieces of Time." Taft Museum, Cincinnati, Ohio.

"Material Evidence: New Color Techniques in Handmade Furniture." Gallery at Workbench, New York, N.Y., and the Formica Corporation.

"Material Pleasures: Furniture for a Postmodern Age." Queens Museum, Flushing, N.Y.

"New Chair." San Angelo Museum of Fine Arts, San Angelo, Tex.

"New Wood, New Ways." Traveling exhibition. Organized at Murray State University, Murray, Ky.

"Tradition and Innovation: Decorative Art by Castle, Chihuly, Paley, Woodman." Laguna Gloria Art Museum, Austin, Tex.

1986

"American Contemporary Works in Wood '86." Dairy Barn Gallery, Southeastern Ohio Cultural Arts Center, Athens.

"Contemporary Art Furniture: Collaborations between Designer/Craftsmen and Architects," Bevier Gallery, Rochester Institute of Technology, Rochester, N.Y.

"Contemporary Arts: An Expanding View." Monmouth Museum, Lincroft, N.J.

"Craft Today: Poetry of the Physical." American Craft Museum, New York, N.Y.

"Forty-four Alumni." Museum of Art, Rhode Island School of Design, Providence.

"Furniture in the Aluminum Vein." Kaiser Center Art Gallery, Oakland, Calif.

"New Art Forms." Annual event. Chicago, Ill.

"New Furniture." Gallery of Contemporary Art, University of Colorado, Colorado Springs.

"New Works." Brockton Art Museum/Fuller Memorial, Brockton, Mass.

"Robert March: Contemporary Furniture." Worcester Art Museum, Worcester, Mass.

"Swain School Program in Artisanry Masters Exhibition." Brockton Art Museum/Fuller Memorial, Brockton, Mass.

"Time and Defiance of Gravity: Recent Works by Wendell Castle." Memorial Art Gallery, University of Rochester, Rochester, N.Y.

1987

"American Contemporary Works in Wood '87." Dairy Barn Gallery, Southeastern Ohio Cultural Arts Center, Athens.

"Chairs as Art." Arts Club of Chicago, Chicago, Ill.

"The Eloquent Object: The Evolution of American Art in Craft Media since 1945." Philbrook Museum of Art, Tulsa, Okla.

"Fantastic Furniture." Lannan Museum, Lake Worth, Fla.

1989

"American Contemporary Works in Wood '89." Dairy Barn Gallery, Southeastern Ohio Cultural Arts Center, Athens.

"Craft Today USA." Organized by American Craft Museum, New York, N.Y., for various venues

"Furniture by Wendell Castle." Detroit Institute of Arts, Detroit, Mich.

"Furniture: Contemporary Expressions." Lyman Allyn Art Museum, New London, Conn.

"George Nakashima: Full Circle." American Craft Museum, New York, N.Y.

"New American Furniture: The Second Generation of Studio Furnituremakers." Museum of Fine Arts, Boston, Mass.

1990

"Art That Works: Decorative Arts of the Eighties, Crafted in America." A traveling exhibition with fourteen venues, organized by Art Services International.

"Contemporary Works in Wood: Southern Style." Huntsville Museum of Art, Huntsville, Ala.

SELECT BIBLIOGRAPHY

A

Adamson, Jeremy. *The Furniture of Sam Maloof*. Exh. cat. Washington, D.C.: Smithsonian American Art Museum, 2001.

Albright Art Gallery, Buffalo Fine Arts Academy. *Designer Craftsmen of Western New York 1957*. Exh. cat. Buffalo, N.Y.: Albright Art Gallery, 1957.

American Craft Museum. *Craft Today USA*. Exh. cat. New York: American Craft Museum, 1989.

———. *Explorations II: The New Furniture*. Exh cat. New York: American Craft Museum, 1991.

———. *New Handmade Furniture: American Furniture Makers Working in Hardwood*. Exh. cat. New York: American Craft Museum, 1979.

———. *Pattern: An Exhibition of the Decorated Surface*. Exh. cat. New York: American Craft Museum, 1982.

American Craftsmen's Educational Council. *Designer-Craftsmen U.S.A. 1953*. Exh. cat. New York: Blanchard Press, 1953.

Arts Club of Chicago. *Chairs as Art*. Exh. cat. Chicago: Arts Club of Chicago, 1987.

B

Ball State University Art Gallery. *Crafts 1967*. Exh. cat. N.p., 1967.

Barter, Tanya, John Dunnigan, and Seth Stem. *Bentwood*. Exh. cat. Providence: Rhode Island School of Design, 1984.

Bayer, Patricia, ed. *The Fine Art of the Furniture Maker: Conversations with Wendell Castle, Artist, and Penelope Hunter-Stiebel, Curator, about Selected Works from the Metropolitan Museum of Art*. Exh. cat. Rochester, N.Y.: Memorial Art Gallery of the University of Rochester, 1981.

Bevier Gallery, College of Fine and Applied Arts, Rochester Institute of Technology. *Keyser: Wood Furniture, Sculpture, and Ecclesiastical Objects*. Exh. cat. Rochester, N.Y.: Rochester Institute of Technology, 1978.

———. *SAC: Faculty and Alumni Exhibition*. Exh. cat. Rochester, N.Y.: Rochester Institute of Technology, 1975.

Bishop, Robert. *The American Chair: Three Centuries of Style*. New York: E. P. Dutton, 1972. Reprint; New York: Bonanza Books, 1983.

Bodine, Sarah. "Handmade." *Metropolis* (April 1982): 18–20.

Boyd, Virginia T., et al. *Contemporary Studio Case Furniture: The Inside Story*. Exh. cat. Madison: Elvehjem Museum of Art, University of Wisconsin–Madison, 2002.

Breedin, Robert L., et al. *The Craftsman in America*. Washington, D.C.: National Geographic Society, 1975.

Brockton Art Museum/Fuller Memorial. *Woodforms: Contemporary Hand-Crafted Furniture of Original Design*. Exh. cat. Brockton, Mass.: Brockton Art Museum/Fuller Memorial, 1981.

Brown, G. Charles. "Happy Birthday Dear Memphis." *Modernism Magazine* 4, no. 3 (fall 2001): 16–23.

Buffalo Craftsmen and the Burchfield Center. *Language of Wood*. Exh. cat. Buffalo, N.Y.: Buffalo Craftsmen and the Burchfield Center, 1975.

Buscaglia-Castellani Art Gallery. *Recent Art Furniture*. Exh. cat. Niagara Falls, N.Y.: Buscaglia-Castellani Art Gallery, Niagara University, 1981.

C

Carpenter, Arthur Espenet. "The Rise of Artiture: Woodworking Comes of Age." *Fine Woodworking*, no. 38 (January–February 1983): 98–103.

Castle, Wendell, and David Edman. *The Wendell Castle Book of Wood Lamination*. New York: Van Nostrand Reinhold, 1980.

Cehanowicz, Laura. "Portfolio: Woodworking Women." *Fine Woodworking*, no. 17 (July/August 1979): 54–56.

Charbonneau, Diane. "Art Furniture in America in the 1980s and 1990s: Assis entre Deux Chaises." Master's thesis, SUNY Fashion Institute of Technology, New York, 1998.

Chastain-Chapman, A. U. "Fine Furnituremaking." *American Craft* 44, no. 6 (December 1984–January 1985): 10–17.

Cincinnati Art Museum. *Change of Pace: Contemporary Furniture 1925–1975*. Exh. cat. Cincinnati, Ohio: Cincinnati Art Museum, 1975.

Clearwater, Bonnie. *Fantastic Furniture*. Exh. cat. Lake Worth, Fla.: Lannan Museum, 1987.

Cochran, Leslie. "To Market, to Market: The Growing Interest in Handmade Furniture." *Craft International* (October–November–December 1985): 13–15.

NOTE TO THE READER

The following bibliography is a highly selective guide to the growing literature on studio furniture. Those seeking more specific information on makers, schools, and galleries will find additional references in the sections devoted to those subjects in this volume. Numerous short articles, advertisements, and other useful material, in addition to the material cited here, can also be found in the pages of *Craft Horizons* (which changed its title to *American Craft* beginning with vol. 39, no. 3 [June–July 1979]), *Fine Woodworking*, *Woodwork*, and occasionally in other journals and magazines such as *Modernism*. Beginning in 1999, the Furniture Society has published an occasional volume entitled *Furniture Studio*, with variant subtitles, devoted to both historical and current aspects of studio furniture, as well as a regular newsletter entitled *Furniture Matters*.

Colorado Springs Fine Arts Center. *Woodworking in the Rockies*. Exh. cat. Colorado Springs: Colorado Springs Fine Arts Center, 1982.

Conway, Patricia. *Art for Everyday: The New Craft Movement*. New York: Clarkson Potter, 1990.

Cooke, Edward S., Jr. "Arts and Crafts Furniture: Process or Product?" In *The Ideal Home, 1900–1920: The History of Twentieth-Century Craft in America*, ed. Janet Kardon, 64–76. Exh. cat. New York: Harry N. Abrams in association with the American Craft Museum, 1993.

———. "Coming of Age in Boston." *Art New England* (December 1989/January 1990): 10–13, 49.

———. "Craftsmen." In *American Decorative Arts and Household Furnishings in America, 1650–1920: An Annotated Bibliography*, ed. Kenneth L. Ames and Gerald W. R. Ward, 333–42. Winterthur, Del.: Henry Francis du Pont Winterthur Museum, 1989.

———. *New American Furniture: The Second Generation of Studio Furnituremakers*. Exh. cat. Boston: Museum of Fine Arts, 1989.

———. "The Study of American Furniture from the Perspective of the Maker." In *Perspectives on American Furniture*, ed. Gerald W. R. Ward, 113–26. New York: W. W. Norton for the Henry Francis du Pont Winterthur Museum, 1988.

———. "Women Furniture Makers." In *Women Designers in the USA, 1900–2000*, ed. Pat Kirkham, 291–303. Exh. cat. New Haven and London: Yale University Press, for the Bard Graduate Center for Studies in the Decorative Arts, New York, 2000.

Creative Arts Workshop. *Circa 1876: American Handcrafted Furnishings*. Exh. cat. New Haven, Conn.: Dorothy Ann Lipson for the Creative Arts Workshop, 1976.

Crocker Art Museum. *Contemporary American Wood Sculpture*. Exh. cat. Sacramento, Calif.: Crocker Art Museum, 1985.

D

Dairy Barn Gallery, Southeastern Ohio Cultural Arts Center. *American Contemporary Works in Wood*. Exh. cat. Athens: Dairy Barn Gallery, Southeastern Ohio Cultural Arts Center, 1984. [See also catalogues published with the same title in 1985 and 1986.]

Daniel, Greta. "Furniture by Craftsmen." *Craft Horizons* 27, no. 2 (March–April 1957): 34–38.

Danto, Arthur C., et al. *Angel Chairs: New Work by Wendell Castle*. Exh. cat. New York: Peter Joseph Gallery, 1991.

Danto, Arthur C., and Nancy Princenthal. *The Art of John Cederquist: Reality of Illusion*. Exh. cat. Oakland: Oakland Museum of California, 1997.

Dartmouth College Museum and Galleries. *Walker Weed: A Retrospective Exhibition, 1950–1981*. Exh. cat. Hanover, N.H.: Dartmouth College Museum and Galleries, 1981.

"Decoration vs. Desecration." *Fine Woodworking*, no. 24 (September–October 1980): 92.

"Designed for Production: The Craftsman's Approach." *Craft Horizons* 24, no. 2 (March–April 1964): 13–33, 61–67.

Designer/Craftsman Guild. *Of Growth and Form*. Exh. cat. Fort Wayne, Ind.: Designer/Craftsman Guild, 1976.

Diamonstein, Barbaralee. *Handmade in America: Conversations with Fourteen Craftsmasters*. New York: Harry N. Abrams, 1983.

Domergue, Denise. *Artists Design Furniture*. New York: Harry N. Abrams, 1984.

Doran, Pat. "Crossing the Boundaries." *Art New England* 12, no. 1 (December 1990–January 1991): 12–13, 38.

Dormer, Peter. *The New Furniture: Trends + Traditions*. New York: Thames and Hudson, 1987.

Dunbar: Fine Furniture of the 1950s. Atglen, Pa.: Schiffer Publishing, 2000.

E

Emery, Olivia H., and Tim Andersen. *Craftsman Lifestyle: The Gentle Revolution*. Pasadena, Calif.: California Design Publications, 1978.

Everson Museum of Art. *Syracuse Collects: Arts and Crafts and Made in Syracuse Today, Contemporary Work in Wood*. Exh. cat. Syracuse, N.Y.: Everson Museum of Art, 1985.

F

Fairbanks, Jonathan L. "Craft Processes and Images: Visual Sources for the Study of the Craftsman." In *The Craftsmen in Early America*, ed. Ian M. G. Quimby, 299–330. New York: W. W. Norton for the Henry Francis du Pont Winterthur Museum, 1994.

Fairbanks, Jonathan L., and Elizabeth Bidwell Bates. *American Furniture, 1620 to the Present*. New York: Richard Marek, 1981.

Fine Woodworking Design Book. 7 vols. Newtown, Conn.: Taunton Press, 1977–96.

Fisher, Marshall Jon. "The Ergonomic Rocking Chair." *Atlantic* 287, no. 4 (April 2001): 93–95.

Fitzgerald, Oscar P. *Four Centuries of American Furniture*. Radnor, Pa.: Wallace-Homestead Book Company, 1995.

Forsyth, Amy. "Jere Osgood and Thomas Hucker." *Woodwork*, no. 69 (June 2001): 24–33.

Fox, Judith Hoos. *Furniture, Furnishings: Subject and Object*. Exh. cat. Providence: Rhode Island School of Design, 1984.

Frid, Tage. *Tage Frid Teaches Woodworking*. Vol. 1, *Joinery*, and vol. 2, *Shaping, Veneering, Finishing*. 1979, 1981. Reprint (2 vols. in 1), Newtown, Conn.: Taunton Press, 1993.

———. *Tage Frid Teaches Woodworking*. Vol. 3, *Furnituremaking*. Newtown, Conn.: Taunton Press, 1985.

"Furniture Plus." *Craft International* (October–November–December 1985): 24–27.

G

Gallery at Workbench and Formica Corporation. *Material Evidence: New Color Techniques in Handmade Furniture.* Exh. cat. Washington, D.C: Smithsonian Institution, 1985.

Greenburg, Cara. *Mid-Century Modern: Furniture of the 1950s.* New York: Harmony Books, 1984.

———. *Op to Pop: Furniture of the 1960s.* Boston: Little, Brown, and Company, 1999.

H

Hall, Julie. *Tradition and Change: The New American Craftsman.* New York: Dutton, 1977.

Hartman, Donna. "Women in Woodworking." *Woodshop News* (August 1989): B2–B15.

Herman, Lloyd E. *Art That Works: The Decorative Arts of the Eighties, Crafted in America.* Exh. cat. Seattle and London: University of Washington Press, 1990.

———. *Paint on Wood: Decorated American Furniture since the Seventeenth Century.* Exh. cat. Washington, D.C.: Smithsonian Institution Press in association with the Renwick Gallery, 1977.

Holmes, Roger. "Color and Wood: Dyeing for a Change." *Fine Woodworking,* no. 41 (July–August 1983): 70–73.

———. "Survivors." *Fine Woodworking,* no. 55 (November–December 1985): 91–97.

Hosaluk, Michael. *Scratching the Surface: Art and Content in Contemporary Wood.* Madison, Wis.: Guild Publishing, 2002.

Huntsville Museum of Art. *Contemporary Works in Wood: Southern Style.* Exh. cat. Huntsville, Ala.: Huntsville Museum of Art, 1990.

I

Ilse-Neuman, Ursula, et al. *Made in Oakland: The Furniture of Garry Knox Bennett.* Exh. cat. New York: American Craft Museum, 2000.

Institute of Contemporary Art, University of Pennsylvania. *Improbable Furniture.* Exh. cat. Philadelphia, Pa.: Institute of Contemporary Art, University of Pennsylvania, 1977.

J

Jackson, A. D. "Good Design in Furniture." *Craft Horizons* 11, no. 3 (autumn 1951): 21–23.

James A. Michener Art Museum. *George Nakashima and the Modernist Moment.* Exh. cat. Doylestown, Pa.: James A. Michener Art Museum, 2001.

Jepson, Barbara. "Art Furniture," *American Craft* 45, no. 5 (October–November 1985): 10–17.

John Michael Kohler Arts Center. *American Chairs: Form, Function, and Fantasy.* Exh. cat. Sheboygan, Wis.: John Michael Kohler Arts Center, 1978.

K

Kelsey, John. "Woodworking in Mendocino: A Close Look at the New Generation of Artist-Craftsmen." *Fine Woodworking,* no. 29 (July–August 1981): 36–43.

Kelsey, John, and Rick Mastelli, eds. *Furniture Studio: The Heart of the Functional Arts.* Free Union, Va.: Furniture Society, 1999.

Kirkham, Pat, ed. *Women Designers in the USA, 1900–2000.* Exh. cat. New Haven and London: Yale University Press, for the Bard Graduate Center for Studies in the Decorative Arts, New York, 2000.

Krenov, James. *A Cabinetmaker's Notebook.* New York: Van Nostrand Reinhold, 1976.

——— *The Fine Art of Cabinetmaking.* New York: Van Nostrand Reinhold, 1976.

———. *The Impractical Cabinetmaker.* New York: Van Nostrand Reinhold, 1979. (Also published as *The Joys of Cabinetmaking* in the same year for the Popular Science Book Club.)

———. *James Krenov: Worker in Wood.* New York: Van Nostrand Reinhold, 1981.

———. *With Wakened Hands: Furniture by James Krenov and Students.* Bethel, Conn.: Cambium Press, 2000.

L

Landis, Scott, ed. *Conservation by Design.* Exh. cat. Providence: Museum of Art, Rhode Island School of Design, and Woodworkers Alliance for Rainforest Protection, 1993.

Lebow, Edward. "Wood/Work/Business." *American Craft* 48, no. 5 (October–November 1988): 44–49.

Lucie-Smith, Edward. *The Story of Craft: The Craftsman's Role in Society.* Ithaca, N.Y.: Cornell University Press, 1981.

Lyman Allyn Art Museum. *Furniture: Contemporary Expressions.* Exh. cat. New London, Conn.: Lyman Allyn Art Museum, 1989.

M

Main, Kari M. *Please Be Seated: Contemporary Studio Seating Furniture.* Exh. cat. New Haven, Conn.: Yale University Art Gallery, 1999.

Maloof, Sam. *Sam Maloof, Woodworker.* Tokyo, New York, and San Francisco: Kodansha International, 1983.

Manhart, Marcia, and Tom Manhart, eds. *The Eloquent Object: The Evolution of American Art since 1945.* Exh. cat. Tulsa, Okla.: Philbrook Museum of Art, 1987.

Mastelli, Rick. "The Designer's Intent: Six Northwest Woodworkers Trace Their Roots." *Fine Woodworking,* no. 39 (March–April 1983): 76–81.

Mastelli, Rick, and John Kelsey, eds. *Furniture Studio: Tradition in Contemporary Furniture.* Free Union, Va.: Furniture Society, 2001.

Mayer, Barbara. *Contemporary American Craft Art: A Collector's Guide.* Salt Lake City, Utah: Gibbs M. Smith, 1988.

Meilach, Dona Z. *Contemporary Art with Wood: Creative Techniques and Appreciation.* New York: Crown Publishers, 1968.

———. *Creating Modern Furniture: Trends, Techniques, Appreciation.* New York: Crown Publishers, 1975.

————. *Woodworking: The New Wave.* New York: Crown Publishers, 1981.

Memorial Art Gallery of the University of Rochester. *Paley / Castle / Wildenhain.* Exh. cat. Rochester, N.Y.: Memorial Art Gallery of the University of Rochester, 1979.

Museum of Contemporary Crafts. *Designer-Craftsmen U.S.A. 1960.* Exh. cat. New York: Museum of Contemporary Crafts, 1960.

————. *Furniture by Craftsmen.* Exh. cat. New York: Museum of Contemporary Crafts, 1957.

————. *Young Americans 1962.* Exh. cat. New York: Museum of Contemporary Crafts, 1962. [See also catalogues for exhibitions with the same title, 1950–77.]

N

Nakashima, George. *The Soul of a Tree: A Woodworker's Reflections.* Tokyo, New York, and San Francisco: Kodansha International, 1981.

"The New American Craftsman: First Generation." *Craft Horizons* 26, no. 3 (June 1966): 15–34.

New Gallery of Contemporary Art. *Furniture as Sculpture: Handcrafted Wood Furniture by Five Contemporary Artists.* Exh. cat. Cleveland, Ohio: New Gallery of Contemporary Art, 1981.

Noll, Terry. "Finding Your Own Voice." *Woodwork,* no. 1 (spring 1989): 36–41.

Nordness, Lee. *Objects: USA.* Exh. cat. New York: Viking Press, 1970.

O

Oakland Museum of Art. *California Woodworking: An Exhibition of Contemporary Handcrafted Furniture.* Exh. cat. Oakland, Calif.: Oakland Museum of Art Special Gallery, [1980].

Ostergard, Derek E. *George Nakashima: Full Circle.* Exh. cat. New York: Weidenfeld and Nicolson in association with American Craft Council, 1989.

P

Parrasch, Franklin. "The Emerging Leaders of Furniture: Sam Maloof's View of the Contemporary Furniture Scene." *Art Today* (summer 1989): 26–30.

Pasadena Art Museum. *California Design.* Exh. cat. Pasadena, Calif.: California Design, 1955. [See also catalogues published periodically with the same title from 1956 through 1971.]

Paz, Octavio, and the World Crafts Council. *In Praise of Hands.* Exh. cat. Toronto, Ontario, Canada: World Crafts Council, 1974.

Peterson, Norman. "California Suite." *Craft International* (October–November–December 1985): 20–21.

Philadelphia Museum of Art. *American Crafts 1977.* Exh. cat. Philadelphia, Pa.: Women's Committee of the Philadelphia Museum of Art, 1977.

Philadelphia Museum College of Art. *Craftsmanship Defined.* Exh. cat. [Philadelphia, Pa.]: Philadelphia Museum College of Art, 1964.

Piña, Leslie. *Fifties Furniture.* Atglen, Pa.: Schiffer Publishing, 1996.

Portland Art Museum. *Works in Wood by Northwest Artists.* Exh. cat. Portland, Ore.: Portland Art Museum, 1976.

Q

Queens Museum. *Material Pleasures: Furniture for a Postmodern Age.* Exh. cat. New York: Queens County Art and Cultural Center, 1985.

R

Renwick Gallery. *Craft Multiples.* Exh. cat. Washington, D.C.: Smithsonian Institution Press, 1976.

————. *Woodenworks: Furniture Objects by Five Contemporary Craftsmen.* Exh. cat. St. Paul: Minnesota Museum of Art and Smithsonian Institution, 1972.

Rush, Michael. "Philadelphia Wood." *American Craft* 59, no. 1 (February–March 1999): 80–83, 94.

S

Sasso, Paul, and Michael Watts. *New Wood, New Ways.* Exh. cat. Murray, Ky.: Murray State University, 1985.

Shea, John G. *Anatomy of Contemporary Furniture.* New York: Van Nostrand Reinhold, 1973.

Simon, Kenneth A. *New England Handcraft Catalog.* Chester, Conn.: Globe Pequot Press, 1983.

Simpson, Thomas. *Fantasy Furniture: Design and Decoration.* New York: Reinhold Book Corporation, 1968.

Simpson, Tommy. *Two Looks to Home: The Art of Tommy Simpson.* Boston: Bulfinch Press, 1999.

Simpson, Tommy, and Lisa Hammel. *Hand and Home: The Homes of American Craftsmen.* Boston: Bulfinch Press, 1994.

Slivka, Rose. "The American Craftsman." *Craft Horizons* 24, no. 3 (May–June 1964): 10–93.

Smith, Paul J., and Edward Lucie-Smith. *Craft Today: Poetry of the Physical.* Exh. cat. New York: Weidenfeld and Nicolson in association with the American Craft Museum, 1986.

Smith, Paul J., ed. *Objects for Use: Handmade by Design.* Exh. cat. New York: Harry N. Abrams in association with the American Craft Museum, 2001.

Society of Philadelphia Woodworkers. *Furniture…by Philadelphia Woodworkers 1983.* Exh. cat. Philadelphia, Pa.: Society of Philadelphia Woodworkers, 1983.

Steinbaum, Bernice, and Nina Stritzler. *Pioneer and Pioneering: Twentieth Century Women Furniture Designers and Furniture Designer/Makers.* Exh. cat. New York: Bernice Steinbaum Gallery, 1988.

Stone, Michael A. *Contemporary American Woodworkers.* Salt Lake City, Utah: Gibbs M. Smith, 1986.

————. "Garry Knox Bennett." *Woodwork,* no. 71 (October 2001): 24–30.

T

Taragin, Davira S., Edward S. Cooke, Jr., and Joseph Giovannini. *Furniture by Wendell Castle*. Exh. cat. New York: Hudson Hills Press in association with the Founders Society, Detroit Institute of Arts, 1989.

U

University Art Gallery, State University of New York at Binghamton. *Master Craftsmen: An Invitational Exhibition, November 7–28, 1971*. Exh. cat. Binghamton, N.Y.: University Art Gallery, 1971.

V

Virginia Museum. *Virginia Craftsmen 1970*. Exh. cat. N.p., 1970. [See also catalogues for exhibitions with the same title in 1972, 1974, 1976, and 1977.]

Visual, Tactile, and Functional: Contemporary Furniture in Boston Galleries, 1989–1990. Exh. cat. [Boston]: Meridien Printing, [1990].

W

Wallance, Don. *Shaping America's Products*. New York: Van Nostrand Reinhold, 1956.

Webb, Aileen O. "American Craftsman's Council/1964: The International Era." *Craft Horizons* 24, no. 3 (May–June 1964): 9.

Whitaker, Irwin. *Crafts and Craftsmen*. Dubuque, Iowa: W. C. Brown, [1967].

Wichita Art Museum. *The Furniture of Wendell Castle*. Exh. cat. Wichita, Kans.: Wichita Art Museum, 1969.

"Women Are Woodworking." *American Craft* 43, no. 1 (February–March 1983): 44–45.

Wood Turning Center and Yale University Art Gallery. *Wood Turning in North America since 1930*. Exh. cat. New Haven, Conn.: Wood Turning Center and Yale University Art Gallery, 2001.

Worcester Art Museum. *Craftsmen of the Northeastern States*. Exh. cat. Worcester, Mass.: Worcester Art Museum, 1963.

———. *An Exhibition of Contemporary New England Handicrafts*. Exh. cat. Worcester, Mass.: Worcester Art Museum, 1943.

———. *New England Craft Exhibition—1955*. Exh. cat. Worcester, Mass.: Junior League of Worcester, 1955.

Wright, Virginia. *Modern Furniture in Canada, 1920–1970*. Toronto, Ontario, Canada: University of Toronto Press, 1997.